The Will To Live

JOHN COLLIER, former U. S. Commissioner of Indian Affairs, invites us here to consider the way of the American Indians. For he sees in their way of life the hope and the fate of mankind. "In the past, only those who knew John Collier intimately," says Solon T. Kimball in *The American Indian,* "were privileged to understand the larger purpose and greater motivation of his effort. Now there is revealed, for all, the intuitive and intellectual achievements of a life deeply immersed in the manifestations of a disturbed world. He discovered a profound sense of living and a new hope in Indian society. He learned that centuries of planned destruction had dimmed but not destroyed the spiritual possessions which kept it alive. There was revealed to him *'that passion and reverence for human personality and for the web of life and the earth which the American Indians have tended as a central, sacred fire since before the Stone Age. Our long hope is to renew that sacred fire in us all. It is our only long hope.'* "

John Collier tells of the American Indian from the Paleolithic Age to the present. He reviews the Indian records of Spain and those of the United States, and gives a moving dramatization of four centuries of Western European impact on the cultures of the Indians of the Americas—both South and North of the Rio Grande—from Inca and Aztec to modern Sioux, Pueblo and Navajo. Collier pays tribute to the great work of Bartolomé de las Casas, and others who have attempted to apply *'the principle of freedom of conscience to the realities of an unfree world.'* He discusses the *'collective corruption'* which until 1933 determined our own spoliation of the Indians, and tells of the newer, more creative policy thereafter put into effect. "But always," says Ward Shepard in the *Saturday Review of Literature,* "the author penetrates to the indestructible spiritual substance of the life-ways and world-view wrought out across twenty millenia by the myriad Indian societies . . ."

MENTOR and SIGNET Titles
of Related Interest

Indians of the Americas

The Long Hope

(Slightly Abridged)

by JOHN COLLIER

A MENTOR BOOK from
NEW AMERICAN LIBRARY
TIMES MIRROR
New York and Scarborough, Ontario
The New English Library Limited, London

TO
LUCY GRAHAM CROZIER
1856-1930

Such, O Mother of Spirits, was our birth,
Our birth long ago, sped by your cosmic ray,
Birth to the meaning of the lasting world.

SIGNET, SIGNET CLASSICS, MENTOR, PLUME AND MERIDIAN BOOKS
are published *in the United States* by
The New American Library, Inc.,
1301 Avenue of the Americas, New York, New York 10019,
in Canada by The New American Library of Canada Limited,
81 Mack Avenue, Scarborough, 704, Ontario,
in the United Kingdom by The New English Library Limited,
Barnard's Inn, Holborn, London, E.C. 1, England.

18 19 20 21 22 23 24 25 26

PRINTED IN THE UNITED STATES OF AMERICA

CONTENTS

Acknowledgments

THIS BOOK is indebted to Fred T. Marsh and to Arabel J. Porter for editorial help both laborious and creative; to B. Ashburton Tripp for the production of the maps; to Laura Thompson for critical and productive help throughout, and for a number of ideas central to the theme; to The Viking Fund of New York for financial aid which made possible a re-study of the Spanish and North American colonial records as part of a wider study of colonialism in the present; to Charles Wood Collier for the thinking and initiative which launched the work of integral conservation in Indian country, and for the clue to the basic polity of the Incas; to Donald Collier for analysis of all the literature on Peyote, for understanding of the social function of the Sun Dance, and for data on Indian cultural areas; to Emma Reh for examination of source documents on the Jesuit Utopia of Paraguay; to the staff of the Institute of Ethnic Affairs, who variously facilitated the book's production; and to The New American Library of World Literature, Inc., through whose initiative and aid the book exists at all.

Since this book is an imperfect rendering of the thoughts and strivings of a multitude, the indebtedness reaches to individuals too numerous to name, yet with hesitation a few are named: Stella M. Atwood, Willard W. Beatty, Alida C. Bowler, Oscar W. Chapman, Pearl Chase, Felix S. Cohen, Lucy Wood Collier, Bronson M. Cutting, Charles de Y. Elkus, Haven Emerson, James A. Frear, Manuel Gamio, Howard S. Gans, Mary A. Gibson, Chauncey S. Goodrich, Richard W. Hanna, Rene d'Harnoncourt, Allan G. Harper, John R. Haynes, Lorenzo Hubbel, Ernst Huber, Harold L. Ickes, William King, Clyde Kluckhohn, Alexander and Dorothea Leighton, Nathan R. Margold, Louis Marshall, Robert Marshall, D'Arcy McNickle, Virginia Mishnun, Luis Chavez Orozco, Michel Pijoan, Maria Rogers, Max L. Rosenberg, Moises Saenz, Emil J. Sady, Ward Shepard, Huston Thompson, Henry A. Wallace, Walter V. Woehlke.

Thanks are due to *Social Research, The Survey Graphic* and *Common Ground* for permission to use, with changes, in three chapters of the book, material previously published by them; and to the other publishers and authors who have generously given permission to quote from their works

CHAPTER I

The American Indian and The Long Hope

THEY had what the world has lost. They have it now. What the world has lost, the world must have again, lest it die. Not many years are left to have or have not, to recapture the lost ingredient.

This is not merely a passing reference to World War III or the atom bomb—although the reference includes these ways of death, too. These deaths will mean the end if they come—racial death, self-inflicted because we have lost the way, and the power to live is dead.

What, in our human world, is this power to live? It is the ancient, lost reverence and passion for human personality, joined with the ancient, lost reverence and passion for the earth and its web of life.

This indivisible reverence and passion is what the American Indians almost universally had; and representative groups of them have it still.

They had and have this power for living which our modern world has lost—as world-view and self-view, as tradition and institution, as practical philosophy dominating their societies and as an art supreme among all the arts.

By virtue of this power, the densely populated Inca state, by universal agreement among its people, made the conservation and increase of the earth's resources its foundational national policy. Never before, never since has a nation done what the Inca state did.

By virtue of this same power, the little pueblo of Tesuque, in New Mexico, when threatened by the implacable destroying action of government some twenty-five years ago, starved and let no white friend know it was starving. It asked no help, determined only to defend its spiritual values and institutions and its remnant of land which was holy land.

If our modern world should be able to recapture this power, the earth's natural resources and web of life would not be irrevocably wasted within the twentieth century, which is the prospect now. True democracy, founded in neighborhoods and reaching over the world, would become the realized heaven on earth. And living peace—not just an interlude between wars—would be born and would last through ages.

My own work for the present is no longer concentrated upon the American Indian. It is no longer confined to the field of direct endeavor which I think of as seeking the renewal of human personality. My main effort now is the United Nations and involves some of the immediate problems which brought the United Nations into being. We must try now in a world of immediate crisis to deal with the hurtling external factors. There are institutional structures to be built, electoral decisions demanding every power of persuasion, aims of statesmanship to be achieved; and for these tasks many thousands of us are needed because our race, with all its lost values and values not yet lost, is wavering on the verge of self-destruction.

True, the deep cause of our world agony is that we have lost that passion and reverence for human personality and for the web of life and the earth which the American Indians have tended as a central, sacred fire since before the Stone Age. Our *long* hope is to renew that sacred fire in us all. It is our only long hope. But the externals we have made our gods are in the saddle now. In our present crisis and out of our inadequacy we must try to sway the immediate event.

Yet now I find myself attempting this book about the Indians, and attempting it in the full consciousness of the world crisis. That is because of the profound, the stupendous fact about them: They were, and in representative areas still are, concentrated upon the attainment, through social ministration, of adequate human personalities, and upon the living, creative union of these personalities with the earth and its web of life—with the universe and the God. We must pursue the long hope even while we attempt emergency actions within our cataclysm. Our emergency actions will be stronger if we dwell on the long hope, too.

Since this first chapter is in a somewhat personal vein, I shall tell how the long hope came to my own life through the Indians. Rather, how it was renewed in my life and brought into the present after I had come to believe that it was only a dream for some far future time.

I was thirty-five years old. I had organized and taught in the fields of social work and community development from New York to California. I had probed, with whatever resource I could command, the effects of machine technology and mass production and mass communication on the lives of peoples. I had studied industrial unionism and distributive co-operation and had worked at adult education, public recreation and racial relations. I had experienced the disillusionments following World War I.

Repeatedly, I had been solicited on behalf of America's Indian peoples; but always I had resisted and refused. It was too late, I believed; that golden age was done.

And any golden age was done! Not in our time was that profound sense of living to be regained by men in groups. I think I viewed accurately, back in those early years after the first World War, the sickness—not a passing one—of our age: its externalism and receptive sensualism, its hostility to human diversity, its fanatical devotion to downgrading standardization, its exploitative myopia, and that world fascism and home fascism which the boundless, all-haunting insecurity and the consequent lust for personal advantage were bringing to fatal power.

So during that year, at thirty-five years of age, I brought abruptly to an end all my professional connections. I had been serving as Director of Community Organization for the State of California. I believed that I was done with public work, and I wanted to make the decision final. With my wife, three young sons and their dogs, I departed for the Sonora Mountains of Mexico. The family would camp there for a year or longer. It was the desert we wanted—the nonhuman wilderness.

We were a month on the journey, camping just above tidemark along the Southern California seabeach. Then came, from Mabel Dodge (now Mabel Luhan) at Taos, New Mexico, a renewed appeal. She had sent the word many times before. Her letters, in mythopoeic imagery, had tried to describe stupendous facts within tiny dimensions at an Indian pueblo concerning whose very existence, except as a show place, I was skeptical. But, "You can detour here, and go on to Sonora so easily," she urged. So the little party detoured; and it did not enter Mexico until eleven years had passed.

We climbed to the Taos plateau in a blinding snowstorm, just before Christmas. Then while great snowflakes descended at

twilight, we watched the Virgin and Child borne from the
Christian church high along an avenue of fires to a vast chanting of pagan song. After two days, the Red Deer Dance began,
and the Sacred Mountain which haunts the sky northwestward
from Taos shuddered, and poured out a cold, flaming cloud to
the sun and all the stars. It seemed that way. And veritably,
within its own affirmation, through a multitudinous, stern, impassioned collective outgiving, the tribe's soul appeared to wing
into the mountain, even to the Source of Things.

Once before—almost twenty years before—I had been storm-
shaken as on that Taos day. That was upon my discovery of Walt
Whitman during my seventeenth year. I was rocked; it was like
an hallucination of earthquake; a sudden dread fear; the time-
horizon pushed back in a moment and enormously; and then the
rebound from somewhere deep within and great without, and
exaltation; and the whole summer forest, viewed from a hilltop,
seemed to sway and leap in a rejoicing dance. That solitary experience of "cosmic consciousness" had been mine, that forever
solitary translation. But here, at Taos, a whole race of men,
before my eyes, passed into ecstasy through a willed discipline,
splendid and fierce, yet structural, an objectively impassioned
discipline which was a thousand or ten thousand years old,
and as near to the day of first creation as it had been at the prime.

Here was a reaching to the fire-fountain of life through a
deliberate social action employing a complexity of many arts.
Here was the psychical wonder-working we think we find in
Greek drama as lived out in Athens four hundred years before
Christ. And here it was a whole community which entered into
the experience and knew it as a fact. These were unsentimental
men who could neither read nor write, poor men who lived by
hard work, men who were told every day in all kinds of un-
sympathetic ways that all they believed and cared for had to
die, and who never answered back. For these men were at one
with their gods.

That year, and over the twenty-five years since, and among
many Indian tribes, I was to witness many times the evocation
of dominions and powers within the soul through their evocation from the universe without. I was to learn something of
the kinds of personality-structures shaped through lifelong,
age-long personal and social striving; shaped to the end that the
tribe was at one with the world—the universe, which called
for this mortal consciousness and which, in turn, delivered itself
into the tribal human will and required the action of that will.

The Taos experience, twenty-six years ago, changed my life

plan. But not immediately, since the view of most anthropologists that the Indian's spirit (and all so-called aboriginal spirit) has to die, stubbornly possessed my mind. After a year or two, becoming familiar with the sheer force of the facts of Pueblo Indian life, I modified my fatalistic position. But then, I thought, these Pueblo Indian city-states are a case apart. They are unique. At the outer margin of the old Spanish Empire in the New World, they had been left in quiet, more or less, and had had time and peace to learn how to "guard the valid old and build the valid new." Most Indian tribes could not possibly have this survival quality.

For years I believed that the long, remorseless course of events, the social destruction piled on biological destruction which the white man had wrought upon the Indians, must have killed, in most Indians, that most profound of their spiritual possessions—the one our sick world most needs. That possession is a way of life at once simple, since it is disciplined, and complex: it involves world-view and sentiment of self; institutionalized tradition and symbol-invested belief, which implicitly or explicitly realizes man as a co-partner in a living universe—man and nature intimately co-operant and mutually dependent. It is a way of life which realizes the individual and his society as wholly reciprocal and both of them as drawing value and power from the racial and cosmic past and transmitting value and power to the racial and cosmic future, and past and future are not only that which in linear time-sequence has been or is yet to be, but are propulsive, efficient, living reality here and now.

This kind of world-view and self-view involves the human personality in "abysmal deeps," since it is one with the cosmos; and the cosmos is eternal depth, being one with the soul.

W. H. Hudson, in that most precious book *Far Away and Long Ago,* wrote of that inherited *animism* which he found to be irrepressible in himself. Indeed, it suffused his whole feeling nature and made life good. His intellect rejected animism, though he knew it was undying in human nature; his intellect viewed "this visible world as what it actually is—the stage to which man has been summoned to play his brief and unimportant part, with painted blue and green scenery for background." Perhaps a dawning age will find itself freed from the imprisoning dichotomies of the Cartesian Century; perhaps not, since that which in our nature and society makes what we currently call fascism may end by turning man wholly inward upon himself emotionally, as the angry devourer of his own soul, and outward on nature as a mechanical exploiter, no more.

I believe that the answer will contain our fate. Their own answer, the Indians still living in their societies continue to affirm. Self-willed, self-wrought personality excellence, empowered by the whole social institution of the tribe and of the race, is more than a merely practical thing, according to their answer—according to their view of selfhood, society and the wide world. It is the very essence of cosmic survival and victory.

As we traverse Indian history from the Conquest down to their present-day strivings, and up and down the two continents, we come upon the Indian affirmative over and over again. We shall meet that affirmative—which this writer, at least, was so slow to understand—all through the record. For through all the slaughter of American Indian biological stocks, the slaughter of their societies and trampling upon their values, strange as it may seem, they have kept the faith. The inner core-value, complex and various, has not been killed.

And since it has not been killed, it never will be. Be it for now or a hundred years from now, or a thousand—so long as the race of humanity shall survive—the Indian keeps his gift as a gift for us all.

Could we make it our own, there would be an eternally inexhaustible earth and a forever lasting peace.

Societies exist. They create a people's temperament, the world-view and the color and structure of personality among their members. They deep-dye the peoples; and myriad are the dyes and juxtapositions of colors with myriad patterns. Present-day men are not everywhere the same; men on the average through recorded time have never been everywhere the same. This is because societies differ one from the other; they make the man. To individuals they are nurture, shaper and fate.

Societies as the shapers and sustainers of life were implicitly, even explicitly, denied to exist by the epoch immediately preceding our own; the assertions or assumptions of that epoch— call it the period of industrial revolution, or the nineteenth century—govern our thinking today. The practical consequences are enormous, are even decisive for evil. Not only our popular mind, but also the minds of most of the workers in the nascent social sciences remain profoundly, unconsciously biased by the nineteenth-century presumptions as to the nature of economic and political man.

What were those presumptions? To state them briefly is to over-simplify, but here are some of them.

The "free market" and laissez-faire doctrines and practices viewed the human world as an aggregation of persons—individuals—each of whom was controlled by a universal, and therefore interchangeable, rational or calculating economic self-interest. The law of the free market was considered to be the law of human life. The free market was lord of all; and if it wrought havoc upon societies, heritages, ethical and esthetic values, family and community life, *and even the natural resources of earth itself,* it remained the overriding principle; it dominated conduct and assured ultimate salvation. It would eventually heal every wound it inflicted.

The Industrial Revolution contained the assertion of a certain complex of "values," made supreme over any other values which might exist. These values were those of wealth as an end in itself and wealth as the means to power; these overriding values were believed to contain within themselves the dynamics of humankind. They were society. Human process was individual process under the stimulus, universally efficient, of physical want and the money-lust or money-for-power lust. True it was that as viewed through these core-values and postulates about the nature of men, there did still exist facts of non-economic culture, institutions, languages, prejudices. They existed to be made use of, or circumvented, or endured, until the core-values of the Industrial Revolution could be made utterly regnant and its postulate as to human nature could be made wholly true through the rearrangement of human conditions and the re-conditioning of men's minds.

And true it was, also, that there were needs to be met, which as yet the free market seemed unable to take care of; especially, there were havocs wrought by the free market which had to be compensated for. These were concerns of philanthropy and the political State; and it was presumed that they could be coped with through a direct traffic between philanthropy and the State, on the one hand, and individuals requiring schooling, health aid, charitable relief, and recreation, on the other hand. So to the pulverizing uniformities of free-market economic operations were added the denaturing uniformities of philanthropic and political-State services.

I am not attempting here a critique of industrial-revolutionary nineteenth-century thinking and actions. I wish merely to indicate how the obliviousness toward, and the intellectual denial of the effective existence of, society and the many societies came to be. Additional factors were also responsible, and these additional factors continue to operate both massively and subtly today.

One of these factors was the mere condition, aside from any theoretical rationalization, which the Industrial Revolution produced—the uprooting of populations, the disintegration of neighborhoods, the end of home and handcrafts, the supremacy of the machine over the man, the immense impoverishment of the age-old relationships between the generations, the increased mobility of the individual, the enormous expansion of commercialized recreation, the quest by mass-circulating newspapers, the movies and radio for lowest common denominators. All this confused, degraded, and even sometimes destroyed the societies utterly.

Because the free market's rationally self-interested man is only a small fragment of the human race, and because if men cannot have good societies they will have worse ones, there took form those new societies, exploitative of the psychotic trends in men, which World War II was waged to suppress. Yet can the psychopathic pursuit of a basic need be stopped through war or force, if the healthful pursuit of basic needs is made impossible by the condition or drift or fanaticism, or the myopia, of a world's age?

I shall mention only two additional, linked factors which helped to make that obliviousness toward society and the many societies which was of the nineteenth century and is of today.

One of these factors was—and is—the urge of science for mechanistic findings, rectilinear cause-and-effect findings, findings which presume that the universe is an aggregation of separate particles moving and moved by next-to-next action. Biology is only chemistry. Purpose is only epiphenomenal. Ideas are masked wishes. Societies are only fixed or drifting aggregations of "traits" which pass from man to man. Even the metaphorical attribution of "organic" inwardness, resourcefulness, reproductive power, personality, where societies are in question, is smiled at or frowned on. With Einstein, Whitehead and their generation, this compulsion of science has been deflected, perhaps reversed, where the cosmos or the atom is the subject of discourse, enterprise or prediction; but the urge of the century gone is still the urge of most political thinking and most social science.

Hence the failure—even the absence of strong urge—in most of social science to view society and the societies with intense, creative preoccupation, with the imaginative boldness which might illuminate our minds and the minds of statesmen and educators everywhere, which might put us on the track of hope and of happiness.

The final factor is that for more than a century the best minds of the Occident have accepted as fundamental the isolation of the individual, have not sought to bind themselves with either the ancient societies or with such emergent societies as labor, the co-operatives, the re-asserting folk-movements. They have not tried to understand, and have not tried to do anything adequate or persevering about, that starvation of the soul within themselves and all of us, owing to that *sheet erosion and gully erosion in human life* which is silently wasting our own society and all western societies into a sea of endless night.

Over-simplification is the price of brevity. I shall not try to brighten the picture through reference to the awakenings and regenerations of ethnic enterprise in many parts of the world. My province here is the Indian of the Americas.

The Indian knew the meaning of society as creator of personality and as organizer of man with universe, through many aeons before ever the white man came. He kept alive, and was made alive by, a multiplicity of contrasting societies.

The white conqueror, for reasons military, economic and religious, pronounced sentence of death on the Indian societies. Through century-long years of slavery, expropriation, physical decimation, and propaganda directed to the Indian against the Indian spirit, the conqueror worked hard to carry out the Indian's death sentence.

A broad view of Indian history from 1492 until recent years shows a death hunt against the Indian societies. To many of the societies, the death hunt brought annihilation, death everlasting. To others it brought wounds that seemed mortal; but with an astounding regenerative power they arose from the rubble. Harried into the wastes, secreted there for lifetimes, and starving, still the Indian grouphoods, languages, religions, culture systems, symbolisms, mental and emotional attitudes toward the self and the world, continued to live on. Not fossilized, unadaptive, not sealed into the past, but plastic, adaptive, assimilative, while yet faithful to their ancient values, these many societies somehow held their own. A few of them burgeoned right on through the centuries, and entered our own day with the noise and shine of waters gushing from their ancient sources. More, many more, sustained only a life covert, indrawn; but they sustained the core and genius of their way of life. When so very, very late, and perhaps for only a brief term of years (none can be sure, as yet) some of the white man's societies lifted their sentences of death from these all but invisible Indian societies, the response was a rush of human energy, a creativity industrial, civic, esthetic. How swiftly, with what flashing brilliance, with what terrible joy, these long-immured, suddenly reprieved little societies demonstrated the truth which our age has lost: that societies are living things, sources of the power and values of their members; that to be and to function in a consciously living, aspiring, striving society is to be a personality fulfilled, is to be an energy delivered into the communal joy, a partner once more in the cosmic life.

So the Indian record is the bearer of one great message to the world. Through his society, and only through his society, man experiences greatness; through it, he unites with the universe and the God, and through it, he is freed from all fear. Those who accept the Indian message and lesson will know how intense, even how awful, is the need for creators and creative effort in the field of understanding and discovery of the nature and meaning of the societies of mankind.

CHAPTER 2

The Indian of Prehistory

THE RED Indian, like other disinherited peoples, is of the present and the future; and he is coming into his own. The Stone Age lives and moves now in his memory. His social energy stems directly from the long hungers and imprisoned strivings of mankind through the centuries. It is not the four hundred and fifty years of ordeal under white domination only that move on in the Indian's soul and in his practical daily living. Farther back are the great cultures and civilizations of his people, ever present in his mind—the Toltec and Aztec consolidations, the Mayan creations, the Inca Empire, the great nations and groups of nations of what is now the United States and Canada. Strangest of all are the unmutilated and undiminished Stone Age societies whose journey through millenniums has brought them into the world's present hour.

Not in kind but only in degree does the Indian differ from other men in the "livingness" of his past. The events that today are shaking and changing our planet bring into view the unextinguished past hardly less than they expose the storms and torrents of change. Out of what time has come the archetype of the German, the Englishman, the Celt, the Japanese, the Chinese? From what far time have come down those values that World War II was fought to save? In India, how enormous is the time and bulk of the continuing past? What hundreds of socially living pasts, going back to the dawn of Asia, are embraced within the confines of the Soviet republics? How much history is contained within the Church? "The dead are not dead but alive." And what is the past of the peoples and their cultures and civilizations of the American hemisphere, on the soil of the two continents of which the white man is only a very recent intruder? Whence did these people come and how long ago?

They came from Asia by way of the Bering Strait at a date so far back that the long extinct horse and camel, the giant beaver and giant bear, the four-horned antelope and the dire wolf and mammoth were their foes and their prey. Their imperishable artifacts (stone arrowheads and spear points, stone knives, hand-worked stone of different shapes) are found in caves and underground in Texas, New Mexico, Arizona, California, Utah, Nevada, Oregon, Wyoming, Nebraska, Minnesota, Colorado, and Saskatchewan in Canada.

The time of their coming was within the Pleistocene or glacial epoch. Most archeologists believe it was near the close of the last glacial period, somewhere between fifteen and twenty thousand years ago, and that their culture was comparable to that of the Late Paleolithic or possibly Early Neolithic in Europe.

The year 13,000 B.C., or perhaps 18,000 B.C., saw these migrant hunters moving across the great central plain of Alaska, which was not ice-covered in the late Pleistocene era, and south-eastward down an open corridor along the eastern slopes of the Rocky Mountains. Their journeys and diffusions did not stop until the whole hemisphere had been traversed and occupied. Their petrified footprints are found beside the petrified footprints of bison in Nicaragua. The bison departed from Nicaragua millenniums ago. In Brazil and Ecuador their imprint is found, and finally in Southern Patagonia. There, in the cave called Palli Aike, within an extinct volcano's crater, have been found bones of the ground sloth and extinct horse, cremation burials of ancient Indians, and artifacts belonging to periods

widely separated in time. The Patagonian remains are estimated to be between 3,000 and 5,400 years old.

The migrants from Asia were of mongoloid stock. The
mongoloid stock includes the Chinese, Japanese, Burmese and
Tibetans, Siamese, Malays, Eskimos and Lapps, Finns, Magyars,
Turks and American Indians. The migration was episodic ,and
trickling, probably over many thousand years. Those who came
were hunters and fishers exclusively; all of the vast development
of Indian agriculture took place in the Western Hemisphere.
They brought fire with them, and at a later time the dog and
their tool-making skills, and nothing else of which a trace
remains. They brought a language, of course, or languages, but
no affiliations among Indian and Asiatic languages can be
demonstrated; so all the multitudinous development of the Indian languages is native to the Western Hemisphere.

In Europe, archaeology finds a gap of millenniums separat-
ing the Paleolithic (Old Stone Age) from the Neolithic (New
Stone Age) man. In America, too, that gap is found, though the
time-period may be shorter. Did Paleolithic man perish, to be
replaced after hundreds or thousands of years by Neolithic
migrants, or did he blend with these new men and societies?
In America, physical anthropology—body-size and head-form
particularly—suggest blending, not replacement; but any sure
answer awaits further archaeological discovery, now fast advancing. Whatever the future answer be, it appears now that
the Old Stone Age and New Stone Age men and cultures were
in their essentials similar, while in general, the movement was
toward technological advancement.

Any conception of uniform speeds of development or uniform sequences of change must be put by. The few Indian
societies of the dawn became hundreds of societies of startling
diversity and contradistinction, over ten thousand years. The
details of change are gone into the past forever, but the inven-
tions which they led to, and the social forms, the tempers of
mind, the spiritual devotions and the world-view of the Stone
Age Indian, marched on into historic time, *and they march on
in our time*.

During the four hundred and fifty years that the white man
has occupied the new world, he has improved many agricultural
products. But, according to Edwin L. Walker of the Southwest
Museum in Los Angeles, the white man has not developed a
single major agricultural product from its wild growth, with
the possible exception of *guayule;* whereas the ancient Indians
developed more than twenty important products. "In addition,"

says Walker, "they cultivated or utilized a great number of wild growths, all of which, acquired by the world, aggregate more than half of our present agricultural wealth."

Maize or Indian corn, for example, probably was developed back in prehistoric times in Central or South America, and its domestication brought a revolution in Indian life on both continents. It brought about the change from wandering to settled life and the possibility of such populations as those estimated for the Inca Empire at its height—ten to sixteen million. Maize was grown in prehistoric time from Canada to Patagonia and from sea level to heights of 14,500 feet.

The development of corn by prehistoric Indians has been called the most remarkable achievement in agricultural history. Of all grains, corn is the most completely domesticated, being the only one that cannot sow itself or take care of itself. It must be husked, shelled, planted, cultivated, usually fertilized, sometimes irrigated and finally harvested.

Let me stress especially a fact upon which all scholars are agreed. Maize, which antedated the oldest of the civilizations that grew up in Mexico, Central America and South America, was the most difficult and one of the most fundamental agricultural creations. Without it, these cultures and civilizations could not have come into existence. It was ancient, tribal man of the primary group who created it.

Just so, the prehistoric Indian contributed to the world the potato and the sweet potato, manioc, from which comes tapioca (a staple today in Oceania and throughout the tropics), pineapple, avocado, artichoke, peanuts, the cultivated strawberry, lima and frijole and kidney and tonka beans, squash and pumpkin, chocolate, rubber, quinine and cocaine, and tobacco. There are over forty lesser crops which were first developed and cultivated by the Indians—for example, mate, maple sugar, pecans, brazil nuts, butternuts, and sarsaparilla. From Virginia to California they processed acorns into an important food.

Much has been made, in very recent years, of the remarkable developments in the hybridization of maize, which is of revolutionary importance in its field. There are those who consider the Indian an unfortunate who needed to improve his corn but lacked the ingenuity to develop "hybrid" corn. Actually, the white man lacked it for 440 years after the Indian, who created it from wild growth, gave it to him. The Indian had created it as his staff of life back in Neolithic, even Paleolithic, time. And his work remains one of the most difficult and important achievements in genetics to this date.

If one stops to consider what all of these crops, and the development of maize especially, testifies to of experimentation, of continuity, of application through seasons, through generations and ages, he will be less likely to think of the Indian as a child-like "savage." Yet the white man's estimate of Indians as "savages" dies hard. And the white man's estimate is important because it dominates consciously and unconsciously his policy and also his manner and behavior toward Indians as toward the other peoples whom he calls "marginal" to his civilization.

What were they like, in inward experience, these dawn men of the Western Hemisphere?

I think the answer challenges the general conception, so familiar even among those who should know better—that of their being "primitive" men and "savages," inchoate men. It challenges even much of contemporary anthropology.

Thousands of years of social striving were behind man already when he entered America. He had long demonstrated, as he went on demonstrating, and continues to demonstrate today in the American southwest desert, the truth that intensity of life, form in life, beauty in the human relationship, happiness, and amplitude of personality are not dependent on complexity of material culture or on that "security" which in the world of today has come to be a controlling objective. The essential goods of life were had by man—were created by man—far, far back in the Old Stone Age; and there are groups of men here and now who know and prove what these essential goods were and are, and how they were and are and can be created and sustained.

This view will waken incredulity, even a suspicion of fantasy, in the minds of many readers. It is hard for us, citizens of an age of giant external power, to conceive that the human, psychic and social values, which on their eternal march are traversing our moment of time, or which perhaps are waning from our society, were not created by ourselves.

Though the facts of anthropology sustain the view which I am taking—the view that many-sided greatness of life very anciently moved through structured personality in structured societies with histories consecutive and evolving—it is not the view of most anthropologists today.

The Stone Age community faced the two worlds of man and nature without any of those impersonal instruments which science has created. It engaged, it grappled naked-handed with, antagonists now banished from civilized life and, more often, with antagonists now relegated to technological specialists. The dawn man's body was engaged in this grapple; his imagination and his mystical perceptions were engaged; his family and his group were engaged with him. That he should feel power, should feel exultation, was a pre-condition of that biological vigor necessary against the possibility of tribal extinction or enslavement. His animistic and magical world-view led him to an assumption which became one of the molding forces of history. That assumption, which he worked over into his institutions, was this: That intensity of consciousness—concentrated, sustained longing and the feeling of power, joy, happiness, beauty, and of union with the sources of being—was effectual in the magical control of nature through co-partnership with the gods.

Hence was built and sustained the life art. The elements of this life art were language, song, dance, ceremonial, craftsmanship, ascetic discipline, fighting, and the chase. All of these, including language, were sustained by unwritten tradition, and the tradition was communicated through the generations by systematized education. Usually the education was aimed toward, and was carried out from, the crisis of adolescence in the individual and the crises of sacred ceremony in the group. The group itself was that kind of group of highest potency, the "primary," or face-to-face, social group.

Our modern Occidental life has submerged the primary social group; the century behind us lost even the memory of its meaning. But in the human background, the primary social group looms enormous in terms of the human nature which it made possible through a hundred thousand years or longer. The primitive primary social group *as actually experienced by any given one of its members* often was more massive and more complex and versatile than a whole nation of today *as experienced by any given one of its members*. For the primitive group required of its members intensity, plunged each of them into much of the whole of the social heritage, applied itself to the personality development of every man, and in immemorial ritual transfigured each of its individuals into a partnership with the forces of the universe.

Indeed, not merely as experienced by its members, but in objective reality, the ancient primary social group often had enormous complexity. It moves through our day unchanged at its core. Any one of the more than twenty Pueblo tribes in the United States could serve as an example. These tribes contain two hundred, five hundred, a thousand members. Their laws and languages, their racial bibles and folklores and poetic literatures, are carried in memory alone. Their vocabularies, universally possessed by their members, in number and range and subtle distinctiveness of words dwarf our print-reading average man's vocabulary. Yet when put into writing, their languages, with all the record they carry, yield but a shadowy sketch of the social life and personal expressiveness of the tribe.

This is because, with primitive peoples, the literally translatable expression of the spoken word is not the revealing expression. Hardly more than a lyric of Blake or Tennyson can primitive speech be translated into prose. Saturated with imagination, formed by imagination, the language enters into its fullness when it is sung, when it is danced, when the visual symbolism of craftwork and of ceremonial drama construe and expand its intent. Then great and ample speech takes form, and every member of the group joins in the amplitude of speech. "They of the earth-grown cities know what Homer knew."

If the primitive group molded its members toward conduct alone (which is tacitly assumed by most anthropologists as well as most laymen), then the group's significance to modern life would not be great. But if there is anything written clear across the almost infinite diversity of primitive society, it is that the group molds its members toward emotion, toward the experience of crises of realization and of conscience, and toward a profoundly romantic world-view which includes a profoundly romantic view of man in the world. Intensity of will, according to the primitive view, exercises in a direct manner effects upon the universe. Spirit, and not mechanical operations alone, enters into every process and is a controlling force even in primitive technology. The gods walk on every road of man, and every road of man is sacred. For the tribe to survive, even for the world to survive, requires intensity—intensity within form —in man. Hence, to an extent hardly imaginable in our modern society and state, the ultimate concentration of the primitive group is upon education—upon personality development. Every experience is used to that end, every specialized skill and expression is bent to that end. There results an integration of body–mind and of individual–group which is not automatic, not at the level of conformity and habit, but spontaneous, essentially spiritual, and at the level of freedom. Many readers will resist this statement, and as in most matters that are essential in human life, the proof that it is true cannot be coercive. Modern man really does not like any suggestion that he has fallen away from a greater good which he once had. But let once the mind be opened, let once a curious and sympathetic interest be born, and then the data of ethnology yields overwhelming conviction on the statement here made. And there are many who, going among primitive groups that exist today, experience the truth, are somewhat wildly moved by joy, and then are moved by a desolating sadness, believing that this mighty significance must die. It is dying in the central Australian desert now, as it died in California eighty years ago; but at least among today's Indians, there are tribes sophisticated in the way of modern life, in daily contact with modernity across centuries, in which the ancient significance has not died.

Man's society since it began has coped with two problems, inseparably related to one another and containing all possible problems. One was to know and control physical and biological nature; the other was to know and beneficently control human nature.

Ancient man in his primary social groups dared not become engrossed in one of the two tasks to the obliviousness of the other, for to do so would have meant extinction. Moreover, his animistic world-view, joined with his belief in the cosmic efficacy of the human will, kept the two problems and tasks involved, each with the other, at every point of life. Technologically, ancient man in his primary social groups advanced slowly. In the control and beneficent development of human nature through institutions he advanced fast and far. Disciplined human nature, absolute in its loyalty to group imperatives, yet possessed by joy and athletically resourceful to meet all tasks and perils, such was the condition of racial survival for this ancient man. In conscious and unconscious enterprises of education on every continent, he met the necessity and he triumphed.

Four main factors aided him. They were the life-shaping potency of the primary social group; the transmitting of heritage mnemonically by planting it emotionally in integrated personalities; the romantic and religious view of man and the world, including the belief in a cosmic potency resident in the human will; and the requirement, which the entire condition of life imposed on the group, of flexibly resourceful personality of great hardihood in the leader and the rank and file alike.

Our present world is rocketing into the infinite in its attempts at control of physical nature; and it is advancing at high speed in its control of biological nature. The direct and indirect results of its technological triumphs have submerged or destroyed most of the personality-forming conditions and institutions which even in our recent age we could rely on. Now we have achieved a weapon which establishes a certain truth. War can no longer be met and controlled through war. Force can no longer be met by force. Nowhere but in the soul can our hope rest now; and the expression of what we call the soul is to be found only in the social art—the art of living. Ancient man could send us a message if he could speak and if he would be heard. For he knew and practiced the truths of the shaping of human nature—truths which we as a society have lost.

CHAPTER 3

The Empire of the Incas

THE INCA Empire of South America has frequently been compared to the Roman Empire. In it we approach mysteries which haunt us the more, now that more facts are known. We meet at least two silent teachings which address themselves to the life problem of our modern world. And we witness the white man's ravin on Indian life. Like Rome, the Inca state died; but like Rome, too, it left its memories, its cultural and physical impress which did not die, which, indeed, is alive today.

This enormous region in South America where the earlier civilizations and the Inca Empire unrolled can be called the mightiest of the inhabited regions of our planet. From the Pacific coast it reaches, in watered valleys and through stretches of desert, to the plateaus at ten and fourteen thousand feet, and on to the Cordillera reaching to twenty thousand feet; then dropping, chasmically, to the eastward jungles embracing the headwaters of the Amazon. In this titanic land, from several centuries before the time of Christ to the Spanish Conquest— some twenty centuries—neighboring civilizations burgeoned from the archaic Indian societies, bloomed into complexity with manifestations of great beauty, diffusing their elements from one to another, then passed their heights and finally shredded away.

There is no written record of any stage of Pan-Peruvian Indian culture except the final one, that of the Incas as told in the Spanish archives and chronicles. "Pan-Peruvian" includes Ecuador, Peru, Bolivia, northern Argentine, and the northern reach of Chile. The Inca stage lasted only three hundred years and the farthest-flung Inca dominion, only one hundred years. The Pre-Inca stages lasted more than fifteen hundred years.

Andean archaeology is today making revolutionary advances. It goes beyond the recorded Inca epoch, and lifts veil behind veil from monumental civilizations that were kindred to one another; the remotest veil until now is that which has hidden the Chavin civilization of highland and coastal Peru. Chavin culture flourished from 100 A.D. to 500 A.D. Nourished from it, but adding different elements, the beginning of the mighty Tiahuanaco, on the shore of Lake Titicaca, took form—initially, a city-state whose influence did not reach beyond the Lake Titicaca neighborhood. Early Tiahuanaco civilization perished from causes unknown as early as 500 A.D. Its conquerors or successors received a powerful new stimulus from the early Nazca civilization of the south-central Peruvian coast; and the so-called Classic Tiahuanacan culture proliferated enormously. After three hundred years, Tiahuanaco fell into decay a second time, and forever, but its symbols and styles, called *Tiahuanacoid,* had become Pan-Peruvian. Meantime, the Early Chimu culture had flowered, reaching to Late Chimu, destined to endure within the Inca Empire until its swift, total destruction by the Spanish conquerors. Finally, the Inca dominion established itself. The relatively crude and quite local Inca system drew strength and form from many, even all of the ancient Andean roots. Viewed sociologically, but not through its fine arts, the Inca dominion fulfilled the epochs gone before; it did not destroy or supersede them. In intensity and in the ways of the spirit it was less than they had been. It added a particular kind of genius of organization and of economic, social and ecological planning; and that same genius, like the Roman genius, imposed a rigidity of benevolent absolutism which somewhat weakened the fountains of life. The Incas were the Romans of the Western Hemisphere.

Toward the earlier epochs,. imagination yearns as toward cloudy mountain ranges where one's feet may never go. Only from their silent artifacts can we try to divine the inwardness of their life. These artifacts are fabrics of the highest perfection, which have outlasted centuries in tombs along the arid coast of Peru; pottery, unexcelled in decorative power and subtlety and in technical process; gold, silver and copper ornaments; and above all, masterpieces of stonework. The supreme craftsmen who wrought these artifacts were not few but multitude; their output over ages was beyond count, and individual creative excellence was not occasional but usual. Only in the later Inca period do evidences of mass and rote production begin to present themselves.

The apex of ancient Andean culture was Tiahuanaco, the

immense. Its name was given it by the Incas and means "City of the Dead." It had been a dead city for hundreds of years when the Incas named it. It was a holy city, and its God was Viracocha, the Uncreated Creator, whom ages later the Ninth Inca, Pachacutec, was to enthrone as supreme over even the Sun God of the Incas. The city occupied the bleak land above Lake Titicaca in modern Bolivia at an elevation of 13,000 feet. Tiahuanaco, to stretch a point, might be called the Athens of Pre-Inca (or Pre-Roman) society.

After three hundred years, about 900 A.D., the Second or Classic Tiahuanacan civilization crumbled or died; but its influence had become Pan-Peruvian. Why Tiahuanaco perished we may never know. The unfinished character of some of its monuments suggests sudden ruin at an invader's hands.

The brevity of these epochs of civilization is impressive, coinciding as it does with the work of these artist-craftsmen who wrought as if within eternity or as though eternity were theirs, and following as it does upon the slowly changing archaic movements of the eight or ten thousand years that had gone before. And not less impressive is the brevity of the Inca epoch—less than three centuries from the first local assertion of Inca power to the destruction of the mighty empire.

The facts about the Incas and their world are so extraordinary that, unless one knows the sources, they have an air of romance, projection or dream. Social anthropology, applied to the living Indians of the Andes, sheds retrospective light, and archaeology enriches our knowledge of the material culture of Inca as of Pre-Inca times; but our main sources must be the same as they were a hundred years ago when William H. Prescott wrote his classic histories of Mexico and Peru. Half blind in a darkened room, Prescott knew, historically, nearly all that we know today—or ever can know. He organized his material with the skill of an artist as well as of an historian.

Because the Incas had not, in the European sense, a written language, they would have suffered oblivion as a nation and empire had it not been for records made by certain scholars, jurists and clergymen who followed in the wake of the Conquistadores. They were Spaniards, mostly, of the early sixteenth century who wrote the histories of the conquests and wrote, also, of the peoples who had been conquered.

In addition to the work of these early chroniclers[1] are the

---

[1]The most important chroniclers were Garcilaso de la Vega, Juan de Sarmiento, the Licentiate Polo do Ondegardo, and Cieza de Leon; the foremost historian was the Jesuit Father Bernabe Cobo.

Spanish archives which even today have not been exhausted.
These consist of royal grants and ordinances, instructions of the
court, letters of the King to his colonial officers, municipal
records, personal diaries, and masses of memoranda and cor-
respondence that passed among the principal actors in the
turbulent drama.

But we are here concerned less with the events of the Conquest than with the way of life of the Inca before the Conquest.
The two eras for a generation overlapped, and coalesced, and
this remarkable fact is to be noted: Whereas the Conquest is
one bitter chapter of ruthlessness and greed, treachery and
cruelty and fanaticism, yet also there went forward, step by
step and year by year, within the Conquest, exhaustive and
objective observation—recorded observation—and a process of
social valuing by priests, jurists, administrators, and emissaries
from the Crown, which in the main was free of racial preju-
dice, and expressive of a mature and rich intellectual culture
resident in Spain. Nor was this intellectual activity indifferent
to justice, or to the welfare of the conquered peoples; rather, it
fed itself into that stream of effort which produced the New
Laws of the Indies and which gave nobility of intent, and in
places and times greatness of humane achievement, to the
Spanish colonial enterprise in the New World.

Briefly, the main characteristics of the Inca society and the
Inca state were these: A communistic or collective absolutism;
a technique of conquest in which warfare was a secondary
means, attraction being the primary one; a body of social legislation unapproached in its humanity in the modern world
before the attempts of very recent times; a land-use technology
which has never been rivaled; administration, very complex in
the absence of a written language, but precise, and reaching
immense distances, no written language, not even a hieroglyphic
record (except for the extraordinary instrument, known as the
quipu); no money in any form; no wheels (although log rollers
were used); a cumulative continuity of government policy and
boldness of administration by a corps of men trained to ad-
minstrate; a monopoly of formal knowledge on the part of
the ruling class under a one-way flow of power from one man
alone—the Inca; religious tolerance in a state which, curiously
enough, made compulsory the official religion—a paradox to be
revealed later.

The span of the Inca dynasty was thirteen generations. Six
of the thirteen generations had passed before the dynasty moved
toward empire. Thus, for practically half its course the Inca

Empire was little more than a local consolidation around Lake
Titicaca. These earlier generations molded the Inca forms;
through the latter generations, which moved so swiftly toward
doom, the forms did not decay. The great expansion of the Inca
Empire may not have commenced more than 125 years before
the Spanish Conquest.

The dynasty's founder was the myth-veiled Manco Capac.
Manco Capac may have been a "culture hero," a composite of
folk-dreaming and of the official poetry of the later time, or he
may have been a highland tribal chief of genius, around whom
folk-dreaming and the later official poetry built their myth.
The earliest historical Inca chief was Sinchi Roca, whose beginning date is fixed at 1105 A.D. by Philip Ainsworth Means and
a hundred or more years later by most scholars. Sinchi means
literally "strong man," or war chief of a highland *ayllu* or tribe.
We have noted that the later, or classic, Tiahuanaco civilization
or consolidation had broken up into its earlier component parts
two or three centuries before; Sinchi Roca may be assumed to
have started his career as war leader of one of these sundered
fragments. He led his own little group to acknowledge his
authority as all-inclusive, and then proceeded by negotiation to
bring the neighboring tribes under his tribe's hegemony.

Without wars, on until his death, Sinchi Roca slowly extended
his consolidation southward along Lake Titicaca. His son,
Lloque Uupanqui, ruled and advanced without war; his grand-
son, Mayta Capac, departed from peace only in local conflicts
which tilted the balance of persuasion. And so through the
period of the next Inca, Capac Yupanqui, and his successor,
Roca II. Then, under Yuhuar-Huaccac, the Incas launched upon
aggressive expansion; but till the end, war was a secondary
reliance, attraction the primary one, and within the empire,
finally extended to 380,000 square miles, a *Pax Romana* prevailed. But war smoldered or flamed along the remote frontiers;
and before the end, dynastic civil war had begun.

The chroniclers dwell much—disproportionately, to my way
of thinking—on the splendors of the Incas' court. When the
Inca traveled through his realm, he did so in great majesty,
seated on a rich litter fitted with loose poles enriched with gold
and silver trappings. There were arches of gold hung with
curtains to afford privacy. The curtains were elaborately dec-
orated with rich ornamentation; on some were embroidered the
sun and the moon; on others great serpents, all symbolical. The
litter was raised on the shoulders of the most important lords

of the empire. Drawing on the source work of Cieza de Leon, Means gives us a brilliant description:

"Around the litter marched the Canari guard, who always surrounded the monarch's person to the number of two thousand. In front of the litter marched five thousand slingers, and after it came two thousand warriors of the Inca caste. All this multitude passed slowly onward in religious silence broken only by the rhythmic shuffle of innumerable sandals. Every little while a halt was made, in order to rest the litter-bearers and to afford the sovereign a chance to admire the view or to hear the plaints of his subjects, who, in vast throngs, lined the roadway to see their divine liege pass on his journey. *They* were not silent, for, as the litter passed along, they shouted, 'Most high Lord, Child of the Sun, Thou art our sole and beloved Lord. The whole earth truly obeys Thee.' "[2]

Let us hold this image in mind when we try to comprehend the mystery of the conquest by Pizarro. When the Inca was treacherously kidnapped and the scores or hundreds of his headmen surrounding him were slaughtered, it was not only the King whom Pizarro held prisoner; it was the Sun God. When the imprisoned Inca forbade reprisals or attempts at rescue, it was the voice which had been obeyed as that of a benevolent god through generations—obeyed absolutely. Such is not the essential meaning of the Incas' downfall; but it is close to the heart of the mystery.

The basis of the Inca Empire, as of other American Indian empires, was agriculture, pursued by the Incas intensively but controlled through long-range planning. The transplanting and colonizing of peoples has been mentioned. It went forward through all the later reigns of the Incas and it served diverse uses—the disposition of groups who might become rebellious, the diffusion of the Quechua language and of the official cult of the Sun. But its prime objective and effect were maximum use of soil, water and vegetative resources, without destroying resources through over-use.

The Incas' practical science of land utilization was rooted in nature-mysticism. No dead earth existed, in the ancient Andean mind. Places lived, not merely existed. The *huaca,* or place-shrine, was everywhere. The whole of the Inca conservation enterprise can be viewed as technology and social organization moved by religion.

The massive public works of the Incas have nearly all perished, but there is one exception, a partial one. That is the

[2]From *Ancient Civilizations of the Andes* by Philip Ainsworth Means. 1931. By permission of the publishers, Charles Scribner's Sons.

erracework which today, in the Andes, reaches from valley floor to the frost line and even higher. The terraces transform steep, even precipitate slopes, into hundreds, thousands of little level fields. Their masonry is rock. With minimum care they outlast the centuries; and it is in soil already ancient at the date of the Conquest, that the Indians of the Andes today do their planting.

For "tribute" work on the terraces, the peoples under the Incas received clothing, subsistence and medicine, and needed raw materials. Labor rotation placed but a light burden on each individual. In the case of the terraces and irrigation systems, the worker's community became the user of the land, and the yield of that part of the land reserved for the Inca flowed back to the community according to need. Thus, it was by nothing resembling slave labor that the immensities of terraces and irrigation aqueducts were constructed.

The Inca's governmental system was constructed on the basis of the *ayllu*, or endogamous tribe, which existed throughout the Andean country as the ultimate social unit. Like the Pueblos of New Mexico and Arizona today, and the village communities of India and Indonesia, the *ayllu* was not merely its people, and not merely the land, but people and land wedded through a mystical bond. Often these ayllus had joined themselves into small states, each ruled by a *curaca* whose authority was hereditary. Rather frequently, these small states had formed themselves into confederacies or compound states, and these, on the Peruvian coast, had become intricately organized kingdoms of the feudal type. All of these facts antedated the Inca's hegemony. Because each state added to the Inca Empire already had its own social structure, ranging from the simple single ayllu up to the large feudal kingdom, the Incas found ready for their use excellent materials with which to strengthen the social fabric of a growing empire. Their genius in such matters as these was great, principally because of their strong tendency toward numerical regularity. The earlier social groupings were irregular, inharmonious as to size, and diverse as to functions. The Incas took them over and reduced them all to suitable places in a symmetrical administrative pyramid.

We can project the Incas' administrative system thus: Ten households under an official, designated from above, from among their own number; fifty households, under an official similarly designated; one hundred households, under a *curaca*, who was one of the nobility; and so on up to five hundred households, one thousand and ten thousand households. Then, forty thousand households, whose officials were called Tucui-ricuc-cuna, or "They who see all." Above these officials were the Apa-cunas, four in number, each in charge of one of the four quarters of the empire, and above these four was the Inca. The officers of the two highest ranks were of Inca blood. Each official chose the one immediately below him in rank, subject only to the overriding authority of the Inca. And below the Apa-cuna level, no *horizontal* interrelation of officials existed; absolute authority flowed down from level to level.

When a state, small or large, became incorporated into the empire, its ruler was made a part of the hierarchy, but each rank of officials was firmly riveted to those above and below it, and the current of authority flowed ever downwards from the source of all earthly power—the Inca—*with no contact between officials of equal rank*.

To this point, the reader's impression will be that of an extremely mechanical organization and a movement of sheer authority. Whence was derived, in such an absolutist system, the continuity of policy, cumulative through centuries, and the benevolence universally diffused? The answer lies in the deliberate building of tradition, through conscious education, among a predestined noble or royal caste, a course which was systematically pursued by the first Incas and those who came after. Those of royal blood were not few but many. The Inca was polygamous—his concubines were hundreds and there were thirteen generations of Incas.

The aristocracy and the administrative class were many more than merely those individuals of royal blood. Pachacutec, the great Inca, found the Incas by blood insufficient in number for the work of the state. He extended the Inca privileges to all inhabitants of the empire who spoke the Quechua language. The headmen of each tribe or state brought within the empire were made Inca noblemen and they or their sons were brought to Cuzco for periods of training. When these local leaders proved to be competent their authority was made hereditary.

The Incas of royal blood, together with the nobility, filled all the administrative posts down through that of the *curaca* or governor of one hundred households; and the royal blood and the nobility monopolized all educational opportunity. The first historical Inca, Sinchi Roca, founded at Cuzco the Yachahuasi, intended to become the national university, and the ninth Inca, Pachacutec, greatly expanded it. Here lived the *amautas*, or philosophers, and the *haravec-cuna*, or poets. They were esteemed by the Incas and by all the people. Many disciples lived with them, chiefly of the blood royal. The philosophers and poets concentrated in their hands the wisdom and the intellectual amenities of life under the Inca regime.

In this school, the Incas and the provincial nobility were taught together, and each Inca monarch in turn received there his immersion into the traditions, ideals and skills, and the policies which became complicated without being fundamentally altered through the three centuries. The "course" of the school lasted four years, of which one year was devoted to teaching the use of the *quipu,* or knot record. Initiation and public examination followed graduation from the school, at sixteen years. "This examination (and initiation)," William H. Prescott relates, "was conducted by some of the oldest and most illustrious Incas. The candidates were required to show their prowess in the athletic exercises of the warrior; in wrestling and boxing, in running such long courses as fully tried their agility and strength, in severe fasts of several days' duration, and in mimic combats, which, although the weapons were blunted, were always accompanied with wounds, and sometimes with death. During this trial, which lasted thirty days, the royal neophyte fared not better than his comrades, sleeping on the bare ground, going unshod, and wearing a mean attire." According to Garcilaso, the candidates were beaten with sticks and forced to stand unflinching while an instructor whirled a club around their bodies so that it almost touched their faces. A single cry or the slightest sign of flinching branded the candidate as a coward.

The first impression, then, of iron authority moving in a one-way track through a mechanized, arithmetical administrative system, must be superseded in part. Within the nobility, education was democratic and intensive. The administrative cast of the whole empire was brought within this education, on an equality at least formal, and probably genuine, with the highest Inca heirs. The teachers were the empire's wisest and noblest men. The details learned were made to flow from a glamorous and mighty mythopoeic source; the epoch of learning was the crisis of adolescence; and the climax of learning was the endurance of ordeals. The future monarch's development unfolded within the learning group. Add the two further facts, that the administrative group was made up of those men or families who had established their leadership previously among the myriad little societies brought into the empire, and that administrative authority during the first centuries of the empire did not descend by primogeniture but was attained through proved individual merit, then can be understood why the Inca autocracy was benevolent and efficient, too, and why within an unlimited absolutism, public policy yet remained undeviating through the generations and was kept experimental and pragmatic. There were Inca sovereigns of manifest personal greatness and others who were self-indulgent and wavering men, but there were none who deviated from the public policies.

All should work, none should work too much or too long, none should suffer want; this was the Inca view. The wealth of the Inca Empire was land and labor. The basic unit, social and economic, was the *ayllu* (tribe). No land of an ayllu could be alienated, and each of its household heads was vested with a right to land. This had been the Pre-Inca system. Under Inca law, one part of the ayllu's land was devoted to the Sun (the state religion), one to the Inca, and one to the local community. All the chroniclers agree that the portion reserved for the local community was ample to maintain its people in comfort. When population increased, the problem was met by grants to the community from the Inca's land, by subsidy from the imperial storehouses, and by redistributions of populations from overpopulated to under-populated lands. These colonizing enterprises were managed with humaneness and skill in the Inca Empire.

Some chroniclers erroneously believed that the State decreed who, among the people, should marry whom. The uselessness of such a policy and the absence of evidence of religious sanction for it make it highly improbable, and I conclude that in general young people chose their own mates, or their parents chose them. Divorce laws for "primary" marriages were severe; therefore, the logical and benign Incas maintained as an institution what we would call the trial marriage.

The penal code of the Incas was sparse but stern; its enforcement was immutable even though it might reach to one of royal Inca blood. However, equity entered into it, as in judging for theft: Did the thief steal wantonly, or because he did not have that minimum of goods which every citizen was entitled to? In the latter case, the judgment reached to the official who had allowed the injustice to arise. The Incas' penal code in its detail was no severer than that of England a hundred years ago, and it rarely needed to be invoked. Outside the entire administrative hierarchy were the "guardians," also called "informers" by the chroniclers. These were of royal blood and were personal representatives of the Inca. They mingled with the people, sought out abuses, examined the workings of policies, and reported directly to the Inca.

Two of the Inca institutions the Spanish conquerors adopted and turned into evil—the *mita* and the *yanacona*. The *mita* was the Inca system of state-required public work, and it was a chief concern of the Incas that this work be duly rotated and be not too demanding. The Spaniards kept the same name and turned the institution into one of homicidal enslavement. The *yanacona*, under the Incas, was made up chiefly of skilled workers (as those in stonework, weaving, metallurgy, accounting) who were exempted from taxes and whose labor was held to be honorable and not to be exploited. The Spaniards changed the *yanacona* into a horde of landless Indians driven from place to place and used without pay for all kinds of personal services.

The Inca unit for measuring land was the *tupu*, sixty paces by fifty. A *tupu* of irrigated farmland was deemed enough for a married couple without children. Each boy born brought an additional *tupu*, each girl a half a *tupu*. Land distribution was in the hands of the officials in charge of ten, fifty or a hundred households. A unique feature of the Inca economic system was the collection of tribute, or taxes in kind, under the control of a principle of moderation, and the subsequent flow of most of these taxes back to the people. Let us note some of the general statutes of the Incas dealing with "tribute." Garcilaso cites them, from a lost work by Father Blas Valera.

1. No person exempted from tribute could ever be called upon for any contribution (to the Inca or the Sun) of merchandise or of work. The exempted classes were: Persons of the blood royal and the nobility; army officers and soldiers while on active duty; all males under 25 and over 50 years (but youths and elderly men were expected to help their kinsmen at their tasks); all women; all sick persons and all incapable persons (but the deaf and dumb were given work suited to them); and all priests of the Sun.

2. Tribute was to consist solely of labor, time and skill as a workman, artisan or soldier. All men were equal in this respect, he being held to be rich who had children to aid him in making up his appointed tribute, and he who had none being considered to be poor.

3. Every craftsman who labored in the service of the Inca, or of his *curaca* (superior), must be provided with all the raw materials, and his employment in this way must not exceed two or three months in the year.

4. A craftsman was to be supplied with food, clothes and medicine at need while he was working, and if his wife and children were aiding him, they also were to be supplied. Thus the tribute-

payer received state compensation for his work. In such work, not time, but a special stint of accomplishment was required of the tribute-payer, so that if he had help from his family, he could finish the task the sooner, and could not be called upon again that year.

5. The surplus of the tribute, after the royal wants had been satisfied, was placed on deposit and drawn upon for the good of the people as required.

6. In special cases tribute was paid in the form of work upon the roads, upon the temples, palaces, aqueducts, bridges, storehouses or other public works. Or the tribute-payers might serve as post-runners or litter-bearers or miners.

Father Valera's record on the subject of collecting the tribute throws illumination on the Incas' administrative system: "At a certain time the collectors and accountants assembled in the chief village of each province, with the *quipu-camoyac-cuna* (knot-record keepers) and by means of the *quipus* and also little pebbles, the accounts and reckonings were cast up in the presence of the officer in charge. They saw, by the knots, the amount of labor the Indians had performed, the crafts they had worked at, the roads they had travelled over by order of their superiors, etc. All this was deducted from the tribute that was due. Then they showed the collectors and the governor each thing by itself that was stored in the royal depots, such as the provisions, pepper, clothes, shoes, arms, and all other things that the Indians gave as tribute, down to the gold, silver, precious stone and copper belonging to the King and the Sun, each item being recorded separately. They also reported what was in store in the depots of each village. The law ordained that the Inca governor of the province should have a duplicate of the accounts in his own custody, to check any error on the part either of the collectors or the payers of tribute."

The quipu was the Incas' sole instrument of counting and also of record. History, laws, vital and other statistics, all were in the keeping of the quipu, which fundamentally was an aid to memory. Its uses were so various that it can almost be termed a form of writing. The typical quipu consists of a long cord from which hang a number of major cords, varying in number from one to more than a hundred. The major cords are about a foot long, and to them are attached minor cords. J. Eric Thompson says:

The reckoning was made by means of knots. Each cord was divided into zones, the lowest representing the numbers one to nine; higher up, the second digits, ten to ninety, were recorded by knots. Higher again was the space for the third digits, one hundred to nine hundred, and if necessary the spaces could be continued indefinitely in the decimal system. Each unit of a digit was expressed by a knot. Thus, 237 was expressed by two knots at the top, a space, three knots, a space, and finally, seven knots.

Colors appear to have indicated the subject of a calculation. Early writers tell us that red cords dealt with war, black with calendar, carmine with the Inca, gray with provincial matters, and so forth. The minor cords apparently must have been used for sub-headings. Thus, if a cord gave the population of a province, town by town, the minor cords may have given the number of children or members of each age-group in the town.[3]

While some quipus were used primarily for numerical record, others amounted to nothing less than complete books. With these quipus the Incas found a way to preserve their history, their laws and ceremonies, as well as their business affairs. The only quipus surviving are those which have been found in graves. It is natural to suppose that legal and historical records represented the last stages of evolution of the quipu as a vehicle of literary expression; that such quipus were few in number; and that, being in the public repositories, they were heavily represented among those thousands burned by the Spaniards. The Spaniards melted down the exquisite art objects of the Incas which were silver and gold in order to transport them more easily. They burned the quipu libraries because of the supposed heathenisms they recorded. The dualism of the impulse of Spanish conquest is symbolized in the burning of the books; for during the identical years of the burning of the books, the great chroniclers were struggling to record, interpret and value the Inca civilization.

The Incas' system of communication, which bound the empire into a physical unity, was one of the wonders of that remarkable civilization. The Inca roads, traversed by runners and burden and litter-bearers, and by the domesticated llama and alpaca, ran from ocean to jungle and from the far south to the far north of the empire. Means points out that, characteristically, the roads ran, whenever possible, in straight lines—for the Incas tended to go straight to their objective.

On the roads, in posthouses, were stationed the highland couriers. Running was greatly cultivated among the Incas as among many Indian peoples; we have seen that it was an element in the initiation ceremony of the Inca elite. The couriers

[3]From *Archaeology of South America* by J. Eric Thompson. 1936. By permission of the publishers. Chicago Museum of Natural History.

were trained from youth, but as in all labor for the state, they were rotated and relieved at short intervals. The posthouses varied in interval from a mile and a half to five miles, according to ascent. Non-stop, all-weather, day-and-night service was kept up on all the arterial roads, primarily for administrative and military reports and orders, but also for transport of light and perishable tribute to Cuzco, to the central storehouses, or the Inca himself who might be on a tour of the empire accompanied by thousands of his train.

Along the roads were also built the *tampu-cuna,* or inns for travelers. These were commodious; their main room was 100 to 300 feet long and 30 to 50 feet wide; and there were private apartments and storerooms in addition. These inns were built, serviced and supplied by the local authorities. In these inns, as we learn from Father Bernabe Cobo's history, "were lodged, wholly at the expense of the Inca, the various classes of official travelers—and there were none but officially sanctioned travelers."

In times of emergency, the running couriers were supplemented through smoke and fire signaling. The smoke and fire code, according to Garcilaso, transmitted news, from as much as 2,000 miles distant, to Cuzco in two or three hours or even less time.

Basic to the civilization of the Incas, and informing it in all its aspects, was the Inca religion—the Religion of the Sun. These were and still remain *huacas,* or place-shrines, many of which used to be temples with priests and priestesses. Above these were the Earth Mother and the Mother Sea, Sun, Moon and Stars. The Inca himself represented the Sun on Earth—more strictly, he *was* the Sun, for Inca means Sun. But that was the symbol, as difficult to explain as the sacred rites of all religions are difficult, if not impossible, to explain.

Stars in the constellation Lyra were guardians over the flocks. The Pleiades were guardians over growing seeds and weather. Certain stars were guardians of wild animals; and the snakes, too, had their guardian stars. Thunder was of the godhead; the Milky Way was a heavenly river whence Thunder drew his rain.

Beyond all other gods—within them and without them—was the Uncreated Creator-God, Viracocha, "ancient foundation, lord, instructor of the world."

The Viracocha concept goes back in ancient Indian society to a time beyond memory. The great chroniclers tell how the ninth Inca came to restore Viracocha to his rightful place, even above the Sun—even above the Inca. But he had existed in the ancient

City of the Dead (Tiahuanaco) from which the Roman Incas had derived their Athenian culture, before Cuzco and the Inca Empire had ever been heard of.

Belief in immortality was explicit and even dominant in Inca life, and carried with it a belief in the on-reaching effects of moral actions. When an Inca died, he was led into the world beyond by his dog, who was slain that he might be there to lead his master. His palace and all the delicacy and splendor that it contained was sealed. Each Inca created his own establishment anew.

The confessional was a developed institution among the Incas, with absolution at the hands of a priest or priestess, and with penances.

There were virgins of the Sun as well as priests of the Sun. At ten years of age, girls were examined and classified by imperial officials; those of greatest beauty, physical perfection and the graces became "chosen women," and were educated in convents near the temples of the Sun. Some returned to their people; some were given as principal or secondary wives to the nobles; some became concubines of the Inca; some, drawn from the nobility, remained the "Virgins of the Sun." But a few were designated at the beginning for sacrifice. These were considered the most fortunate ones. Though the chroniclers assert that in the ceremonies of the Sun there were no human sacrifices, or that the sacrifices were very rare, archaeology has established that human sacrifices did take place. In the cemetery of the sacrificed women at the Sun Temple at Pachacamac, Max Uhle after the year 1900 found many burials of women and children. They were honored and cherished burials, for with the dead were laid the objects dear to them in life.

The Incas were state-builders of a social wisdom and benignancy greater than that of the Antonines of Rome. They built human good through methods of benign absolutism in their brief time (less than 300 years)—yet in the end they were helpless to defend themselves. To an extent that seems to have held good of no other truly ordered society that has ever existed, they enforced a one-way flow of power and responsibility, and they projected the myth that this flow was from the God himself, the Sun. They established for everyone security, and for everyone a sentiment of deep and willing submission to an authority that did in truth furnish kindly protection, lifelong security, even plenitude. All this in a universe where gold and silver were only elements in an art, where money and interest in money, and accumulation, and power, and prestige through accumulation, were non-existent; where the only material value was land, and land was assured to all. Yet when the fierce conqueror came with gunpowder and horse and steel, with a faithlessness unimaginable, and ambitions and motives unimaginable to the Incas and their subjects alike, the Inca state and society were blown into dust.

With the Inca caste there perished the culture and the social energy which had been silently sucked away from every group—local ayllu and feudal kingdom alike—that had been brought within the empire.

Knowledge and wisdom, glory and power, responsibility and self-activity—these, said the first historical Inca, should be for the elite alone. For the people, there should be peace and security, but no longer a local self-determination. And when, in the Inca great century, the Indian genius flowered, as it did flower, the glory of it was for the elite alone. The Inca Sinchi Rocas' thought did not reach on to foretell how in an extreme hour of the peoples' and the rulers' need, the rulers would find the people unmoved to help their benefactors. He did not know that the people would have been impoverished through the usurpation by their rulers of all that makes strength of will, greatness of soul.

Unintentionally, as it were, the Inca system operated toward the sterilization of genius, toward mass mediocrity. It was the deficiency inherent in an absolutism—however benevolent. In the long view, the very benignancy of the state absolutism, its de-socialization and particularly its de-personalizing effects, resulted in death for both the society as a whole and for the intricate system of societies of which it was composed. Probably it would have been conquered in any case eventually through the armed might, ruthlessness and savage brutality of the white man; but it need not have lost its soul in the process.

Almost there is a suggestion of sleep-walking in the manner in which the Inca and his counselors and staff met the Spanish wolf when he came. The plain people could only dimly know what was happening because they had had no representatives and had been methodically excluded from intellectual partnership in the empire. Actually the great Conquest was a kind of palace revolution.

Historians, even recent ones, have, I think, attributed too much to the circumstance of a dynastic civil war which coincided with the arrival of Pizarro. It seems to me that they have the Mexican analogy in mind. Mexico and Peru were very different mpires. Pizarro had no need to use rivalries, had they existed. He needed only to use the godlike absolutism of the kidnapped Inca.

But in one respect the Inca civilization may be tried in the balance and not found wanting. That is a matter of perennial and, as of today, very great significance—the maximum use and conservation of land.

Babylonia and Assyria, Carthage, Greece, Rome and, more recently, Spain destroyed their basic resources (soil and water) through policies which exploited the earth under them without giving the equivalent in return. This also happened in northwestern China; is even now happening in the United States and most of the Western Hemisphere as well as most of Africa.

Second only to the issue of ending war is this world issue of ending the havoc being wrought on the world's food potential. Later in this book we shall witness contemporary Indian tribes struggling to meet this world issue in their own regions. Only in the last fifteen years has the awareness, even, that the issue exists, dawned in the general mind.

Saving and making perpetual the food potential of nations is only subordinately a technological task; predominantly it is a task of social policy and of a re-ordering of the perspectives of men.

It is this task which the Inca Empire made its central one; all policy and action was focused toward it; success was complete, for the first time in history; and the Inca Empire in this matter still challenges, still prophesies, still shows the way.

A population possibly denser than that of today in the same area used the land and its water. None were in want, where today millions are in chronic want. From generation to generation the soil and water resources became more, not less. Today, as ever since the European conquest, the Andean area marches with most of the rest of the world on its way to the destruction of these resources.

Maximum human use of the land and water, with total conservation, was the dominant long-range policy of the Incas. This is their living, increasing meaning to the world.

CHAPTER 4

The Dominion of the Aztecs

DIFFERENT from the Inca civilization were those long gone civilizations of Mexico and Guatemala— Mayan, Zapotec, Toltec, Aztec. The strength and the weakness of the Incas are wholly relevant to our modern issues. The comprehensive achievement of the Incas—harmonious reciprocity between society and earth, sustained through technologies and through administrative practices both subtle and massive— speaks to us imperatively. Their comprehensive error, denial of liberty and responsibility to the people, has its monition for us today. In contrast, the ancient civilizations of Mexico seem to us today to rest rapt in magic dream; and in the dream is blood.

Was it thus in reality? The ancient peoples of Mexico lived *in their own now,* not in ours which may seem as remote as theirs, and as without sequence, to a future time. What was *their* world-view, and what values *to them* did it yield? May it not be that we, in our imagination and understanding, are more time-bound than we know? May it even be that these ancient Mexican and Central American civilizations are doing a work in this very present of ours? For in their silence and their strangeness of light and darkness they attract our modern mind with fascination; they baffle and repel us, but their fascination is renewed. They invite us to dare to cast aside our inhibitions and positive values in the process of trying to understand—inhibitions and values salutary and profound in us but which they did not have. They invite us to a strenuous effort at empathy— at knowing the inwardness of another society which seems so utterly different from, even antipathetic toward, our own. So, they may give us a deepening awareness of that house of many mansions, life in societies. And precisely such a deepening, it may be, is now the world's greatest need.

What is the dominating first impression, made by the archaeological record and the Spanish records alike? It is that of peoples of restless, even explosive, energy and of rich, very versatile artistic endowment, whose statesmanship was also a priestcraft, and who yielded themselves both splendidly and terribly to the allurements and dominance of magical religions. This is the paramount impression, from the beginning of Mayan recorded time, some three centuries before Christ, to the Spanish Conquest and the sweeping ruin the Conquest brought.

I do not refer here to human sacrifice, a phenomenon of the Aztec domination which occupied a mere two hundred years out of two thousand. The Toltec age lay far behind these. It built and rebuilt Teotihuacán, that far-flung harmonious city of temples. Yet farther back reached the Mayans, lavish builders of priestly cities, who were preoccupied through generations with astronomy and with perfecting a marvelously accurate calendar.

Again, at Monte Alban, above Oaxaca, one finds a whole mountain hewed and leveled to be the base of a vast complex of religious structures where the Zapotecs were to repose their hopes. At Cholula, near Puebla, the average man thinks he is climbing a mountain to reach the Catholic church at its summit, but he is climbing a Toltec pyramid built by hands. At La Venta, in the State of Vera Cruz, religious sculptures weighing up to thirty tons, carved out of igneous rock, are found. The nearest source of the rock is fifty miles away. How were these immense blocks of stone moved this long distance down rivers and across great stretches of swamp to where they are now? They were moved by manpower alone; the Mayans had no draft animals and did not know the principle of the wheel.

Do not imagine a priestcraft, dominating kings, who by armed might achieved these vast religious works through the sweat and blood of races of slaves. Through much of the Mayan era, war and the weapons of war hardly existed at all. Among the Aztecs slavery existed, but none were born into slavery. The slave had his own status and rights; and as a rule tribute, whether of manpower or goods, was exacted only with moderation from the subordinate peoples. No, it was the will of whole peoples which built the mighty religious structures and which maintained them.

The power of the religious motivation which swayed these Mexican peoples is better realized if we hold in mind these facts: For the massive work on the religious structures they had only stone tools, supplemented by copper for the more refined tracings. They had no beasts of burden. The land, owing to their husbandry, became densely populated. On the plateau, then as now, rainfall was barely enough, always uncertain. Nothing but profound faith in the utility and necessity of their religions of endless efflorescence, along with the emotional satisfactions derived from their religions, could have given these peoples the strong propulsions, derived from the religions, to carry on the enormous work of construction and to maintain it willingly from age to age.

The expansion and complications of the religions were both continuous and cumulative. Mayan cities were built and then abandoned utterly. Whole populations trekked to new regions and built their templed cities all over again. There were century-long subsidences in Mayan civilization, but the religious continuity was never broken.

The Aztecs' life was one of efficient, many-sided agriculture; of craftsmanship unexcelled in the Western Hemisphere or the world; of much democracy in human relationships. Its social base was the exogamous clan, and within the clan, leadership was achieved and kept through proved individual merit. Clans united into tribes, with equal representation on the tribal council; and the council chose the tribal functionaries on the basis of demonstrated merit. There existed rank, but not caste, the only exception being the quite fluid, shifting slave class. The slave controlled his own family and could in turn hold slaves; none were born into slavery; murder of a slave brought the death penalty to the killer; slavery became a temporary status while a man expiated a crime. Often, families of the poor would rotate their children, one at a time, into temporary slavery.

Productive resources were communally held; but there were lands whose produce was set aside for the religious organizations and other lands whose produce was set aside to pay tribute. Where one tribe established dominance over another, moderate tribute was taken. The bulk of such tribute went to the whole of the dominating tribe through its clans. For distinguished services, as in war, life-tenure of lands, and sometimes the right to the labor of subjugated vassals, was bestowed on individuals, from time to time.

There existed no coinage or other currency, but through the institution of the market, exchanges went on locally and across all Mexico and down as far as Panama; and there was an intertribal, international guild of merchants whose persons were immune even in war, and who penetrated everywhere.

The institution of the judiciary was fully developed, justice was even-handed, and venality or favoritism on the part of judges was punished ruthlessly. Restitution to the injured individual, rather than punishment of the wrongdoer, was a guiding principle. The more extreme punishments were aimed at antisocial acts, whether secular or supernatural, such as preventing a fugitive from seeking sanctuary. Drunkenness on the part of the young and those of working age was severely punished. Violation of the ethics or ceremonial of war-making brought the death penalty, and it was applied even-handedly to the sons of kings. Violation of the safety of embassies and of merchants was a major crime. Faithlessness of a guardian toward his ward was a major crime. There was no imprisonment except for those awaiting trial and captives awaiting sacrifice, but the making of restitution to a wronged person might entail temporary enslavement to him; he, however, was accountable for the life of his slave. Thieving brought the death penalty, as it did in England two centuries ago. Houses had no bolts or fastenings of any kind; and along the roadsides, corn was planted for those who might be in need. The judiciary was independent of the executive; but on its side, it advised the legislative-executive branches on laws and policies.

The institution of the confessional existed, and it functioned in the judicial system. The secrets of the confessional were inviolable as in Europe, but the priestly confessor could furnish a certificate of the confession of a crime, and this certificate carried immunity from secular as well as supernatural punishment for the crime. Confession could be made but a single time, and therefore was reserved until late in life as a rule. This suggests that the grimness of Aztec justice was more in the word than in the deed.

There were schools for training in the general business of life, called *telpuchcalli,* or "houses of youth," maintained by the clans, or *calpulli,* for the children of their members. The houses of youth taught citizenship, war, arts and crafts, tradition and history, and the religious observances of common men.

There were special schools, called *calmecacs,* for training in priestcraft. The *calmecacs* were connected with the temples of various important gods; and in them was taught also the Aztec writing system, which was pictorial and hieroglyphic, but which included the beginnings of phonetics. The Aztec writing system lent itself but rigidly to the expression of the dramatic and abstract, and was supplemented by a mnemonic wealth of that rhythmic recitative which was the real vehicle of Aztec literature. However, the writing system served adequately in the courts of law and in most state business, and was accepted for purposes of legal record and evidence by the Spaniards. There existed many thousands of books, often of exquisite, even radiant beauty, in parchment. The first Christian Bishop of

Mexico gathered them up for a huge bonfire in the plaza of Mexico and over the whole land they were sought out and destroyed; only a handful have survived until now.

Life in the *calmecac* schools was severe but also romantic. The students shared common eating and sleeping quarters with their teachers, who were priests of a subordinate status, called Tlamacatzons. These priests were supervised by an assistant to the two supreme priests. Though in one aspect democratic, Aztec society in its profoundest aspect was a theocracy, and the novices in the *calmecac,* often devoted by their parents from infancy to their careers, were destined to become the interpreters of the gods, and mediators. The pantheon of the Aztecs included several hundred gods, who in their totality constituted the powers of the universe, and who interacted with one another within the framework of the Aztec calendar.

So it was into a wilderness of mythology and a vast complex of ritual that the student had to be led; and he learned the chants which contained the esoteric lore, and the organization of the great dramatic pageants. He joined the ceremonial fasts, lit the incense at midnight, and journeyed at night alone and nude to a neighboring mountain, carrying incense, a torch, a conch-shell trumpet, and a bundle of the aloe spines used in ritual self-torture.

The highest of the priesthood ultimately would be chosen from among those who had passed through the *calmecac;* and in the choice rank or birth played no part. For the sacred priesthood, merit alone was considered. Although in its latter years, as we shall see, Aztec society was moving far away from that equality of opportunity which had guided it until near the end, the priesthood never moved away from these virtues or values. It recruited from the whole of the Aztec peoples; it nurtured equally the lowly and the mighty who entered its service, and performed its romantic, mystical, and often bloody tasks under the open sky, in the view of all. Sections of the *calmecac* schools were devoted to the training of girls. However, the woman's role in Aztec ceremonialism was a subordinate one, and the girls when they reached marriageable age could leave their convents.

In the Aztec state, land was a clan property, and the clan officers saw to its even distribution and beneficial use. That portion of the clan's holding which was devoted to the religions and to the "king" was worked by the clan members in common. Craftsmanship of a very high order, and various, was almost universally diffused. The market was important socially as well as economically, even as it is today in Mexico and Guatemala; and through the merchants' guilds it brought the wide world to the common folk of Tenochtitlán and Texcoco.

Land shortage in the Valley of Mexico became acute in the later cycles, and the Tenochas solved this difficulty by creating their own land. They went out into Lake Texcoco and scooped mud from its marshy borders. This mud they held in place by thin walls made of reeds, and later by trees whose roots bound the earth together. Between these artificial islands the water flowed in narrow canals. Great sections of the marshlike lake were thus transformed into land of extreme fertility. The *chinampas,* as these islands were called, exist today, on a greatly reduced scale since the lake has been drained. They are farmed as of old by Aztecs who speak their own ancient language. Visitors to Mexico know them as the "floating gardens." As Tenochtitlán grew larger the *chinampas* served as foundations for buildings, and agriculture was pushed farther into the lake. Throughout Middle America, the rural dweller had as his community center the city with its market place and temples; in Tenochtitlán, the farms were practically within the city.

Warfare rested not very onerously upon the people of Mexico, since for a hundred years before Cortés a military alliance between the three city-states of Tenochtitlán, Texcoco and Tlacopan had made them all but irresistible. All men were trained for war and were available as warriors, but the sometimes rather frequent wars lasted in each case only for days or weeks. Battles were events of gorgeous pageantry, waged with a minimum of bloodshed since the object was to capture the foe, not kill him. Indeed, no honor was paid for killing men in battle, while their capture was a prerequisite to the civic advancement of a warrior. Capture was for sacrifice, and to be sacrificed was public service.

Craftsmanship was not an isolated utility. It passed into architecture of stern beauty, and into the dramatic ceremonies of mass participation keyed to the universal rhythms of life.

But of course in the Aztec civilization there were also debit items, particularly those that belong to the last century before the Conquest and which prepared the way for the Conquest.

The league of the three Nahuan city-states, mentioned before —Tenochtitlán, Texcoco and Tlacopan—was formed about the year 1432, after the three states had joined to overthrow the Tepanecs who were then dominating Texcoco. By agreement, the military leadership of the league was reposed in the Tenocans, newly come into power. The Tenocan king, Itzcoatl, divided the land of the conquered Tepanecs not among the clans but among individual warriors who had distinguished themselves in the war. He also gave these warriors the right to make serfs of the Tepanecs. Thus was established the beginning of a caste system and the private ownership of the land. And that system grew with the succeeding decades, encroaching heavily on the communal lands of the clans. Through these same decades, population increased and the land-base deteriorated; so that before the Spaniards arrived, masses of the people in the Valley of Mexico were in the process of becoming disinherited and permanently impoverished. A revolution was in process and destruction of the ancient communal and democratic system was under way.

The Tenocan god was Huitzilopochtli, the God of War. The Tenocans were by policy predatory. They had fought their way to the top, immature newcomers to the ancient civilization which they adopted as their own. Now having power, they did not adopt moderation. They went on conquering; and they exacted heavy tribute, giving nothing back. Mexico needed unification and was ready for it; the Aztecs had the chance to accomplish it; but their statecraft was inadequate to the task. Finally, the immense increase of human sacrifice by the Aztecs created a vicious circle; sacrifice–war, war–sacrifice.

Before the end, human sacrifice to the gods was carried to such an extreme that as many as twenty thousand lives were offered up on a single occasion. Difficult as it may be for us at the present time to understand such rites, they were not held in abhorrence by the sacrificial lambs of ancient Mexico. Human sacrifice empowered the gods—of whom there were very many. We know of cases where tribal headmen delivered themselves willingly, even gloriously, to be sacrificed; where parents delivered over their children.

Warfare among the peoples of ancient Mexico would strike us as strange—also, most certainly, would ours strike them. Theirs was exceedingly ceremonial; but ceremony was not the whole thing. The main principle was this: Do not kill your enemy but capture him, not only for your own glory but also for his, since he will be sacrificed and thus pass as renewed might into the gods who make for fertility upon the earth and move the sun and the stars. When there were no wars—often there were none over long periods of time—the people in the Valley of Mexico inaugurated the institution they called "The Battle of the Flowers," the sole purpose of which was to enable each of the contending tribes to capture victims for sacrifice.

It is well to keep in mind that human sacrifice has been

familiar at one time or another to nearly all peoples—in ancient India; in Greece and Rome; in Africa, especially the West Coast; in Polynesia, Tahiti and Fiji, and elsewhere.

Diverse significances and motivations have been discerned in these institutions of sacrifice, the generic one being the renewal of the union between God and Man. Within our Hebraic–Christian tradition, we have still the symbolism. Our Christian faith, in history, flows down from the most solemn of all human sacrifices; and in the central ritual of our Christian faith, bread and wine are transformed into the body of Christ and are then eaten by men. Yet Aztec human sacrifice was used by the Spaniards to justify every atrocity of Cortés and those who came after him; though one notes that the atrocities were equally extreme in those areas where there was no human sacrifice.

The people gave themselves to the religion as a whole, but not as so many lay preachers. Priesthoods came into being early and were the keepers and developers of the great religious traditions. Ritualism elaborated itself endlessly, and the priestly life came to be one of extreme rigors and disciplines. Energies of imagination, splendid, sometimes terrible and sometimes, seemingly to us, hideous, were poured through century after changing century, into great dramas of life and death. These dramas, which were not merely artistic but reinforced the mighty efforts of upholding the world, called for mass participation. The literature of the Conquest, in particular the writings of Friar Sahagun, gives us long accounts of some of these dramas. They were dramas by the gods, not only for them, and the gods constituted an immense hierarchy.

One of the dramas was called the "New Fire Ceremony." This was a calendrical ceremony, and it occurred once in every fifty-two years. The end of the fifty-two year cycle brought the death of one whole order of the universe and the birth of a new order; and failing the ceremony, there might never again be new life. The altar fire that had burned unbrokenly for fifty-two years was put out. For five days the people let their fires die, and destroyed their household goods, and fasted and mourned, for they awaited possible extinction. Then at sundown of the eve of the new year the priests who represented the whole pantheon of the Aztecs, accompanied by representatives of all the surrounding cities, started in procession toward the summit of Huixachtecatl, the "Hill of the Star." They reached the temple at its summit at midnight and scanned the heaven. When a star not certainly identified (one of the Pleiades, or Aldebaron) approached the zenith, expectancy grew breathless. Would it cross the zenith? That meant life. Would it cease to move, or tremble into darkness? That meant the end of the world. Then—

The star crosses the zenith. Immediately the priests seize a fire-drill, and within the breast of a newly slain human victim they kindle the fire. Then from the new fire, runners kindle torches, and bear the flame to the temples of every city, and the people rekindle their home fires from the temple fires. Then universal rejoicing takes place; homes are renewed; sacrifices are made through voluntary bloodletting as well as through the slaying of human victims as sacrifice. Existence is sure for another fifty-two years.[1]

Prescott, intellectually the most understanding, emotionally the most sensitive of all the later historians, did not escape the point of view of his culture and civilization. The thought of human sacrifice and, even worse, ceremonial cannibalism, deeply pained him, though he recognized that the Aztec human sacrifice had "nothing in it degrading to the victim." But the inwardness of the sense of sacrifice in the Aztec soul has been better comprehended, it seems to me, by the modern anthropologist, Herbert J. Spinden. Dr. Spinden in his chapter in *American Indian Life* re-tells the story of the sacrifice of Tezcatlipoca, and his comments, along with his explanation of the story as others have told it, seem to me to come close to what was the underlying truth of the matter.

He shows the "victim" to have been no victim in his own esteem, but rather a god-favored hero, moving through elevated and ecstatic dramatic emotion to an ultimate transfiguration in the service of the world and his race. The extravagances of human sacrifice were contained within the far older complexities of faith and ritual, proliferated across the generations, over centuries, which to the Aztec mind, as to the earlier Toltec or Mayan mind, were inseparable from the universe itself. Like the huge travail of temple building, human sacrifice and self-torture and ceremonial bloodletting were not imposed upon the basic and never-questioned world-view and life-view, but were logically consistent with it; they were functional within the universe of time and place.

Shortly before Columbus discovered America, Nezahualcoytl, the great Texcocan king, state-builder, lawgiver, and patron of all culture, tried to put a stop to the exaggerated display of human sacrifice. One of the great Indians and one of the great

[1] *The Native Races of the Pacific States,* edited by Hubert Howe Bancroft. 5 vols. 1874–75. Doubleday & Company, Inc.

leaders of recorded times, he was near to those fountainheads of the people's spirit, whose waters became blood-tinctured in the Aztec dominion, and near to the loftiest religious consciousness of mankind. Nezahualcoytl resisted the institution of human sacrifice, but yielded to over-persuasion by the priesthood and countenanced it. Then once again he revolted profoundly, within his own spirit, against human sacrifice and all ritual and belief whose pattern it held, and against all magic which was not directly cosmic. But he knew that symbolism and ceremonial were essential in even the highest regions of the spirit of his race. He built a new temple, in the established pyramidal form, and on its summit a tower nine stories high, representing the nine heavens; and then a tenth story, with a roof painted black, gilded with stars on the outside and radiant with precious metals and stones on the inside. He dedicated this temple "to the Cause of All Causes, the Unknown God." Musical instruments were placed on the top of the tower and their sound, accompanied by the ringing of a sonorous metal struck by a mallet, summoned to prayer at regular seasons. No image was allowed in this temple, and no blood sacrifice was allowed, but only the offering of flowers and scented gums.

But Nezahualcoytl failed to curb the human sacrifice of the Aztec people. And the reason for his failure was simply, as near as we can make out, that the people would not have it. I do not think that even the great Nezahualcoytl opposed human sacrifice solely on ethical or humanitarian grounds, but rather, primarily, for reasons of secular utility.

This is the way Nezahualcoytl, I believe, would have viewed the Mexico of 1450: Cohesion for mutual aid and defense had never been achieved among the tribes in and around the Valley of Mexico. Hence, again and again tribes comparatively barbarous had overrun rich civilizations. Now pressure of population, on natural resources severely diminished, had emerged as a constant war-breeding influence. The priesthood, wrapped in their myriad channeled religious romance, were steering the people and the civil leaders toward an increasing, exclusive, magical preoccupation. Into this situation the Tenocans and the Texcocans, who then dominated the Valley of Mexico and beyond, had brought exaggerations of the rituals of human sacrifice. Precisely because human sacrifice represented a logical fulfilment of the religious view of the whole Valley of Mexico, and carried that view to its highest intensity, the Tenocans in a hundred years were able to spread this exaggeration of human sacrifice to all the other tribes. Human sacrifice required the capture of foes; so to all the other war-making and divisive tendencies and factors, human sacrifice was added; and the Aztec calendar called for these sacrifices many times each year. They were the despair of statesmanship, the final reason why there could be no peace in Mexico. Nezahualcoytl's counsel of moderation failed. His dominating ally, Tenochtitlán, predatory and proud, was not to be reached with influence, nor could Nezahualcoytl even extricate his own state from the vicious circle of war—sacrifice, sacrifice—war. His domestic laws were adopted by Tenochtitlán too, but those laws were silent on human sacrifice, and they furnished no restraint on predatory war-making. Nezahualcoytl's immediate successor, Nezahualpilli, joined with Ahuitzotl, the Tenocan chief, in a raid into the Oaxaca region which captured 20,000 "enemy" soldiers, and with their own hands he and Ahuitzotl tore out the hearts of the first ones, leaving the remainder of the 20,000 to the priests, who immolated them all.

But Nezahualcoytl's voice was not the only voice that had been raised against human sacrifice. Dim centuries before, the great god Quetzalcoatl had enjoined the people against blood sacrifice. The myth of Quetzalcoatl is the most diffusive of all the presences of Middle America—diffusive and multiform but always benignant. Viewed as history, Quetzalcoatl was a man who existed, "the Toltec king, priest, astronomer and culture-hero extraordinary," according to Herbert J. Spinden. He reduced the Mayan calendar and some of its appurtenances to a system of signs and ideographs which fitted all languages equally well. He died on April 5, 1208.

Myth and symbol from much older time flowed over the man Quetzalcoatl, and subsequent myth-making changed his apotheosis. The man Quetzalcoatl, who visited the Mayans and brought their calendar to the Toltecs, or the symbol Quetzalcoatl, representing the conquest by the Toltecs of the late-Mayan civilization, became enveloped in the more ancient, abstract and elemental myth and symbolism, and then the myth took this form: Quetzalcoatl in a time long gone (the Toltec time) descended from heaven where he had been the God of the Air. He became man, and taught all art, wisdom and kindness to the people. He brought a golden age to nature and to man alike. But he incurred the wrath of some greater god, and war forced him to flee; and on his way toward the eastern ocean he stopped at Cholula, where the mountainlike temple, today still undestroyed, later was built in his worship. He went on to the sea, and promising that he would return, embarked in a wizard skiff made of serpent skin for the fabled land of Tlapallan.

Historically, the "greater god" who drove Quetzalcoatl from the Toltec country was the Chichimec people who overwhelmed the Toltecs of Teotihuacan. In their mythology and that of the Acolhuas and Aztecs who came after them, Quetzalcoatl lived on. He was the patron of learning among the Aztecs, the god of the *calmecac* (the school) and the arch-patron of magic; the Aztec chiefs or kings were installed as his representatives; the most revered priest in Mexico was the priest of Quetzalcoatl at Cholula, who led the most austere of lives. Quetzalcoatl became, too, a subordinate god, being the god of a conquered people; and his injunction, delivered at Cholula, against any sacrifice beyond the offering of fruits and flowers, was rejected. He was the god of the solar calendar. His promised return might not come to pass at *any* date, but only at a periodically recurring date in the Aztec time-cycle.

Actually, the Spaniards reached the coast of Mexico in the year of the predicted return of Quetzalcoatl. Montezuma II, the Aztec king, had been trained as a priest; and his paralysis of decision, with its fatal results, was in part at least a palsy resulting from the prophecy.

Nezahualpilli, Nezahualcoytl's successor, became father to a son, Ixtlilxochitl. According to the chronicler Fernando de Avila, the birth of this son Ixtlilxochitl, was accompanied by unfavorable astrological patterns, and the astrologers advised the king to destroy his son, because if he lived, he was destined to unite with the enemies of his race and to overturn the institutions and religions of the Aztecs. But Nezahualpilli replied, "The time is near when the sons of Quetzalcoatl will return from the east to take possession of the land, and if the Almighty has selected my son to co-operate with them in his work, then His will be done." So Ixtlilxochitl lived, and as the Texcocan king he joined with Cortés in the overthrow of the Indian civilization.

So runs the vast religious myth of Quetzalcoatl, reaching through all the civilizations of Middle America and far north to the present Pueblos of the Rio Grande in the United States, and reaching from its cosmic level too high for any but symbolical representation, to clothing the Spanish invader with divinity and fate, and to the obliteration of a great Indian age, whose most universal symbol and core-belief Quetzalcoatl had

been. The cycle was finished; that genius of romantic religion
which had wrought a wondrous two thousand years of Middle
American life, at its end prepared all of that long life for an
almost unrecorded extinction.

CHAPTER 5

The Spanish Conquest

THERE is always a gate to any history. The
Indians entered a certain gate, one which Columbus opened
when he presented to Castille and to Leon a New World. On
this imagined gate there was to be carved the line from Dante:
"Through me you enter in to endless dole."

For those among the great Red Indian civilizations who
entered the gate, the line remains as their obituary. Enormous
groups and cultures perished to the last Red Indian. But today
thirty millions of American Indians on our hemisphere testify
to the strength of the certainty that, having been admitted
through the gate and undergone their purgatory, they shall rise
again. Unless, indeed, doom is predestined for all of us; unless
world ruin builds a vaster entrance into which all of us, like so
many herds and flocks, shall go down an endless way—to endless dole; unless we are through as a biological race (and that is
a possibility), we might very thoughtfully consider the way of
the American Indian.

No perspective one can get on the Conquest can make it appear as anything other than bitterly sad and desperately ignoble.
It is all the more tragic, from one side, and ignoble from the
other, because of this: From the first beginnings of the Conquest there were great hearts on both sides; there were fine
intelligences and profound understandings. The great writers
whose source material is the chief thing we have to lean on, and
many others quoted by them, knew that the horrors of the Conquest (and those were rugged days when it came to horror)
were not only unnecessary, but wholly impractical. Not only
writers but great governors and great churchmen pointed out
the errors. But the tide of exploitation rolled on.

It is a record of adventure without parallel in historical an-
nals, and probably of destruction without rival in its implacabil-
ity and swiftness. Broad-based, earth-rooted, symbol-clouded,

timeless and dreamful Indian life was confronted by an enemy with a new life, a new way, one with passion of purpose; one narrow, insatiable, intense and of fabulous hardihood; one driven by motivations which were wholly outside the experience of Indians—by the lust for gold, not as a metal but as a symbol of power; and by an equal passion for proselytizing.

The Spanish were the conquerors. They were men of a feudal age not yet ended; an age in the throes of transition entering into the Age of Discovery, along with the burgeoning of Europe's second great imperial order. They were, individually, adventurers who for the most part financed their own expeditions, selling stocks and shares and signing bonds for as much as they could get in advance; men who staked everything on the throw. At the same time they were emissaries of the Crown and the Church. Cesare Borgia planned a new Roman Empire in Italy. Cortés planned to take over an established empire in the New World.

They knew with great exactness what they wanted. What they wanted was plain and simple and they wanted it ruthlessly. In the cases of Mexico and Peru they knew they could win only through desperate measures, their own lives, individually, thrown into the pot. Something of the pain they caused they also endured.

Their natural abilities, as also their luck, varied widely and some of them were obvious incompetents, while at least one of them was a man of many-sided genius; their sophistication ranged from that of the unlettered and criminal type like Pizarro (perhaps the boldest adventurer of them all) to that of the worldly-wise, subtle, meditative Cortés, who, like Caesar, was superlatively a man of action, too. But no one of them deviated from the broad pattern; all had those qualities which under the circumstances made for their short-term success—overpowering lust for gold, religious fanaticism, hardness toward self and toward others, including heroic discipline; and with rare exceptions, through the duration of their crises, faithfulness to comrades; above all *encore de l'audace, toujours de l'audace.*

Confronting men of this type of motivation, how did the Indians appear in the light of the Conquest events?

They were peoples of diffused and nonaggressive purpose, and of a life ceremonially lived; of hospitality as a law of personal and social life; unused to money economy and to the traits that money economy brings to birth; peoples whose nonproselytizing religions of nature-mysticism were also religions of ceremonially regulated conduct; who were not orientated toward war as Europe waged war; to whom horses, iron, and gunpowder were unknown. In the West Indies (except for the Caribs), they were people of somewhat indolent, dreamful peace. In Peru, they were peoples living under a benevolent theocratic absolutism whose immediate roots struck into a decentralized agrarian base and whose mild art of war had become an imperial pageantry.

But as one reads and rereads the Conquest records and sadly broods over them, it becomes apparent that such factors are not enough to explain the historical results. Nor do the Spaniards' gunpowder, steel, armor, horses and man-killing dogs explain them.

The Indians in the fatal first decades of the white man in America were conquered because they could not conceive what it was that the white man was after, and what manner of man he was. The white man's concentrated, obsessive ruling passions, with their abolition of all limitation and all scruple, were unknown to the Indians and inconceivable by them. This remains a fact even today, after four hundred and fifty years of the Indians' contact with our devouring race; it was a more absolute fact at the beginning. The blend of single-tracked predatory energy accompanied by audacious, conscienceless guile, which these ruling passions—the passions for gold and for proselytizing—produced in the white man, took the Indians off guard. On the Indian's side of the Indian–white equation in those first years, the dislocation and shock were as profound as life itself allows. The situation was as if a mysterious stranger, announcing himself with words of love, welcomed with delight as a guest, embraced as a friend, given the run of the house and taken into the family's bosom, had suddenly revealed himself as no man at all but a devouring werewolf.

The record begins with Columbus. He found the natives of Española (Haiti, Santo Domingo) to be gentle beings, souls of hospitality, curious and merry, truthful and faithful, walking in beauty and possessors of a spiritual religion. All of this he put in his own writing. Yet, with no seeming awareness of incongruity, he seized these natives to be sold as slaves in Europe. Soon thereafter he established the *encomienda* in the New World. This was a grant of land with accompanying unpaid, forced, Indian labor for life. Queen Isabella ostensibly disallowed the Indian chattel slave trade; but it continued and increased, and with her approval. Cortés as a young man was a slave raider; indeed, Mexico was discovered through the voyage of a slave-hunting party, after which Cortés enters the picture.

But in the West Indies it was not decimation that befell the Indians—the peoples whom Columbus had found to be gentle, merry and walking in beauty—it was annihilation. Since the supply was supposed to be unlimited in the beginning, these chattel slaves were worked to death. So terrible was their life that they were driven to mass suicide, to mass infanticide, to mass abstinence from sexual life in order that children should not be born into horror. Lethal epidemics followed upon the will to die. The murders and desolations exceeded those of the most pitiless tyrants of earlier history; nor have they been surpassed since.

On his second voyage, Columbus spent several months in subduing the island he called Española, which we now call Haiti. He imposed tribute on individuals (from fourteen years up), on families, on communities, on districts, that would have been terrible to any people. But to these Indians of the West Indies, unaccustomed to work beyond the needs for their "gentle, merry" way of life, the burden was intolerable. They retired to the mountains, hoping that their enemies, with no Indians to feed them, would perish from hunger. But in this state of siege it was, of course, the Indians who suffered most. Not only could the Spaniards bring supplies into the island in their white-winged ships, but they could import other Indians by force. Natives from the Bahamas and other "useless" islands, as officially denominated, were kidnapped for Española where they died off faster than the original inhabitants. There have been none of the original native stock, nor any of these importees, in Haiti for over 300 years. According to Peschel, the ethnologist and historian, the population of Española in 1492 was less than 300,000 and more than 200,000. In 1508 the number of natives was 60,000; in 1510, 46,000; in 1512, 20,000; in 1514, 14,000. In 1548 it was doubtful if 500 natives of pure stock remained, and in 1570 only two villages of the Indians were left. A similar fate befell all the islands.

The Bahama Indians were sold for four pesos apiece. The Indians of the various islands who resisted were hanged or burned, and those who escaped were hunted down with man-killing dogs. In the sixteenth century the depopulation of the West Indies Indians was over. Mexico had been conquered, beginning in 1519.

The night which engulfed the Caribbean Indians was to have no dawn. Yet within the very pit of that night, the flame of Las Casas started to burn—Bartolomé de Las Casas, the first Christian priest to receive consecration in the New World, and the greatest of reformers in behalf of Indians. For the Caribbean Indians, Las Casas' torch served only to illumine the horror in which they gasped toward death, but for the Indians as a race it was not a torch lit in vain. Las Casas bore the torch high until he died at ninety-two years. It passed to many other hands, and passes now to other hands.

If looked on as adventure only, the deeds of Cortés are supreme. All other true adventure stories grow a little pale when matched against this one, and no fictioned adventure has been so daringly imagined. The Spanish Conquest record in the Antilles is a structureless depravity; in Peru, it is a desperate piracy rushing too quickly to triumph. Cortés had aristocracy and intellect. He moved complexly to his ends. He destroyed cruelly and almost immeasurably, but thereafter, he constructed, too. Surely it is true that the level of life went far down as a result of Cortés' success, that a golden house of beauty was ravaged and many sources of the spirit were killed. But the Toltec great age was long since done when Cortés came; the Mayan great age was centuries ended; and there were seeds of death in the less noble Aztec order. Spain, or Europe (since Las Casas could not prevail) would have worked ruin on Mexican life even if Cortés had never been born. So the drama he wrought—the tragedy he wrought—can be viewed without too much pain; and just as drama and tragedy, it is resplendent.

Cortés with his armada reached land at what is now Vera Cruz, in 1519. He had disembarked on the Yucatan coast, but had met hostile Indians. At the island of San Juan de Ulua the natives had welcomed him, and there the indispensable Marina, a female slave, had been given to him. Bernal Diaz tells of her origin, which in subsequent years he was able to verify. Her father, a rich and powerful chief in the province of Coatzacualco, bordering the Aztec Empire, had died in her infancy. Her mother had remarried and had borne a son. In order that the son might claim Marina's inheritance, the mother had feigned that the daughter was dead, but in fact she had delivered her to an itinerant merchant, and he had sold her as a slave. Marina was perfectly at home in the Aztec language, and she was witty, wise, kind, and beautiful. She became Cortés' interpreter, his informant and adviser, and his mistress; she was at his side in all the adventures to come.

At the future Vera Cruz, the Aztecs gave every help and hospitality; and the chief, or governor, agreed to send couriers to the Aztec emperor, Montezuma, at the Capitol. This chief,

Teuhtlile, construed literally the words of Cortés' address, that "the Spaniards were troubled with a disease of the heart, for which gold was a specific remedy." He could not look beyond and know that the enslaving of the whole race of Anahuac would not be enough to cure this disease of the heart in the white man.

Teuhtlile's couriers bore gifts to Montezuma, and the message that Cortés desired to visit the Capitol and to present the friendly greeting of a mighty king from across the eastern sea. Montezuma committed the first of an uninterrupted series of blunders so uniform that they had the look of destiny. He sent a hundred runners, led by two of his noblemen. These bore enormous treasure, wrought into myriad objects of fantastic beauty, and the message from Montezuma: He could not, would not, receive the Spaniards; he begged them to return forthwith across the sea.

In Mexico, as later in Peru, the Spanish conquerors melted the silver and gold art treasures into ingots for convenience of transportation; and while the commentator Bernal Diaz roughly catalogs the objects which were presented by the Aztec ambassadors, he concentrates on their cash value simply as precious metal, estimating the gold as distinct from the silver at $170,000. These first acquired treasures were not melted into ingots, but were sent by Cortés to Spain to prove that his expedition was going to be a collector's, as well as a money-making success.

In 1520 Albrecht Dürer viewed the treasures and thus described them in his diary: "Also I saw things which were brought to the King from the New Golden Land: a sun entirely of gold, a whole fathom broad; likewise, a moon, entirely of silver, just as big; likewise sundry curiosities from their weapons, armor, and missiles; very odd clothing, bedding, and all sorts of strange articles for human use, all of which is fairer to see than marvels.

"These things are all so precious that they were valued at a hundred thousand gulden worth. But I have never seen in all my days what so rejoiced my heart, as these things. For I saw among them amazing artistic objects, and I marvelled over the subtle ingenuity of the men in these distant lands. Indeed, I cannot say enough about the things which were there before me."[1]

We must try to account for Montezuma's actions at this point

---

[1] Albrecht Dürer as quoted in *Medieval American Art*. 2 vols. Copyright 1943 by Pal Keleman. The Macmillan Company, Publishers.

and on to their tragic end. Montezuma at this date was past middle age. He had displayed military and administrative energy; then he had begun to change. He had moved into priestly occupations and imaginings, brooding upon omens and prophecies; and in the same years, he had immensely enlarged the pomp and luxuriousness of his court, and had laid heavier and heavier demands for tribute on the vassal states.

The myth of Quetzalcoatl magnetized the soul of Montezuma. Sometime far gone, perhaps in the Toltec age, the all-wise, all-benign Quetzalcoatl had said his farewells and departed over the eastern sea, promising to return and to heal and illuminate the people once more. In the latter years of Montezuma, for whatever reason, the feeling seems to have prevailed that the period for the return of Quetzalcoatl was near at hand. Something approaching collective hallucination appears to have been diffused in the Valley of Mexico. Strangely, its emotional tone was fear, not hope—strangely, because the return of Quetzalcoatl, according to the myth, was to have been the beginning of an age of happiness.

Then the bearded white man came, and with him four-legged giants with human bodies on their backs. Runners brought the news of this arrival to Montezuma, along with drawings of the ships, the horses and the iron-clad men. Palsy of decision ensued, affecting not only Montezuma but his councilors.

Practical facts reinforced the deficit of will. Montezuma knew that the Tlascalan tribe, an embittered enemy never subdued by the Aztec confederation, occupied a zone through which the Spaniards would march if they insisted on continuing their enterprise. He knew that none of the tributary tribes nor city-states entertained love for Tenochtitlán, his dominating city. He knew, as Cortés mounted from the seacoast, that the season was harvest time, when the Aztec groups customarily did not wage war.

Whatever the cause, Montezuma and the clan leaders of Tenochtitlán faltered in decision again and again, and through faltering, lost all. When later, far too late, confronting hosts of Indian allies of Cortés, the great Guatemozin, successor to the dead Montezuma, brought adequate decision and energy to bear, the Aztecs were already doomed. Far less of decision and energy would have destroyed the Spaniards in the critical first months. It really appears that prophecy, working itself out through the soul of a king, did overturn Mexico.

The first Indian city entered by Cortés in his march toward the capitol was Cempoalla, near the Gulf coast, with probably thirty thousand inhabitants, a member of the Totonac nation. The Spaniards were received as friends. Its headman, or *cacique,* gave to Cortés an account of the divided condition of the Aztec Empire. The Totonacs were prepared to revolt, but they dared not.

The Spaniards journeyed on to the city of Chiahuitzla, thirteen miles distant on the coast; four hundred *tamanes,* or carriers, were furnished them by Cempoalla. At Chiahuitztla, the Spaniards encountered five Aztec tribute collectors, men richly clad and haughty, who moved with bunches of flowers in their hands and were followed by attendants with fans, who brushed away the flies. These tribute collectors chided the Totonac chiefs for rendering assistance to Cortés, and demanded as punishment twenty young men and women for sacrifices. Then Cortés spoke violently and insisted that the Totonacs throw the tribute collectors into prison; and the Totonacs, with divided mind, complied.

Then, in the night, Cortés procured the escape of two of the collectors, had them brought to his own quarters, voiced regret at the action of the Totonacs, and promised the release of their companions as well.

The Totonacs, angered by the escape of the two collectors, proposed to sacrifice their three companions. Cortés manifested horror and insisted that the collectors be transferred to his fleet. This was done. Then he sent all of the five on their way to Montezuma. Thus, for the Totonacs, the die was cast; Cortés had successfully betrayed them. They had no choice except to go forward with Cortés.

Why did not the Indians counter guile with guile, lies with lies, and the planned monstrousness (which we shall soon behold) with planned monstrousness? The answer rests in the fact that men and groups cannot swiftly recondition themselves in fundamental attitudes and reactions. It rests in part on the hypnotizing wonder awakened by the unpredictable behavior of the Spaniards, and by their armament and horses, amid the powerful suggestive effect of the prophecies now seemingly being fulfilled. But in addition, no Mexican Indian could have foreknown what it was that would ensue after the Spaniards had become their masters.

The Spaniards climbed to the plateau of Mexico and there, as Montezuma had dreaded, they encountered the Tlascalan nation. After some bitter and inconclusive fighting (had the Tlascalans kept it up, they would have worn down and exterminated the Spaniards), Cortés, the master diplomat, persuaded the Tlascalan nation to join him for the overthrow of the Aztecs. What Montezuma had feared had taken place; Cortés was now the leader of a major civil war in Mexico.

The Spaniards marched on to Cholula and were welcomed there; the Cholula nation had invited them to come. Cortés wrote that Cholula contained twenty thousand buildings within its walls. Now we come to the first deed of startling monstrousness on the part of Cortés.

To the great square of Cholula he invited the headmen of the Cholulan nation.

They came and brought, not armed warriors, but *tamanes* and numerous retainers, totaling several thousand. Cortés' armored men with their cannons, crossbows, arquebuses, horses, were posted invisibly around the square. The signal for the onset was to be the firing of an arquebus; and by secret prearrangement, the Tlascanan army was to assault Cholula at the instant when Cortés started the massacre. The arquebus was fired; what had been so carefully planned followed. Amid the thousands of dead, the Spaniards looted the city.

None but the Spaniards themselves have told the Cholula tale. Their chroniclers assert that Marina had gained information that a plot to exterminate the Spaniards was being carried forward, under Montezuma's instruction, and they assert that some of the Cholula headmen confessed it before they were massacred. Many times thereafter the Spaniards were to sanction monstrous deeds by alleging that plots were being hatched against them. Thus they sanctioned the mock trial and murder of the last Inca emperor, the murder of the last Aztec emperor, and the massacre in Tenochtitlán. In the particular case of Cholula, Cortés' real motive probably was strategical and political. Through a sudden and frightful deed, he sought to paralyze the Aztec will.

The Spaniards entered Tenochtitlán, the Aztec capital, the Mexico City of today. Montezuma received them as the ambassadors of a great monarch overseas. He housed and entertained them royally, and gave them the freedom of the city. Then Cortés forcibly abducted Montezuma, and applied to his royal prisoner-host that Spanish epithet, "dog," which in the Laws of Burgos in 1512 the Spaniards had been forbidden to use toward Indians. The psychological torture which followed was a coldly ruthless, calculating, cumulative murder of a personality.

At Vera Cruz, where Cortés had left a garrison, two Spaniards were slain, treacherously, by the Aztec headman, Quauhpopoca,

he governor of a neighboring province. The abducted Montezuma was ordered by Cortés to command the presence of Quauhpopoca at Tenochtitlán. Montezuma obeyed, and Quauhpopoca
arrived, borne on a litter and accompanied by his son and by
fifteen of his headmen. Quauhpopoca did not evade or apolo-
gize; yes, he had ordered the two Spaniards killed. Cortés condemned the whole party to be burned alive in the area in front
of the palace where Montezuma was confined. While the stakes
were being driven by Cortés men, and the faggots piled, Cortés
entered the room where Montezuma was imprisoned and man-
acled the Aztec king by the ankles. Quauhpopoca and his son
and his fifteen headmen were burned.

Montezuma's physical end came when his usefulness to
Cortés had been exhausted. He was struck on the head by a
stone hurled by an outraged Aztec. Reports vary as to whether
he died of this wound or whether the Spaniards, having used
him up, murdered him. It is immaterial; Cortés had already
murdered him in spiritual torture.

Six months after entering Mexico City, Cortés departed with
a portion of his forces, to negotiate with, and then to fight and
defeat, Panfilo de Narvaes, who had reached Vera Cruz from
Cuba to insist upon a share in the Mexican adventure. As head
of his forces left in Mexico City, Cortés appointed Pedro de
Alvarado, a man of conquistadorial capabilities and a personal
friend, a cavalier of high family, gallant and chivalrous.

A few days after Cortés' departure, the time for the yearly
festival of Huitzilopochtli, the war god of the Aztecs, was at
hand. Most of the Aztec nobles, as well as the priests, engaged
in this yearly festival of dance, song, and sacrifice, and its place
was the court of the great temple of Huitzilopochtli, adjacent
to the princely quarters which had been assigned to the Spaniards and where the abducted Montezuma was then confined.
As a part of that temple had been taken over for Christian
worship, the Aztecs requested Alvarado to permit them to use
their temple, and he assented.

They gathered—nearly all of the highest nobility—on the
sacred day, all clothed in their ceremonial garments and with a
wealth of gold adornments and symbolic implements of silver
and gold. They were unarmed, of course. The engrossing ceremonies began, and then, at a prearranged signal, Alvarado and
his men rushed upon the throng, and hewed it down. Those
who tried to escape were impaled on long pikes by Spaniards
stationed at the exits of the court. Every man of the Aztec throng
was slain. Alvarado's stated reason for this deed was that he

believed that the nobles, though unarmed, had secreted their weapons at some place nearby.

When Cortés returned, he found the Aztec temper completely changed, and his forces in Mexico City ringed by a wall of siege, the public market closed, and starvation in the offing for the Spaniards. The murderous slaughter was the immediate cause of this change, and Cortés chided Alvarado for indiscretion. But it was upon the imprisoned and helpless Montezuma that he poured his wrath and his insults.

The Spaniards evacuated Mexico City when the assaults of the enraged Aztecs became unendurable. They retreated at night along the causeway of Tlacopan. The Aztecs had begun to learn something of European warfare, and they cut the causeway, then attacked the Spaniards from boats. The retreating forces of Spaniards and Tlascalan allies numbered seven thousand. Accounts differ as to the losses of the Spaniards and their Indian allies; the probable number was four to five hundred Spaniards killed or missing, and three to four thousand of their Indian allies. Many Spaniards were drowned through the weight of the gold which they had tied about their bodies. Much armament was lost. This was the battle of the *Noche Triste*, remembered by the Aztec peoples and told in many of their chronicles.

Cortés with his surviving forces took refuge with the Tlascalans and awaited reinforcements from Cuba. Then was commenced the final assault on Tenochtitlán. By this time, the Aztec Empire or confederation had dissolved; numerical superiority in the civil war had shifted to Cortés' side. With forces now overwhelming in manpower as well as in equipment, he isolated Tenochtitlán from its food supplies. On the shoulders of Indians he transported the parts of ships which had been assembled more than twenty miles away. The final act against besieged Tenochtitlán was a land and naval operation. The Aztecs went down fighting with a stern bravery that held no hope. A prolonged massacre followed the collapse of the Aztec resistance.

Montezuma, the weak or spellbound, whose torture and whose dissolution of soul furnished the symbol and prophecy of that which the Spaniards were to do to the whole race of Indians in Mexico and Peru, had been succeeded by Guatemozin. Guatemozin, too late, had summoned and organized and led the resistance of the Aztecs. He surrendered to Cortés when all was lost. Cortés had promised him, if he surrendered, honor and protection.

Promptly, Cortés put Guatemozin to the torture in an effort to force him to reveal where gold might be hidden. The Cacique of Tacuba was tortured alongside Guatemozin, and confessed his anguish through groans. Guatemozin, from out his own torture, rebuked him saying, "and do you think, then, that I am enjoying my bath?"

Then Cortés marched into Honduras. He took along with him Guatemozin and the Cacique of Tacuba. Cortés became suspicious, or pretended to be, that in some indefinite, unspecified, and in fact impossible way, Guatemozin was "plotting" against him. He ordered Guatemozin, the Cacique of Tacuba, and the nobles accompanying them, to be hanged. "I knew what it was," said Guatemozin when the noose was placed on his neck, "to trust to your false promises, O Malinche (Cortés); I knew that you had destined me to this fate, since I did not fall by my own hand when you entered my city of Tenochtitlán. Why do you slay me thus unjustly; your God will demand of you to know." The Cacique of Tacuba declared that he desired no better lot than to die by the side of his lord.

Cortés killed Guatemozin because he feared him. He had the power to kill him. He need not have "framed" him and killed him ignominiously. The facts speak for themselves when we attempt to appraise the one man among the Spanish conquerors who had the loftiest mind and the greatest genius.

Cortés immediately instituted the *encomienda* in what there-after was to be called New Spain. He himself took land and serfs on the scale of a kingdom. He established the *encomienda* in defiance of the Spanish Crown, and continued it in face of a stern, even impassioned order from the Crown to abolish the institution. And the Crown surrendered, as it was to do in Peru twenty years later; surrendered, and then became the leading partner in that enslavement which it had condemned, and which it persevered in condemning through the generations, until the Spanish rule of the New World was no more.

The next example comes from the tremendous story of the Conquest of Peru, ten years later, by the brothers Pizarro. Ferdinand de Soto (later to lead his own expedition into what is now the United States) was there, too. And so were, according to the best authorities, exactly 177 soldiers and officers, foot and horse, come to challenge a nation numbering, to use a median figure, fifteen million. Prescott, citing the chroniclers Ovideo and Naharro, says that everywhere they were received with hospitality all along the route.

At any stage of their advance toward Caxamalca, where the Inca with his court was then staying, Francisco Pizarro with his handful of men could have been annihilated through a mere gesture of the Inca's hand. Instead, they were given royal hospitality all along the way. They arrived at Caxamalca, and the Inca ceremoniously welcomed them. The Inca was urged in flowery language to be a most honored guest for a day and a night in the spacious quarters which he had assigned to Pizarro's party. The Inca accepted. He came with a numerous army, but halted the army at some distance away. With the heads of his government and altogether with some thousands of his retinue, all unarmed, he entered the great square.

But the Inca's host, Pizarro, was not awaiting the Inca in the great square. He was hidden with his men and their cannon, arquebuses, lances, and horses, in the rooms surrounding the square. Only the Friar de Valverde came forth to welcome the imperial guest; and the Friar, in a long and aggressive rigmarole, through his interpreter, went on to demand that the Inca be baptized a Christian then and there, and yield his land and people to the Pope and the King of Spain.

Atahuallpa, the Inca, at first bewildered by the Friar's gaucherie and by his talk of the trinity of three Gods and then a fourth God who was all of them, after a while became affronted and said: "The God who is my God still lives in His heaven, and looks down on His children," and he pointed to the sun, and flung aside a breviary which the Friar had thrust into his hands.

Then the Friar rushed to where Pizarro, the host of the Inca, waited concealed, and shouted, "We are wasting our breath talking to this dog, full of pride as he is." Pizarro waved a white scarf in the air, the appointed signal; the cannon was detonated, and the armored Spaniards on horseback charged upon the weaponless throng. Wild confusion ensued; the exit from the square was blocked with the dead; the Spaniards shot, stabbed, slashed, and trampled; and the massacre went on for several hours. Atahuallpa himself, as planned in advance by Pizarro, was taken alive, to serve as a hostage, to instruct the delivery of a huge quantity of gold (fifteen million dollars' worth, according to Prescott; five millions dollars' worth, according to more recent computers) as a ransom, and then, having delivered the ransom, not to be freed, but to be murdered—garrotted— by Pizarro after a mock trial.

CHAPTER 6

Spanish Rule and Las Casas

WE PASS into hundreds of years of almost voiceless agony for the millions of Indian peoples under Spanish rule. Splendors there were, but they could not be sustained. Only the future can make good those purposes which Las Casas, Vasco de Quiroga, the Jesuits in Paraguay and other enlightened leaders laid down with imagination and the greatest practicality.

Yet, there is another possible view. There were great ideas put forth, great efforts made. And although these failed in their own age, they are valid for ours. An ideal, dynamic and outlasting, a practical philosophy, moved in those extraordinary men whose achievement in their own time seemed to be written on water. The policies for which they strove—and in times and places made effectual—entered into the great traditions of European culture, into the apologia of Christianity, into the basic Indian law of the United States, and, even more especially, into the burgeoning new and fresh approach toward the Indian masses by the southern republics. Their program as it developed between three and four hundred years ago contained much of the program of today and tomorrow for the thirty odd millions of surviving Indians.

There have been three great records of ethnic guardianship—the Roman, the British and the Spanish. I think the Spanish is the saddest of the three. Yet, it is the one where ideals, if we follow the record, reached their highest levels. For nearly four centuries now the ideals have been unfulfilled; the century and a quarter of the republics leave them yet unrealized. The record, for all its sadness, is not one of tragedy. Nothing so tremendous, as a living thing, could be called tragic, but it was portentous.

With the discovery of the new hemisphere, a new epoch came into being. Within the next four hundred years, Europe was to control the world, not only its own civilized world in the European sense—European economy, economic exploitation and economic forms; European evangelism, religious, cultural, political

67

(displacing or subjugating native Europeans along the way)—but the European system was to dominate, first the Americas, then all of Africa, all of Australia and Oceania, and most of southern Asia.

From Columbus on, colonization and with it exploitation of savages—since everyone not a European was a savage—continued. In this revolutionary process Spain for two centuries was the leader. In Puerto Rico and Cuba, in the Philippines and Guam, Spanish authority controlled until 1898. From Patagonia to the Rio Grande, and even northward throughout our own great Southwest, the effects of the gargantuan Spanish colonial enterprise crowd the thresholds of the present and the future.

In deeply etched relief, the Spanish record exhibits the dualism and ambivalence which have beset the colonizing and dependency-ruling enterprises of the several European nations and of the United States; they beset them today. At the one extreme, uninhibited exploitation, ravenous and unconcealed, annihilating the labor supply in exchange for quick returns. At the other extreme, ethical and humanitarian judgment and purpose, battling and laboring through lifetimes, renewed through centuries. Within the first extreme, struggle (within the Spanish Crown itself) between the short-range interest which was willing to consume whole populations in order to win quick gold, and the long-range interest which for permanent revenue took the well-being of subject peoples into account. Within the second extreme, there was the drive toward root-and-branch reforms and greatly imagined humanitarian programs, warring against the entire system of exploitation, secular and ecclesiastical, and efforts at reform (idealistically motivated) which sought to work within the exploitative system.

Antinomies like these, and similar conflicts within the antinomies, can be found in the records of nearly every colonizing power of modern times. They project, as it were, upon the hundreds of millions in the dependencies the conflicts between ideologies, value judgments and ultimate tendencies which rend the brain and heart of the modern Western world. In no record are they more greatly emphasized than in the Spanish record in the Americas.

The total result was the failure of exploitative and humanitarian statesmanship alike; the depopulation and the social degradation of the native masses; the retardation and distortion of the development of those of the conquering blood within the colonies; the secession of the colonies, followed by a renewed ferocity of oppression by the resident white minority upon the surviving natives; and the internal decay of Spain.

In the rule of modern nations over ethnic dependencies, the missionary usually has had his role. With Spain, his practical and official importance equaled that of the secular conquerors. Church and State were functions one of the other; through Papal grants, the Spanish Crown was head of the Church in all except doctrinal matters. The Spanish Conquest has been termed the "last crusade." Secular and ecclesiastical ambitions clashed at times, united at times. The conflicts of motives within the monastic orders and the secular clergy duplicated the conflicts within the Crown. In the first century of the Conquest, one and another of the religious orders, and sometimes all of them together, spoke and worked for the ideal policy; they helped, in fact, to make it the theoretical, formal policy of Spain. Thereafter, on the whole, zeal and intellectual purpose faded; yet in regions like California and Paraguay it did not fade. As it came about, the Church became one of the largest of the property interests.

Religion as a Spanish Conquest motive and continuing colonial motive was predominant. The secular conquerors were religious fanatics; even the many-sided Cortés was a fanatic.

It followed that the assault against native religion was more impetuous and more sustained than in any other epoch of colonial enterprise save only in the Plains Indian area of the United States. Because the Indian societies were saturated with and structured by religion, the killing of the native social soul went deeper than in any other colonial record, ancient or modern, with the possible exception of the subsequent one in the United States. The systematic destruction of Inca quipus, of Aztec temples and of Mayan records, was but the manifest part of a destruction which reached to the intangibles of institution and personality.

Of yet wider effect was the obliviousness of the Spaniards toward the man–nature relationship which, if they had but known it, they came upon in exquisite balance almost everywhere; but they blasted to fragments this man–nature relationship and the inclusive ecological complex within which the relationship was a productive and reciprocating part. The age-wise native institutions, which took account of the indirect consequences of things done and things omitted within the web of life, were deliberately destroyed. Spain made no effort to develop a *de novo* science of the conservation of the resources of nature; the result impoverishes the present and clouds the fate of the regions where she ruled; the impoverishing result is mounting with each decade. This aspect of the Spanish record was but the forerunner of the disruption of the man–nature relationship which was to come in many parts of the earth.

Spain's method of rule was authoritarian and hierarchical. Its administrative ideal was rigidity. All authority flowed immediately from the Crown; the Crown presumed that it was operating by immediate rule all governmental processes in the vast New World. Furthermore, its agents in posts of power (State and Church alike) must all be Spaniards of Spain. Even the Creoles, Spaniards of pure blood born in the New World, were excluded from power; Mestizos, or mixed-bloods, and Indians, were shut out from all except subordinate local functions. Communication between Spain and the far-flung New World was slow and irregular. Within an administrative organization of this kind—centralized, authoritarian, and conducted through agents who moved from place to place—absolute authority became an illusion of authority, and did not know it was illusion. The Crown, where all formal power resided, came to represent retardation, inhibition, and ineffectual counsels of avoidance and of perfection. The gulf between policy as verbalized and policy as executed became wider as generations passed. "I obey, but I do not execute," became a universal by-word in the Spanish colonies.

Historians of the Spanish colonial record dwell frequently on the inadequacy of the Crown's administrative means to its stated ends, especially in the field of the protection of Indians. They were grotesquely inadequate, quantitatively, especially in the first century of Spanish rule. For example, in the decade of 1530, when ravening abuses were being practiced against the Indian masses of New Spain (Mexico), the Crown depended on a single ambulatory commission, traveling as a body, to hear and to rectify Indian complaints in a region four times as large as Spain. But fundamentally it was the *qualitative* inadequacy that frustrated the Crown's will, the fact of absolute authority remotely stationed, of rigidity as a standard, and of the refusal, sustained till the end, to admit into policy-making or into responsible administration the permanent inhabitants of the New World, white, mixed-blood and pure Indian alike.

This particular aspect of Spanish rule in the Americas is

stressed for the reason that the Spanish Crown accented, and pushed to an extreme, a legislative and administrative concept which later was to be applied by modern imperial colonialism as a whole. With some shifts of emphasis and a few interpolations, the record and consequences of the Spanish Crown's colonialism can be transposed to British India, to Indonesia and French Indo-China, even to the rule by the United States over the central Pacific islands today.

Close to the end of its rule of the New World—within fifty years of the end—the Spanish Crown did reorganize its administrative machinery, but the change was only one of mechanism. Mechanism was rendered more efficient; principle and spirit remained unaltered. Spain never passed from a one-way to a two-way flow.

Thus it befell that when the Creoles and Mestizos broke their provinces free from Spain, they had not in three centuries acquired any legislative or administrative experience. The condition however went far deeper. Spain's colonial method as here characterized—authoritarian, remotely centralized, rigid, and non-indigenous—in its decisive effects had squarely prohibited the development of such social integrations within the New World as would have made successful governments possible after independence was won. Chasmic contrast between ideal and abstractly stated intent, on the one side, and actual conduct and events, on the other, had been projected to the very core of the nascent public mind of Latin-America. A hundred years of building on sand was the inheritance of the new governments, newly freed from Spain.

Through tribute to the Crown, the Crown became a partner of the holders of *encomiendas* and *repartimientos;* and as debt-slavery of Indians gradually superseded the labor-draft, the Crown by virtue of tribute remained a partner to the farming, mining and manufacturing groups whose peons the Indians were. Concurrently, the Crown strove to mitigate the extremities of Indian oppression. It tried to protect, and often did protect, the landholdings and the local communal institutions of hundreds of Indian groups. The protection of Indians was a function solely of the distant Crown. With independence, the function perished, and only now is the function being re-created in most of the southern republics. The Creoles of the freed provinces, by legislation and by direct violence, rushed the Indians' lands and trampled what remained of their institutions. Independence brought deepened darkness, more hopeless homelessness, to most of the Indians. Yet the ideal aspects of the enterprise of Spain remained deep in Latin-American memory, and were intellectually resisted no longer, since Spain as the tyrannous ruler was no more.

It was the Spain of the Spanish Inquisition which ruled the New World. The antinomies, the dualistic ambivalence of Spanish policy and conduct, had their seat within the personality of the Crown itself. Under such conditions, and when Spain was at war with the Protestant world of Europe, one would have anticipated that exposure of the terrible things actually being done, and criticism of lethal policies, would have been sternly suppressed. The very opposite proved to be the case.

How did it come about that Bartolomé de Las Casas, a member of the Dominican order which had founded the Inquisition, was permitted not merely to go where he would in the tracking down of horrors against Indians, and to lobby at the Court in the Indians' behalf, but to preach and to write into books his gigantic and detailed descriptions and denunciations of the evils being wrought on the subject peoples by soldiers, clerics, encomenderos, governors, all of whom were direct instruments of the Crown itself? Las Casas, the most famous, was only one of many, and he had successors through the centuries of Spanish colonialism.

The answer is a significant one. Within the very decades of the Conquest—commencing, indeed, within a few years after the discovery—a philosophy, metaphysic and ideal, of Spanish Indian policy had been set forth by the popes, executed by the monarchs themselves, and elaborated by the great Spanish humanist Francisco de Victoria, the friend of Erasmus. Twenty-two years after the conquest of Mexico, this metaphysic and ideal had been written into the Laws of the Indies. Factually speaking, the philosophy and ideal—later, the law—did not control events except in times and places which were not representative; but the controlling *intended* policies, the legally incorporated policies of the Crown, were based on a philosophy and ideal made explicit many hundreds of times and never, in theory, repudiated.

Las Casas and his co-workers and successors stood upon these principles, which the Popes had declared to be the principles of Christendom, and the Crown had declared to be the principles of Spain. They campaigned as defenders of Christendom and of the Crown against acts which violated papal and crown policies. At one point only were they silent. They did not spell out the fact that it was the absolutist Crown, itself, which was

he chief rebel against the Crown's protective policies. Las
Casas did not need directly to accuse the Crown.

The record in all its fullness, the honest cogitation and de-
ate, the apparently unlimited freedom of criticism—all these
houted for the world to hear. All the great voices and even
ittle voices were permitted to be heard within absolutist Spain.
They were permitted because Crown and Church acknowledged
hat the Indians were free men under God, the equals of Chris-
ian Spaniards—that is to say potentially; they had to be converted first. The province of the Church was to make them
Christians. The province of the Crown was to make them
workers.

The theory was this: By conversion you saved their immortal
souls. By training them to work at their daily tasks (under
your dispensation) you taught them how to live under the
European way of life.

It is no mere hypocrisy, no simple venality, that the record
reveals over the years. It was Spain herself, not her enemies,
who told for the whole world to hear, down to the last agony,
the tragedy of unfulfilled intention. And it was the Friar Bartolomé de Las Casas, as no other man, who understood the great,
rejected opportunity which Spain had passed by. He, for all
time, is the master voice, the fountainhead, of the American
Indian cause. More than any other interpreter, through the
present, he understood the Indian within a frame of reference
valid for the whole Race of Man. But he was, too, a man of
practical affairs. He labored concretely for the Indians through
his ninety-second year. He told Spain's record as none can ever
tell it again.

Las Casas looms in titanic dimensions at the very gateway of
the effort toward liberty and racial understanding in North and
South America. His philosophy is one of those fixed stars which
must guide the hopes and thoughts of striving mankind across
our own time and times far beyond ours.

Las Casas was born in Seville in 1474. In his young man-
hood he was a slave owner of some of the earliest Indian slaves.
He became the first Roman Catholic priest consecrated in the
New World.

Still subsequently, he took to himself, in Cuba, an *encomienda*
—a body of land seized from the Indians, with the natives
forcibly attached to it as serfs. Then, in 1514, through the immediate stimulus of certain Dominican monks, he experienced
a profound spiritual upheaval—a "second birth." Self, man and
God became apprehended in a new, utterly compelling vision.

The vision on its social side was that of freedom without an
bound, but freedom under God, for all the inhabitants of th
New World.

Perhaps no man ever has attempted a more exhaustive appli
cation of the principle of freedom of conscience to the realitie
of an unfree world than Las Casas. This, because freedom o
conscience to Las Casas was no mere precept of tolerance an
avoidance, but was the self-willed striving of the whole mar
toward inner freedom and toward a society made free; an
that striving was a striving toward the free will and the mysti
love of God.

From the depths of the Spanish Inquisition, and from withir
the court of the authoritarian Spanish Crown, the voice of La
Casas rose, proclaiming a different and opposite world. Th
scourge of Las Casas was plied, lashing out at the wrongs being
done by State, Church and private adventurers upon the native
of the Caribbean, of Mexico, Middle America and Peru. Al
Europe heard the voice and watched the scourge; and the Span
ish Indian record became a horror in the mind of Europe. Ye
never did the Inquisition or the absolutist Crown move to sup
press the voice. Generations passed, and Las Casas spoke oh.

He was a polemical pamphleteer, one of the most brillian
who ever wrote. He was a lobbyist of great persuasiveness
When past his sixty-fifth year, he framed the Spanish Indiar
code which was to become part of the New Laws of the Indies
promulgated by Charles V in 1542. He rejected the covetec
Bishopric of Cuzco, in Peru, but accepted the Bishopric of sor
rowful Chiapas, in Mexico. There the Spanish colonial popu
lation resisted him en masse. And when he denied the sacra
ments to Spaniards who persisted in murdering, mutilating
enslaving Indians, his own clergy deserted him. He went far of
to an unsubdued warlike tribe in Guatemala and in two years
brought it to Christianity through reason and love alone; and
departed leaving the tribe free.

Las Casas, when Bishop of Chiapas, was nearly seventy years
old. At that time, he elaborated his philosophical position in ar
800-page Latin document which historians, preoccupied with
Las Casas' enormous enterprise and adventure, long ignored.
Indeed, this massive work did but elaborate that which had
come to Las Casas whole and finally in the crisis of his conversion. His argument, flowing from his vision, rejected that dominant scholasticism which bears the great name of Saint Thomas
of Aquinas, and went back to Saint Augustine.

Man, said Las Casas, is a spirit, a spark from the cosmic fire,

who needs to burn toward God. (We of today can change the
terminology if we need to, and in place of God can speak of the
Universe, the God unencompassable yet finite Who strives
within the Universe, the Web of Life, the Race, the Society,
or the sentiment of the good, the just, the true, that "cold,
unchanging gleam" which age transmits to age.) God, said Las
Casas, burns toward man, and that union is the "far-off divine
event" in the terms of which "the whole creation moves." But
there is no union except in perfect freedom, never, except when
the will and love in the free soul are travailing to bring the
whole man, body and soul, and the whole society, in freedom,
to the mystical, cosmic altar.

Thus rejecting scholasticism, as he would have rejected philosophical positivism today, Las Casas proclaimed that the first
and last reality and law of human life, and therefore the supreme dynamic mainspring of society, was *impassioned spiritual
inwardness*. Such inwardness was the gift of creation to all men,
he held, and its realization was the master-instinct, the master-
duty, the one eternal social task which included all tasks.

This was the City of God, Las Casas said; and the good, the
successful human society could be nothing less nor other than
the free, co-operative commonwealth—the commonwealth
which systematically relied upon, and made itself the minister
to, that impassioned inwardness whose first and last law was
freedom. Such would be the *practical* society, Las Casas affirmed,
and nothing else could be practical for the genius of human
life.

When, in his middle manhood, the conversion and vision
came to Las Casas, he had witnessed the ravin which the Spaniard unloosed upon the gentle natives of the Caribbean islands.
The swift depopulation of the West Indies had been almost
completed when Las Casas, through his own inward crisis, was
propelled into his vast endeavors. But all of the continental
mass of North and South America was virgin still. He urged on
the Spanish Crown a course of action which, had it been
adopted, would have insured a different history for the Western
Hemisphere and for Spain.

Las Casas urged that the Crown forbid the entry to the continental American mass of any secular adventurer, of any mer-
cenary or soldier, of any missionary seeking to proselytize
through over-persuasion or force. Give entry, he said, to none
save ecclesiastical agents of the Crown, but let these be rigor-
ously chosen. Let only those priests go who can demonstrate that
they are moved by love and that they believe in freedom. Thus,

urged Las Casas, all the millions of America would be brought through love to God; and thus Spain would grow great in spirit, and as an earthly state would prosper and become impregnable.

Such was the utopia of Las Casas. Events after he had gone from this earth were to demonstrate that it was a wholly practicable utopia. But Crown and Church alike were engrossed in European dynastic intrigue, and the Crown was embarked on costly European wars. The flow of gold from America to Spain was already a dominating motive in Spanish policy, and soon was to grow into an all-consuming madness, with the conquest of Mexico and Peru. The entire spirit and momentum of Spain, hierarchical, exploitative and absolutist, was set against Las Casas' vision of freedom and its life-releasing power.

For nearly seventy years Las Casas fought on. The City of God was not allowed to be. So he fought, and not alone, for crumbs of protection for the desperate Indians. There were great spirits in Spain and in America who joined with Las Casas in building that tradition of noble, sad, defeated endeavor through which he is chiefly remembered. Las Casas died; and then, after fifty years, beginning in 1609, the Jesuit order, in a vast and remote region of South America, undertook to make a reality Las Casas' utopian dream. The Crown gave its consent, for there was no gold in Paraguay; and for a century and a half the Crown and Spain tolerated the most exhaustively wrought-out utopia the world has yet seen.

On the river La Plata, and back across pampa and rain-forest to the Andes, the numerous Indian tribes were unsubdued, but they knew the white man; his slave-raids had plagued and sometimes decimated them. Few, and unarmed, but marvelously equipped with numerous musical instruments and great chanting voices, the Jesuits came. They were not Spaniards alone, but Jesuits from many lands. Fear was not in them, and ascetic discipline to a productive purpose had imbued them with an exhaustless spontaneity of joy and resourcefulness, as such discipline, self-imposed toward purpose, can do. They were not whipped into haste by the thought of the brevity of life or by opportunism. They had equipped themselves with every technology of seventeenth-century Europe.

A number of books have told how one by one their *congregaciones* increased. At maximum expansion probably one hundred and fifty thousand Indians, with fewer than one hundred white men to assist them, were realizing a fusion of work, play, worship and art, and of personal and communal advantage, just as Las Casas had foretold. What all of the documents dwell on is the winging, blossoming joyousness of the life of these communes, and their many-sided, abundant economic productiveness within an abbreviated work-week borne upon music and ceremony. The Crown received its full tribute, and was content. The communes were virile enough; they manufactured their muskets, cannon and gunpowder; and their militia beat Portugal back from the utopian boundaries for a hundred years.

The historians account for the downfall of the Jesuit utopia, commencing in 1768, through external events exclusively. European political conflicts caused the Jesuits to be expelled from Spain and from all Spanish-America; leaderless, the communes were over-borne by Portugal, and the Indians dispersed to the wilderness. The city-states went back to the earth; the golden age was done. The historians are accurate; but they miss a point, and that point is at the center.

Las Casas, and those who followed in his path, perceived profoundly *the individual*. His depth and burningness of perception of the individual, like that of Saint Augustine, his theological master, were such as to make the perceptions of Rousseau, Thomas Jefferson, John Stuart Mill and Emerson appear thin by comparison. Whence the impelling power of Las Casas' doctrine of liberty. Those who worked in Las Casas' tradition perceived as he perceived. They perceived the individual Indian—potent, sweet, practicable, resourceful, co-operative and often splendid. But *they did not perceive the societies which had formed this Indian personality*. They could not know what none in their age guessed. How could they, when even in our time, after centuries, those of us who have been educators or administrators—in our own American Indian country, in Africa, in Oceania, in Asia—apprehend but timidly and, in the main, negatively, *the ineluctable potency of the native society*.

The role of leadership in the native societies; the ways that leaders are chosen and trained for the two-way flow between leaders and people; the educative processes of native societies, often unformalized, sometimes even secret, which are so infallible; the ways through which innovation is embraced by the societies—these are profound mysteries still.

But Las Casas' followers substituted *fiat* leadership for native leadership, *fiat* forms for native forms, *fiat* motivation for native motivation—they substituted, in fact, a *fiat* society for a native society. What they substituted did take into account,

and build on, the native propensities, temperaments and socially inherited genius; but the transposition was comparable to
the substitution of a hothouse, with ecologically untrained
gardeners for the age-formed complexities of a forest. That
which they achieved, within these conditions, could endure
only if they, the Las Casas disciples, endured. It is precisely the
almost unapproached greatness of their achievement—the love-
liness joined with virile power within freedom—which makes
intense, solemn and immortal their lesson to the world.

*Colonizer, missionary, moralist, idealist, crusader for causes,
it is to the hurt of all that you love, to the defeat of your own
purpose and the ruin of men, if you, plunging toward your
aim in terms of individuals, aggregations of individuals, or external material results, ignorantly or impatiently by-pass the
society.*

CHAPTER 7

The Continuing Spanish Record

THE SPANISH record with the Indians is not
concluded yet. Queen Isabella believed that she loved and
cherished her Indians. Her last will and testament very mov-
ingly voices this sentiment. Thus do the schoolbooks speak;
and in his *Life of Las Casas* Sir Arthur Helps, speaking of
Isabella, exclaims: "Could the poor Indians but have known
what a friend to them was dying, one continuous wail would
have gone up from Española to all the Western Hemisphere."

It was, however, Isabella who confirmed the vicious system
of *repartimiento*—the *encomienda* with its accompanying
forced labor—which Columbus set up in the West Indies.

Ferdinand, after Isabella's death, wrote in 1511, "Our Lord
is well served in the bringing of the Indians from the outlying
islands to where gold is." Because of the scarcity of Indians
due to the exterminations in Española, Ferdinand spurred on
the slave-taking raids in the Bahamas and in regions farther
west by suspending "for the present" the payment to the Crown
of tribute for each Indian seized. But he entered the note that
he had learned that the slave-taking expeditions were not being
efficiently conducted; transportation and starvation were killing

so many Indians before their delivery to the Española mines that "it is somewhat burdensome to the conscience and not very profitable to the business."

Business considerations and conscience united in discrediting Indian chattel slavery. Indians who were not branded as chattel slaves paid yearly tribute to the Crown; chattel slaves did not. Other forced-labor arrangements proved more efficient and somewhat less homicidal. The Dominican order threw its weight against chattel slavery. In the year 1542, when the number of chattel slaves still ran into the hundreds of thousands, Las Casas wrote the articles (numbers 26 and 27) for the New Laws of the Indies, abolishing chattel slavery.

From the conquistadores came wails of woe. They pointed out that they held their slaves from the Crown. Indeed, they had bought their slaves from the Crown. Bernal Diaz, the chronicler of Cortés, at that time very favorably fixed in Guatemala, was sent to Spain to lobby against the iniquitous enactments of 1542—iniquitous to the conquistadores.

But the Crown, under advisement, stood firm and went even further. "No person, in war or in peace, may take, apprehend, use, sell or exchange as a slave, any Indian." This dated from 1548 and the prohibition was all-embracing.

As we have seen, other methods of forced labor were replacing chattel slavery. In the whole of Spain's New World, except as a military or punitive measure, chattel slavery had practically ceased to exist. It did not pay. What has since become known as peonage—comparable to serfdom in the old world sense but generally without the ameliorations of true serfdom—took its place. I have used before the terms *encomienda* and *repartimiento*. Let me define them again here—and along with them certain other terms, because they strike at the roots of the Spanish-American system.

An *encomienda* was a grant to a Spaniard, as a trustee of the Crown, of a body of land, with the Indians attached to the grant as serfs.

A *repartimiento* was a grant of Indian forced labor, whether to a land user, a mine, a factory, a monastery or for public works. In Peru, the Quechuan term *mita* was used in place of *repartimiento;* in the Spanish domain north of the Rio Grande, the word used was *la semana.*

An *encomendero* was not the owner, but the trustee of the land granted him. After one, two or three generations, the *encomienda* would be escheated to the Crown. The Crown then administered it directly through *corregidores;* and *repartimientos* of Indian labor were assigned to the Crown's land.

The chattel slave paid no tribute; he was simply a tool, used for life by his owner. The Indian forced laborer, on the other hand, in *repartimiento* or *mita,* paid tribute both to the Crown and to the Church. The fundamental quantum was Indian tribute. Tribute maintained the caste and status of the Europeans to whom *encomiendas* had been awarded. From this tribute, all public works, religious instruction, monastic foundations, institutions of learning, hospitals and civil salaries came. To the individual Indian, the payment of tribute came to be the core of his economic life. It was death and taxes and nothing else.

Charles V was a strong prince, stubborn and obstinate, with a dominant sense of what to him seemed right and wrong. But the record is filled with his vacillations. He believed that the *encomienda* and the *repartimiento,* though wrong in principle, could be controlled and changed into institutions which would not be harmful to his Indian subjects. And, at the least, their souls had been saved.

Gold was a matter of necessity to him, as he viewed his empire—a continual flow of it. His ambitions demanded it. Even apart from his economic and strategic conceptions, gold had a fetish value in his mind. To him, I think, the question was whether the *encomienda* and *repartimiento* brought home the best results in terms of gold and labor convertible into gold. The priests were there to take care of souls. And a Las Casas, after all, even if things were not quite as they should be, should mind his own (and very important) business.

Arguing in general along these lines, Charles entered into partnership with the conquistadores (which is to say the many little emperors of the New World), became himself, indeed, the chief conquistador. He made the *encomienda* and *repartimiento* into his own instruments.

Meanwhile the stream of ordinances for the protection of his Indians poured forth—as they were to continue to pour forth for three centuries. These ordinances were not merely statutes. They were also arguments, expostulations, pleadings; they recited the conditions that made them necessary; they begged patience.

The Crown received one-fifth of the gold and silver seized from the Incas and Aztecs and later produced from the mines. This royal fifth, according to the estimates of Humboldt, totaled one billion pesos, or about two billion dollars, between 1493 and 1803. The record of Indian forced labor in quicksilver mining is as revealing as any, and suggests why the Crown's benignant intentions failed. Mercury was important in silver mining. In 1601, Philip III directed that Indians be congregated at the quicksilver mines. In 1616-19, Juan de Solorzano, in his capacity of *visitador* and governor, examined into the effects of mercury mining. He found that the life expectancy of the Indians was four years. "The poison penetrated to the very marrow, debilitating all the members and causing a constant shaking, and the workers usually died within four years." Solorzano reported fully to the Council of the Indies and to the King; but in 1631, Philip IV decreed that the *repartimientos* at the quicksilver mines be continued; and his successor after 1665, Charles II, renewed the decree.

From Charles V to the Viceroy Mendoza in Mexico, while the New Laws of 1542 were being formulated, went an instruction: That he should forbid the Indians to pay tribute in kind; he should accept tribute only in cash; and since the Indians possessed no cash, they would have to work out the tribute in the mines.

In 1574–75, the Viceroy and the Audencia (the court of administration and of judgment in Mexico) found themselves meditating. The "natural viciousness" of the Indians troubled them deeply. Work was the cure for the Indians' wickedness; and work in the mines was the best cure. This meditation, in the form of a lengthy report, went to the Crown. It was supererogatory since the Indians already were in the mines and would stay there. But in 1609 the Crown received a full report on the moral gains of the Indians through the mining *mitas*. It was reported by Messia that Indians, sent in *mitas* to the mines of Potosi, in Peru, frequently had to travel a hundred and fifty leagues each way. Twice he had watched them start from the province of Chutquito. Seven thousand departed; about two thousand returned. Five thousand died or were unable to make the return journey. Each worker took his family with him, and eight or ten llamas, and some alpacas for food. They took mats, for they slept on the ground and it was very cold. The journey each way required two months, for the animals were slow and the little children had to walk. When the *mita* ended (the forced-labor assignment lasted six months) often the Indians had no pack animals or food for the homeward journey; also, they knew that when they reached home they would be seized for other forced labor. Sometimes they would be re-impressed at once and sent back to the Potosi mines. Some provinces had become so depopulated that they did not have enough Indians to meet the quota. In such cases the *justicias* (procurers of the *mitas*) and the mine owners forced the Indian caciques to hire the Indians from other districts at the expense of the caciques.

The Indians in *mita* worked twelve hours a day, going down as much as six hundred feet, working by candle light in stifling air. Ascending, they had to carry the metal on their backs; the trip out took five hours, and a false step might mean death. Reaching the surface, often they would be denounced by the overseer for idling, or for bringing up so light a load, and would be sent back into the mine. Their wage was so low that it failed even to supply the bare necessities of life.

Surely, the reader will be moved to exclaim, these conditions could not have been representative. The Indians would have been annihilated utterly.

They *were* annihilated. In the Audencias of Lima and Charcas, for example, the Indians declined from 1,490,000 in 1561 to 612,000 in 1754. And prior to 1561, the depopulation had been enormous. In 1553, Francisco de Victoria, of the Council of the Indies, had reported that "the abominations cried to heaven." Men and women, young and old, he reported, were being forced to work in the mines without rest; and for food they were allowed one pint of maize a day. As the Indian manpower died off, the Indian women were put into the mines more ruthlessly, working in knee-deep water through the coldest season of the year.

Finally the Crown itself showed distress. In 1581 Philip II addressed the Audencia of Guadalajara. One-third of the Indians had been destroyed already, the Crown stated. Those yet living were being forced to pay the tributes for the dead. They were being bought and sold. They slept in the fields. Mothers killed their children rather than let them be taken to the mines. Thus wrote the Monarch himself to his subordinates.

The problem beckons us out from the New World, and back to Spain and Europe. Charles V had resisted the *encomienda;* the *repartimiento,* the *mita;* then had yielded to them; then had made them his own instruments for tribute. He believed that he could curb their ferocities through regulation. But he and his successors failed to curb themselves.

Philip II had warred with the Netherlands. The Moors had revolted and the ensuing Civil War in Spain had desolated Granada. The Barbary pirates were scourging the coasts. The Crown's treasury, practically non-existent, had been inadequate for the building and maintaining of naval forces sufficient to suppress the pirates. The years around 1581 when Philip addressed the Audencia of Guadalajara were crucial. That year he annexed Portugal, placating the rival claimant with an immense grant of land. Then he proceeded to build the Armada. The Barbary pirates could not be crushed; but England, the heretic, must be crushed.

Whence was the revenue to come? In the quest for it, extreme totalitarian regulation had been imposed on all industry within Spain. By the end of the century, the country had been reduced to a state of Byzantine regulation in which everything had to be done under the eye and subject to the interference of a vast horde of government officials, all ill-paid, often not paid at all—all, therefore, necessitous and corrupt.

Such was the condition within Spain. In the New World, whose effectual existence in the Crown's mind was that of a feeder of the bankrupt treasury, "Byzantine regulation," remotely controlled, was also the method of governance. With deliberation the Crown had shunted into the New World the criminal elements of Spain. A death sentence could be commuted to a two-year indenture to the Caribbean islands. The dissolute and neurotic among the clergy were got rid of by assignment to Peru or Mexico.

Like the Crown, the Church had united itself with the *encomienda* and *repartimiento;* and its demands on Indian labor put all moderation aside. As Indian depopulation intensified, the secular and ecclesiastical pressures on the residual labor supply intensified correspondingly; and always the overriding demand for tribute drove the local exploiters on and on.

These factors and conditions aggregated to a fatality. And what seems noteworthy is not that the Crown's regulative efforts in the New World failed, in the main, but that they were persisted in at all. Rather frequently, historians seek consolation in the thought that after all, the *mita* in Peru and the *encomienda* in New Spain did but continue the pre-Conquest oppressions. The consolation is wholly fictitious with respect to Peru. In the case of Mexico, the late years of Aztec rule did tend that way. A landowning class took its rise, many Indians became share croppers, and the Aztec overlords exacted tribute without returning equivalent service to the peoples. But light burdens, borne by the individual as a member of a cooperative and largely autonomous community (the pre-Conquest fact) became, under Spain, burdens which crushed to death, borne by staggering individual Indians whose communities had been tossed into fragments and whom alien masters drove with the lash and held in chains.

We have defined the word *repartimiento*. In the institution's evolution, the word took on an additional meaning; it was used to denote the process whereby debt-slavery was substituted, gradually, for the earlier methods of labor-forcing. A market was needed for all sorts of manufactured goods, produced in the New World and also exported by Spain. These, the Indians were forced to buy; and often having no use for the goods, and always having no cash to pay, the Indians became debtors. The operation was a continuous one across the generations. The debts being everlasting, the Indians found themselves enmeshed in a wage-slavery which held no hope at all. And such was the situation when independence came—but for the Indians no independence, since debt peonage moved on, into and across the nineteenth century.

As debt-slavery became gradually all-embracing, the Crown limited the scope of the *repartimiento*—the labor-draft. For example, the legal grant of *repartimientos* was denied to the *obrajes,* or factories; in its place, debt-slavery chained the Indians to the factories; but in addition, the factories kidnapped the Indians outright and imprisoned them. Friederich A. A. von Humboldt, who visited these workshops near the end of the time of Spanish rule, observed not only a great imperfection of technical process, but also the unhealthiness of the situation, and the bad treatment to which the workmen were exposed.

One tries to find something to mitigate this dreadful record —the record which stamped its melancholy on nine-tenths of all the Indians of the hemisphere. Mitigation—a very, very little mitigation—is found in the working of three factors.

One factor was the increasing labor scarcity, due to Indian depopulation. This brought competition for Indian labor, and within the seventeenth century it put the mining *repartimiento,* in Mexico at least, practically to an end. Wages in the mines crept up; and as the labor was skilled, or semi-skilled, some faint tendency to conserve its supply began to operate. Similarly, on many an *encomienda,* where the labor was attached as serfs, it became expedient not to drive the Indians to extinction.

The second factor was the inner resourcefulness of the Indians. Through some miracle of self-adjustment, they were able to keep their sweetness of spirit. The bleakness externally viewed, the bleakness in all except spiritual fact, was not quite matched by bleakness within the soul. Here, religion was a saving force; the Indian built himself a new religion, genuinely synthesizing pre-Conquest components with Roman Catholic components. The Indian did this, not the Church; it was the Indian's own creative accomplishment; yet the Church did allow it; and in the Church, even though he knew from heavy and mounting experience that the Church was one of his most avid exploiters, the Indian rested his hope and found his home. And the great myth of the soul, the eternal dream which has its truth mightier than fact, did hold many, many of the Churchmen in its embrace, along with the Indians.

The third factor was the continuing effort by the Crown to make effective the spirit of the Laws of the Indies. Though bankruptcy mounted and mounted in imperial Spain—bankruptcy financial, moral, intellectual and political—still that other part of the Spanish mind, whose representative voice for all time was Las Casas, strove on. The effort had its greatest intensity and duration in Mexico; and one of the reasons for this is to be sought in the creation, probably by the Viceroy Don Martic Enriques, about 1573, of a special Court of Appeals called the *Juzgado General de Indios* for all cases involving Indians. Apparently no such institution existed in the other parts of the Spanish dominion, yet if the *Juzgado* had been established earlier and made universal and consistent throughout Spain's New World, the situation might have been quite different.

This is how the *Juzgado* operated: The Indians of three Pueblos, who had been required to furnish a *repartimiento* to the mines at Zacualpan, complained. They said they were paid only one *real* a day instead of the legal one and a half; that they were forcibly detained at the mine for two weeks; that the *Alguacil* had sold Indians to an *hacendado* on their way to the mines.

In the trial the charges of the Indians were shown to be substantially correct. It was learned that the Indians were sometimes forced to work naked in water; that they were brought to the mines tied together by the neck; that they were sometimes beaten; that the *Juez Repartidor* had been guilty of selling them for two and one-half pesos apiece to the Jesuits for work in the sugar mills; and so on.

The *Fiscal*, reviewing the case for the *Juzgado General*, recommended the suspension of the *repartimiento* for two years, the punishment of the *Alguacil* with one hundred lashes, and the restitution of the money he had extorted from the Indians. No punishment for the Jesuits was recommended.

The *Juzgado* thereupon ordered the *Alcalde* (mayor) of Malinalco (one of the Pueblos) to proceed against the operators of the mines. The *Alguacil* was sentenced to pay a fine of two hundred pesos, was exiled from the province and prohibited from ever holding any public office.

Now to follow the case through: Three years later the operators of these mines at Zacualpan petitioned for a restoration of their *repartimientos*. They pleaded that the denial of them was as much a penalty for the royal treasury as for the operators.

Two years passed and the operators renewed their petition. It now came out that, except for the removal of their *repartimientos*, none of the penalties imposed upon the operators had been executed. The *Fiscal* now recommended that the petition of the operators be granted, while the Indians of Malinalco still opposed the restoration of the *repartimientos*.

Two more years passed. The case was again argued before the *Juzgado General*, which at long last decided to renew the *repartimientos* to Zacualpan. But now it ordered that the *repartimientos* must be changed every fortnight; all Indians must be personally accounted for upon the return of the quota; the men must be paid in silver, not in goods; the *repartimientos* must be escorted by Indian *alcaldes*. *Justicias* failing to enforce these provisions were to be deprived of office and fined two hundred pesos; and the operators were warned not to abuse this concession, for at their next offense they would not only lose their *repartimientos* but would be exiled to the Philippines.

We do not know whether the *coverage* of the *Juzgado General de Indios* was adequate. But the integrity and persistence of the Court's activity are beyond doubt; and, in comparison with their lot in Peru, the Indians' lot in Mexico was eased.

Another institution introduced by the Spanish—that of the *reducciones* and *congregaciones*—was variously carried through in nearly all parts of the Spanish New World. The idea itself dated back to the Spanish Laws of Burgos of 1512–13. For purposes various and sometimes contradictory, the Indians were to be assembled into permanent reductions or congregations. The purposes were evangelization, accessibility of Indian forced-labor supply, protection from white slave-raiders and marauders, ease of administration, removal of Indians from land which the whites wanted for some other use. Sometimes the process of *congregación* was handled by the civil, sometimes by the religious arm. Generalization concerning the results is hardly possible at all. Little utopias were created and nurtured in the State of Michoacan, starting within a few years of the Conquest, by Bishop Don Vasco de Quiroga. These *hospitales* scarcely outlasted the great Bishop's lifetime. In Mexico the massive establishment of *congregaciones* was undertaken as a Crown policy by the civil arm. After abortive efforts commencing in 1590, whose effects on the Indians were disastrous, the Count of Monterey sent out a hundred expeditions to determine what places to use for *congregaciones* and what Indians to concentrate in them. The Friar Juan de Torquemada reported that, though the intention was to congregate Indians who were scattered in many places without order or government, the policy was so interpreted that even well-organized villages were seized as well, their houses burned and the people themselves driven to a new place.

Modern historians believe the Friar Torquemada's indictment to have been over-severe. Leslie Byrd Simpson quotes from various reports which tell of the establishment of these *congregaciones;* they have the ring of truthfulness, and they indicate a conscientious effort to do the thing required with as little hurt to the Indians as possible.

In brief, sometimes the *congregaciones* merely added other Indian groups to a large group in an existing village where excess land was judged to exist; and sometimes they forcibly amalgamated numbers of existing villages into one large new one, and burned the old villages; while sometimes they aggregated into one place Indians who had been living widely separated in the mountain country. The detailed results of *congregación* therefore were not uniform. The general and unintended effect, however, was clear to contemporaries. Epidemics were intensified through crowding the Indians together; social dislocation, already driven profoundly into Indian life in the eighty years since the Conquest, was further extended; and the dwindling Indians were fed more easily into the systems of forced labor.

In Peru, the establishment of *reducciones* was a task of the civil arm. It was carried out more massively than in Mexico, and was one of the main drives of government during the viceroyalty of Don Francisco de Toledo, 1569–81. Multitudes of Indians had fled the ferocities of the earlier colonial years into jungle and mountain fastnesses. The mines were devouring Indian life swiftly, and new concentrations of Indians from regions far from the mines were constantly required. Toledo built the new *comunidades* upon the structure of the *ayllu,* the Inca social unit. In general, the *comunidades* were placed upon, or through migration placed themselves upon, the poorer, higher, more barren lands. When they were located, or found already existing, in the richer valleys, they were placed in *encomienda.*

The Crown granted lands to the Indian communities of various kinds, its rule being to grant that amount of land which the given community already was using, or an amount deemed enough for minimum needs. Often, a square league was granted. In New Mexico, the Pueblos received by grant all lands within one league of the plazas, to north, south, east, and west. The titles were in the communities, these communities being "of the nature of municipal corporations," as the Supreme Court of the United States has since described their status. These lands could be alienated only with the consent of the Crown. With a good deal of perseverance, the Crown protected these Indian communal holdings—with greater success in North than in South America. As generations passed, the numbers of Mestizos and Creoles increased enormously. These relatively landless multitudes pressed against the *encomiendas,* the Church and Crown lands and also against the Indian grants. Their land hunger was a major cause of the revolutions which brought independence.

The second flow of events was the hypertrophy of landholding by the Church. Through grants from the Crown, through bequest and mortgage, through purchases with vast sums derived from tithes, alms, etc., and through the confiscations by the Inquisition, the Church became the largest of all landholders, rural and urban.

The Church was economically privileged throughout the Colonial era. Its functionaries were not under the civil jurisdiction, and ecclesiastical capital was exempt from taxation in the early times and virtually exempt in the later. But the Church's economic dominance did not go unchallenged. The Crown and *the higher Church authorities* made periodic attempts to curb it. The Church nevertheless held to its earthly own and *as a landlord* fell away from its vision and its mission. Only at the margins of the Spanish New World did it remain faithful to the ideals of its great spiritual leaders and, I think I can say, to its trust.

CHAPTER 8

The Indians and the Republics

NAPOLEON invaded Spain in 1808. The Spanish King, Ferdinand VII, capitulated. The Spanish people resisted and, fighting on, proved to be the first great obstacle in the path of Napoleonic world conquest. But the wars for independence broke out in all of Spain's colonial America. These were civil wars as well as wars of independence. Independence finally came in 1826, but in the intervening years the Creoles and Mestizos had ruled on their own; and they were in the saddle for a century to come. The Indian, except as his blood was intermingled with the Mestizos, was still, for the most part, an unemancipated serf.

In Mexico, the struggle for independence began as a social revolution. It was led by two great Roman Catholic priests; and it was waged by the Indians. The first of these priests was Miguel Hidalgo, who was in his middle fifties when the struggle began. Hidalgo had worked in the spirit of Don Vasco de Quiroga, and by his methods, establishing among the Indians co-operative textile and pottery works, bee culture, silk culture and grape culture. The civil authorities tore up the Indians' grape orchards at Dolores, near Queretaro, where Hidalgo was stationed. Then, as the historian Zarate tells, the church bell at Dolores tolled, summoning the Indians, and "what had been quiet New Spain during three centuries rose in arms at the magic words, liberty and emancipation, and the shout of war resounded throughout the soil of Mexico from the vast deserts of the north to the shores of Ussmicinta."

As his standard, Hidalgo used the image of the Indian Virgin of Guadalupe. In six weeks he headed an army of 80,000, armed with machetes, pikes, slings, and bows and arrows. His army was met by well-armed soldiery, and by degrees was cut to pieces. Hidalgo rejected pardon, and ordered the emancipation of all bondslaves, the end of tribute and the restoration of land to the Indians of the Guadalajara district. He was killed by treachery, and another village priest took up the leadership.

But the Bourbons were back on the Spanish throne, and the, poured reinforcements into Mexico.

The second priest was Father José María Morelos who, in the years between 1808 and 1813, was the leader of a goodly portion of Mexico. He summoned a national congress which formally declared independence. But with the return of the Bourbons he was overwhelmed. His people suffered horrors beyond description. He himself was captured in 1815, and, having been denounced by the Inquisition as "a heretic, pursuer and disturber of the ecclesiastical hierarchy, profaner of the holy sacraments, schismatic, lascivious, a hypocrite, enemy of Christianity, traitor to God, King and Pope," he was turned over to the secular arm and was killed.

To trace the evolution of the struggles for independence is beyond the province of this book. At the end of years of strife, ideals of political liberty had been written into the South American constitutions, particularly into those which the great Bolivar inspired.

In most of the remainder of Spanish colonial America, independence was from the start an affair of the native-born whites and some of the Mestizos, Cholos, Ladinos (mixed-bloods); the Indians fared as in Mexico.

Throughout, the Indians not merely "secured no benefits" but were pressed deeper down. The entail upon the Indians' community lands was lifted; the lands were individualized; individual faithless Indians were permitted to sell their own and their groups' lands; encroachment went unrebuked and uncurbed; in Peru, the *comunidades* were legally declared to be not persons or corporations, and thus were forbidden to defend themselves in the courts. Only here and there, brief intermissions of dispossession took place. In Bolivia such an intermission came in 1871. The Bolivian dictator Melgarejo had abolished the *comunidades* by decree, individualized their communal lands, and authorized their sale to whites. But in 1871 Melgarejo was overthrown. The new government annulled such sales, compensating the bona fide purchasers of Indian community lands. The *comunidades* as reservoirs of labor-supply had economic importance; this gradually won for them a minimum of tolerance and protection.

Such is the fact. Yet, there is an anomaly which must be reported. The Indian population curve, both in Mexico and Peru, started to rise. Neither past nor present statistics are exact; but between 1805 and 1910 (when the Revolution commenced which was to ease their lot), Mexico's Indians increased from about 2,500,000 to about 6,000,000; between the same years, Mexico's Mestizos increased from some 2,000,000 to some 8,000,000. In the Andes, since independence was won, the Indians have doubled in numbers at the least. These increases cannot be accounted for through material factors alone, because the material factors remained almost constant. One cannot help but wonder whether the Indian soul, at its deep unconscious level, entered into hope through independence from Spain. Perhaps it knew, or hoped, that after one more century of anguish, the lifting of the Indian's doom actually would begin, so that the will to live, and not to die, became the Indian's will. Possibly the Spaniard, in the Indian mind, had become the symbol and announcement of death, and the Spaniard's overthrow broke the lethal power of the symbol and announcement. The population curve swung upward with independence from Spain—that is all we know.

Yet the Porfirio Diaz regime in Mexico built up those intensified, unbearable pressures on the Indian which insured that the next revolution would be a mass revolution and a social revolution. Expropriation of the Indian communities, under forms of law or no forms, was pressed throughout Mexico. The Yaquis were deported to Yucatan as slaves. On the more generous of the *haciendas* the Indian peons earned eight cents a day; they supported their families on that. But the miseries of the *haciendas* reached beyond their own peons to the whole of Mexico. They used no more than a small fraction of the arable land contained within them; their immense holdings were not for use but for monopoly of the Indian labor supply. Protected by high tariffs on grains, they hoarded their produce, speculating on the scarcity market. They resisted all improvement of agricultural method.

In addition, under Diaz, Mexico as a whole saw the passage of great areas of land to non-Mexican, absentee ownership; saw its mineral and oil wealth pass to foreign concessionaires; saw the looming of a new "Yankee" bondage to take the place of the bondage to Spain.

All of these factors, with many others, entered into the prolonged, tortuous revolution in Mexico which followed the overthrow of Diaz. The Indians' own pressures forced agrarian reform into the very center of the revolutionary program. By 1915, the legal basis for a redistribution of land had been laid; by 1917, the Constitution had sanctioned this redistribution.

Mexico was, and still is, overwhelmingly agricultural in its economy. The mass of the people depend on agriculture, the Indians almost entirely. The *comparative* facts as to crop production greatly emphasize the picture.

Of the area planted to 34 crops in 1930, 58 per cent was planted to corn. Of this total of corn acreage, two-thirds produced only 6 quintals or less per hectare, compared with 15.5 quintals in Spain in the same year; 14 in France; 22.7 in Canada; 20.9 in Austria. For wheat, occupying 9.4 per cent of the cropped land in Mexico, and planted on the irrigated land, the yield was 6 quintals per hectare as compared with 13 quintals in Italy, 9.7 in the United States and 11.5 in Canada. For frijoles, one of the staples of Indian diet, the average yield per hectare was running at *less than one-fifth of the average yield in Spain*.[1]

Why these severe deficit figures? Counter-revolutionary spokesmen in Mexico and abroad have attributed them to the break-up of the great holdings and the re-vestment of the Indians with land. On the contrary, it is the *encomienda* and *hacienda* systems which built the cumulative deficits through hundreds of years. Exploitative and non-reciprocating toward the Indians, they were the same toward the land. They mined it, did not farm it. Through the century before 1910, the Indian communities, on landholdings constantly shrinking yet with rising populations, had no choice but to work their already marginal lands to death. The communities possessed no working capital and had no access to credit or to agricultural advice; the *hacendados* with very rare exceptions ignored agricultural science, content to let peon labor take the place of improved agricultural tools.

Not merely was the soil nurture mined out through one-crop, unfertilized use; it was washed out and blown out through water and wind erosion. What went forward, and what goes forward still, was and is a process of silent catastrophe which, unless it can be reversed, dooms most of the Mexican plateau to agricultural extermination within the century ahead. There remains Mexico's tropical belt; but the costs of development, and the uprootings of Mexican life, will be enormous, when or if the tropical belt becomes the only unexhausted agricultural area. It must be understood that Mexico is no case apart, and that analogous factors have brought, for example, hundreds of millions of acres in the United States into a state comparable to that of the Mexican plateau.

[1]*The Ejido—Mexico's Way Out* by Eyler N. Simpson. 1937. University of North Carolina Press.

One other basic fact must be reiterated here. Rural Mexico—Indian rural Mexico—for unknown ages has had as its ultimate unit the local community. It has been a world of villages, of pueblos. Prior to the last Aztec years, the thousands of pueblos possessed each its own land. In the century before the Conquest, what may be called a tribute-title was bestowed on warriors and others who conspicuously served the State. When, under Spain, *encomienda* and *repartimiento* were imposed, still the pueblos remained as the basic Indian-life units. Spanish law and administration recognized and incorporated them, and tried to protect their landholdings. Independence variously took their landholdings away, and through the Diaz regime expropriation was pressed to virtual finality. *But the pueblos remained.* Very profound in the mass mind of Mexico was the concept of the Indian pueblo and its aspiration; and the pueblo stood as Mexico's everlasting fact.

In 1910, when the Revolution got under way, 10,632,000 pure Indians and Mestizos lived in 61,284 rural pueblos. All but a handful of these pueblos and of their inhabitants were, for all practical purposes, dependent upon the large estates for the means of holding body and soul together. When the agrarian revolution came, there could be no doubt as to the way the land would go. Idealogically, sentimentally, administratively and practically, it would go to the pueblos. Thus was insured one of the great endeavors of decentralized democracy of our age, the *ejidal* program of Mexico.

From what individual source, within the Revolution, came the *ejidal* program, which was so very much more than the mere program of restoring land to the people? Madero, the humanitarian *hacendado* who led the Revolution in 1910–11, did not conceive of the program. It was no part of the rather inchoate, primarily political, agenda of the Revolution at the beginning. The individual source which announced the program and fought it through was a poor peon, or share cropper, who could not read nor write. Emiliano Zapata supported Madero ardently. When Madero lagged in the agrarian program which he had accepted from Zapata but had not genuinely affirmed, Zapata went into rebellion; the Indians thronged to his support, and soon he controlled the states of Morelos, Jalisco, Guerrero, Puebla and at times the Federal District of Mexico itself. Madero endeavored to break Zapata with the army. Zapata struck back with the *Plan de Avala:* The lands should be redistributed now, and the *ejidos* should receive them; if the government did not act, the people would take the lands by direct action. The people—the Indians—proceeded to take them. This was in 1911.

Then the Huerta counter-revolution overthrew Madero. Venustiano Carranza launched a revolt against Huerta; Zapata joined Carranza. In 1914, Huerta was driven out, and after five weeks of chaos, Carranza assumed the executive power. Carranza had pledged himself to Zapata's platform; and under Zapata's pressure—almost, Zapata's bludgeoning—he promulgated the *Plan de Vera Cruz,* involving the distribution of the land to the *ejidos.*

But Carranza failed to act for the *ejidos.* From 1915 to 1920, only 190 pueblos received land; only 180,000 hectares were distributed to 48,000 *ejiditarios.* Zapata went into revolt again.

In 1920, General Obregón and his followers in Sonora declared war; their pledge was to make good on the Revolution's commitments. They swept the country; Carranza perished; Obregón became President.

Still the agrarian revolution was pressed falteringly. Twenty years after the enactment of the *Plan de Vera Cruz,* in 1935, fewer than eight million hectares had been returned to the pueblos. The *ejidal* plan through which the villages obtained their land is, with slight modifications, the present way; hence, at this point it is outlined.

Through its Executive Committee a village petitioned for a restitution, or, as the case might be, a *dotation* (a *de novo*) grant of land. The petition went to the State Agrarian Commission, which took a census, surveyed the available lands, and made other needed investigations. The State Commission reported to the Governor, who was required by the law to render his decision within five months. If the Governor's decision was affirmative, the village was given provisional possession; if the Governor's decision was negative, the village could appeal through that Commission to the President of the Republic. On receiving the recommendation of the National Commission, the President (if acting affirmatively) made definite and final the village's possession. The village received its land as a matter of legal right, not of privilege.

Where a village could prove title, the village received all land covered by its regenerated title, with minor exceptions. In the absence of proved title, enough land was expropriated to insure to each family and every person over 18 years of age from three to five hectares of irrigated or "humid" land, or four to six hectares of good dry-farming land, or six to eight hectares of dry-farming land less good. In totaling the land which should go to a village, the professional class, government employees, persons whose wealth exceeded 1,000 pesos, and persons whose salary exceeded 75 pesos a month, were omitted from the count.

Under usual conditions, haciendas or other landholdings of only *moderate* size could not be expropriated.

The expropriations were not paid for in cash but in special government bonds. The bonds were negotiable, and could be used to pay certain classes of taxation. The face value of these bonds equaled the declared value of the land as sworn to by the owner for tax purposes in prior years, plus 10 per cent. In practice, the expropriation was a mitigated confiscation; but these same *hacendados,* and their predecessors in interest, had confiscated the land and also the lives of the people for generations or hundreds of years.

The *ejidal* lands were inalienable, and the title was communal. The *ejido* could use its lands through collective enterprise or through granting use-rights to its members; but it could not convey title to an individual member.

The *ejido* built its schoolhouse. The State or the Federal Government supplied the teacher. "Cultural missions," serving groups of *ejidos* for periods of weeks or months, toured the Republic. Modest public works of every kind were carried out by *ejidos* here and there. Eight hundred thousand heads of families, more than four million individual Indians, lived on the *ejidal* lands, ruled themselves there, breathed freedom.

Yet in 1935, twenty years after the *Plan de Vera Cruz* had been enacted, clouds of doubt brooded over the *ejidal* movement. For two-thirds of the big *haciendas* of Mexico had yielded not a hectare of land to the *ejidos;* land distribution lagged; and among the 4,500 *ejidos* (approximately), were thousands whose land and water supply was too meager to permit a contribution to the national economy.

Education, though depending, by and large, on the school and the school alone, advanced only haltingly. No adequate credit system existed to make possible the acquisition of capital goods by the *ejidos.*

Mexico needed, desperately, production *with conservation* from all of its agricultural lands. *Ejidal* economic planning, in the absence of capital goods, was handicapped. *Ejidal* enterprise was suffocated.

Among those who knew that there was greatness in the *ejidal* movement, there was a strong intensity of hope and of fear. I quote here from an unpublished notation of my own, written after a third visit to Mexico, in 1936.

"The regenerated *ejido* is not comparable to the Pueblos of New Mexico and Arizona. These United States Pueblos have existed in unbroken continuity as complex, autonomous societies. Their land-base was impaired in the nineteenth century but never destroyed. Their flow as co-operative commonwealths has never stopped. By contrast, the Mexican *ejidos* have behind them four centuries of white rule; their members have just now emerged from being forced-labor slaves, with no freedom of choice, no chance to take responsibility.

"Transition from native co-operative living to co-operative economic enterprise of present-world type is not automatic, and usually is not swift. Its feasibility, in the case of Indians, is being demonstrated in hundreds of places in the United States and Alaska today. Mexico will make the same demonstration; but if, somehow, capital-goods credit, within a credit system designed to be educational, could be furnished in Mexico, the transition would be accelerated. And the *time factor* is tragically important. The future of the structure and spirit of Mexico may be determined in early years by the intensity of success and the rate of spread of the *ejidos*. The entire Western world should give attention and encouragement to the *ejidal* movement; for it is a movement in behalf of us all.

"The *ejidal* movement is, of course, only one component of the Mexican revolution, though it may be the profoundest one. And it has values and results going beyond the statistical and tangible. *The spirit of the Indians of Mexico is now once more facing the sky.* We who first went into Mexico in 1930 will always remember the experience. Utterly poor men, these Indians yet were touched with light. Nothing could exhaust their merriment, their hospitality. After hundreds of years of enslavement, they had made themselves free. In those years, and just recently visiting this and that *ejido*, this and that rural school, one glimpsed what thousands of others have glimpsed—the vista of a sweeter, deeper day for the Western world. The *ejidal* program has not failed; and it is one element in a mighty event which has not failed. But those who know its greatness should also know its desperate difficulties. The *ejido* is Mexico's road to a better and lasting time. It is the kind of road that the other Republics with massive Indian populations must travel. It is a road to be built with great creative striving. The Indians are building it, but they cannot do without help."

New revolutionary energy was the need. New passion, new vision, new administrative will. Lázaro Cárdenas supplied them. He became President at the end of 1934. In the six following years, he established the agrarian revolution. He did very much besides. He established, once and for all, Mexico's national dominion over its natural resources, including oil. Working with the intellectually subtle, the brilliant, audacious Vincente

Lombardo Toledano, he built organized labor into unity and power. Through millions—actually millions—of personal, face-to-face contacts with the Indians in every Mexican state, he built confidence and power into them. In 1940, though overwhelmingly the people's and the nation's choice, he refused to violate the constitutional clause against presidential self-succession; and he refused, and refuses still, to seek to dominate his successors from behind the scenes.

There has been no greater leader of any people in this age than Cárdenas; perhaps there has been none whose heart was so rich and so pure. Future time possibly will measure his achievement on behalf of the Indians as being second only to that of Las Casas.

He is linked, too, with Miguel Hidalgo and José Maria Morelos and Emiliano Zapata; and far back in time, with Don Vasco de Quiroga of Michoacan. Michoacan, incidentally, was Cárdenas' home. He was governor of that state before he became president.

Cárdenas resumed the distribution of lands to the pueblos. By the end of 1938, 13,000 Indian communities had been revested with land. There were 1,600,000 *ejiditarios,* representing nearly 8,000,000 beneficiaries of the *ejidal* lands. Twenty-three million hectares had been confirmed to *ejidal* possession and these made up one-third of the crop land of Mexico.

The problem of credit was a difficult one, not wholly solved by Cárdenas. The beginnings of the *Banco National de Crédito Ejidal* were made in 1935. This bank operated through Ejidal Credit Societies, membership in which was voluntary and which were collectively liable for the credit obligations of their members. The bank was much more than a lending institution. Its personnel of 2,350 technicians worked with the credit societies in the formulation of farm and industrial plans, and only on the basis of such plans were loans made at all. The bank stored the commercial products of the societies in regional warehouses; the loans were repaid from the sales of these products, and the profit was turned back to the societies. Long-term loans for capital goods were made; in 1938, of the total loaned, 9 per cent went for capital goods equipment. Groups of *ejidos* were federated for loans going to public utility needs.

Under the statute, the credit societies were required to set aside 5 per cent of their gross returns as a "social fund." The credit societies controlled their social funds, but the bank advised them. They were used for health services, for the installation of water supply, for the purchase of the material for school buildings, community halls, and so on, built through contributed labor; for the financing of distributive co-operative enterprises, and for any common benefit. The social fund of the credit societies totaled 3,500,000 pesos in 1938.

The credit problem of the *ejidos* was met, but never fully met. In 1939, of 13,000 *ejidos*, only 5,200 had credit societies or were receiving loans; of the 1,600,000 *ejiditarios*, fewer than 500,000 were members of credit societies. The reason lay in the operating rule of the Ejidal Bank, a sound and necessary rule. Loans were made to credit societies only on the basis of farm and industrial plans which on analysis were deemed adequate to insure the repayment of the loans. Thousands of *ejidos* possessed lands so inadequate, or so remote from markets, that valid loan applications simply could not be formulated. In practice, the Ejidal Bank did frequently make loans which were not economically justified; it pushed beyond the margin of safety, so that its delinquencies ran as high as 12 per cent a year. Basically, this incompleteness of the *ejidal* credit system, and its high delinquency rate, was the result of the fact that Mexico did not have enough good land to go around, and that the land program, enormously extended as it was under Cárdenas, still was unfinished. It is unfinished today.

Mexico entered dubious times after Cárdenas. But he left the *ejidal* movement too strong, too proud, and too well implemented to be destroyed. Before Cárdenas, the faces of the Indians were turned toward the sky. Through him, they traveled far on the road of their hope.

CHAPTER 9

The Indians of the United States

To KNOW the spirit of the Indians of the United States is to know another world. It is to pass beyond the Cartesian age, beyond the Christian age, beyond the Aristotelian age, beyond all the dichotomies we know, and into the age of wonder, the age of the dawn man. There all the dichotomies are melted away: joy requires sorrow, and sorrow, joy; man and society and the world are one; fantasy and the old, hard wisdom of experience join in the rituals, the moralizing tales, the songs, the myths; idealism and ideality are joined with searching and undeviating practicality. And the child is joined with the man.

The story of North America's Indians, down the centuries, brings into relief three Indian characteristics, attainable by average men only through the application of a profound social art. They are psychological maturity, many-sidedness, and intensity within tranquillity. The tranquillity includes, not excludes, life abundant and the awareness of tragic fate.

The night he died, in the Danubian marshlands where the barbarians advanced on the Roman Empire, Marcus Aurelius gave to the army its watchword: *Equanimitas.* But this was an equanimity withdrawn from the press of life, from all the splendor and terror of it. The tribal Indian's equanimity is poised within the press of life and rejects nothing of the glory and doom. It is poised, too, between the "twin eternities" of a racial past not dead and a future already alive, on-drawing and event-commanding through the action of the human will implanted far onward within future time.

I had supposed that the tracing of the Indian record in what is now the United States would be the easiest part of this book. I had lived with its subject matter for twenty-five years; it was home ground. But as it has turned out, it is the most difficult part of all. I have searched myself to find the reason for this difficulty. It does not lie in the prolixity of material or in anything controversial in its nature. Prolix the material is. But the movement of events was fairly uniform, fairly explainable, on the whole simple. As for controversy, it scarcely exists in the usual historical sense. What the events were, together with their causes and consequences, are hardly in dispute, whether among scholars or popular historians.

The events are hardly in dispute—but right there lies the source of the difficulty. It is not a matter of controversy among historians. It is an utter disparity between, on the one hand, the impressions made by the events on the historians, and, on the other hand, the personal and social inwardness of Indian life. The events seem to rush in one dark bloody avalanche, then to switch to a still gray monotone, then to hesitate. Thus history sees the facts; thus they were; yet within the Indian, so long as his societies endured, they were not thus.

Whence my difficulty, finally resolved within myself. It was a resistance against being one more narrator about the Indians, that stopped me. For I felt that I would do again what so many narrators had done before me. The problem was to catch what I could of the other side, and, in catching it, to relate it to a meaning for all of us. Let us remember that the Indian's societies did in fact endure until well past the middle of the nineteenth century; that many of them endured through the whole dark age, on into the present day of comparative brightness; and that even when societies, viewed as describable institutions, are destroyed from without, their persuasiveness may go on for a long time within the soul, even for many generations.

European contact with the Indians north of Mexico set into motion events very different from the Caribbean, Mexican, Central American and Peruvian histories. One European epoch encountered two Indian epochs. South of the Rio Grande the Spaniards encountered the epoch of imperial consolidations. But north of the Rio Grande, in what was to be the United States, six hundred Indian national societies existed, each complete, many-sided, self-reliant, profound in its social–spiritual endowment.

This contrast led to subjection and enslavement in the one area, and in the other to hundreds of years of warfare, with no successful enslavement and even, to the end, no yielding by the Indians to anything but the sheer fact of being physically overwhelmed. The cultural events contrasted, because their bases of origin contrasted. South of the Rio Grande, the empires had set into motion a trend toward homogeneity. White conquest accelerated the trend. North of the Rio Grande, no such trend had been established at all; and as physical conquest by the white world advanced over the bloody marches of Indian resistance, Indian social individuality held its own, and even deepened its consciousness of itself.

Is it to be wondered at that the Indians north of the Rio Grande have always awakened a strange yet intimate excitement in the white man's soul? They speak to us from out of our long foregone home, and what hears them is the changeless, eternal part of us, imprisoned and immured by our social epoch even as the Indian societies were imprisoned and immured by us in the century behind. Just as our own buried depths predict a world future and belong to it, so these outwearing, ancient Indian societies predict a world future and belong to it.

At the time of discovery, the region that is now the United States contained some one million Indians. The total for both North and South America was perhaps 30 millions. Today, of the 25 to 30 millions of Indians in the Hemisphere, the United States (including Alaska) count 400,000, or one-seventieth of the world's Indian population. By the quantitative test, therefore, this book should devote only four or five pages to the Indians of the United States, their history past and present, and the white man's traffic with them. Their numbers are fewer than those of the city of Rochester, New York, and many historical works treat of them accordingly. In their *Basic History of the United States*, Charles and Mary Beard concede to the Indians seven references in three pages out of five hundred.

But I shall disregard the quantitative test here, and this not merely for the reason that I know the Indians of the United States better than the other Indians. Nor is the reason that more is known, historically and in the present, about the United States Indians than about the far more numerous other Indians, for the data upon the others are abundant. The true reason, I hope, will appear through this brief record.

The million Indians of the United States and Alaska were formed within more than six hundred distinct societies, in geographical situations ranging from temperate oceansides to arctic ice, from humid swamps to frozen tundras, from eastern woodlands to western deserts. In peace and war these hundreds of societies acted and reacted on one another over ages, and large numbers of them possessed a secondary language that was international among them, the sign language. But no vast consolidations, like those of Mexico, Middle America and the

Andes, ever embraced them, transposing power, leadership and responsibility from the primary, complete societies into centralized nations to be destroyed by time or conquest. Unbroken and unwaning, the primary social group in what is now the United States lived on, worked on, evolved on, from Neolithic or Paleolithic time to the white man's arrival.

At the time of white arrival there was no square mile unoccupied or unused. The six hundred or so Indian dialects were vehicles of more than that number of tribal societies. These societies existed in perfect ecological balance with the forest, the plain, the desert, the waters, and the animal life. These societies desired population totals large enough to insure their continuance; this desire was one among many factors which assured caution and moderateness in their warfare. Beyond wanting enough members to insure tribal continuance, the tribes did not have statistical ambitions. They valued quality, not numbers, in men.

In what is now the United States, warfare, like predation in wild life, functioned toward the ecological harmony; and more complexly than predation in wild life, it functioned toward the shaping of virile, structured, unafraid, truly noble personality, which counted one's separate life and fate as of no great moment.

Yet while Indian warfare was limited, not unlimited or excessive, the Indian and his society "lived dangerously." The extreme of effort, of discipline and resourcefulness, hardest of realism, might at any time be demanded of every member of the little society. The Indian made it his business to have fullness of life within material meagerness, and within a deep insecurity which his wisdom did not even want to see terminated. The abode of this insecurity was not within his own soul or within his group life, but within the world of war, drought, flood, storm, and pestilence. He made, through his social institution and social art, this *external insecurity* into the condition of *inward security*—individually-inward and group-inward.

The white invasion came. Indian warfare enormously increased and Indian insecurity became incalculably intensified, but that profound training and conditioning, and that affirmation of the will to live dangerously while living in impassioned tranquillity, did not collapse. Only with the actual dissolution of his societies could the Indian's life-power start to fail; and this life-power knew how to control the effects of all bad events, within the soul and within the human relation.

Through historical accident, the region now the United States

became possessed by no single conquering white nation but by
the Spanish, Dutch, French and English. These competed with
one another, and the Indian tribes were essential factors in the
rival imperialisms across three centuries. So it came about that,
though intertribal wars were incalculably multiplied, and Indian warfare was perverted from its ancient ecological, educative and moderate rules, and changed into total war driven by
irrelevant, white-imperialistic aims, yet the Indian societies were
not at first proscribed. "Indirect rule," and a severely limited
indirect rule, with high status for the native societies, was the
calculated policy of the trade-competing and warring imperialisms, particularly those of England and France. This policy had
become standardized and codified in treaties and statutes at
dates long prior to the American Revolution; and the United
States incorporated it as the basic, theoretical law of Indian relations.

After the day of rival imperialisms was over, however, there
remained only one expanding empire, race-prejudiced and with
a boundless land hunger. The former policies toward Indian
societies and Indianhood became reversed; a policy at first im-
plicit and sporadic, then explicit, elaborately rationalized and
complexly implemented, of the extermination of Indian societies
and of every Indian trait, of the eventual liquidation of Indians,
became the formalized policy, law and practice.

But it was not until the white centuries had five-sixths completed themselves that the planned, implemented destruction
of the Indian societies as the means of breaking the Indian's
soul began. The full intensity of this policy and practice of social
destruction against Indians lasted only sixty years and then was
stopped. Its policy of mutilation and starvation reached deep;
but it had not time enough to kill a thing so strong.

If the reader holds in mind these considerations, he will
find only the more distressing the deeds of the white man in the
United States toward the Indian, and the presumptions and
lusts which inspired the deeds. But he will know that in his true
citadel and home—his tribal society, and his soul—the Indian
went on, transmuting hard and faithless events into spiritual
good. The Indian's spiritual and social hygiene remained triumphant. Pain beyond any possible telling, depopulation, the
loss of homeland, the loss of any foreseeable future—all these
he endured, and did not try to tell himself that they were less
than they were. He kept his humor, his pride, his values of
aristocracy, his power of love and his faith in gods who do not
hate. Betrayed, overwhelmed, subjected to scorning hate, he was

never inwardly defeated. So the bleak record did not mean, to him, what it meant externally and what it must mean to you and me. Sadness deeper than the imagination can hold—sadness of men completely conscious, watching the universes being destroyed by a numberless and scorning foe—such sadness the tribal Indian knew through the long event. His spaciousness of life, the slow, immense rhythms of it, its tidal inflow and outflow of the boundless deep, and its spontaneity of joy which suffused the wise old, the earnest young and the child—these never failed.

Are we willing to know the Indian's secrets? The creative potency of human societies encounters, in most of social science, a glassy eye.

Yet what is there in our world like the achievement of the Indian? Perhaps thus the Druid society met its fate; we do not know. William Morris depicts such an achievement by a Teutonic society, in his *The House of the Wolvings*. Some Christian monastic orders, men and women, have now and then attained this creative potency. In the United States, it was hundreds of tiny Indian societies which held themselves and their individuals at such a level through hundreds of years on to the last hour; and among these hundreds, a goodly number of the societies triumphed past the end of the ravening age, and are operative today.

In *Black Elk Speaks,* one of the classics on Indians, John G. Neihardt[1] records the memories and thoughts of Black Elk, an illiterate, aged Dakota Sioux. Black Elk was speaking thirty years after the final crushing of the Oglala Sioux society as an entity, but during the time when the fragments of that society were being pursued into the very fastnesses of the soul.

"And I," said Black Elk, "to whom so great a vision was given in my youth—you see me now a pitiful old man who has done nothing, for the nation's hoop is broken and scattered. There is no center any longer, and the tree is dead."

Black Elk had just been describing, circumstantially, but without any taint of hate or bitterness, the Wounded Knee massacre of 1890 which had taken place when the Indians had assembled to witness a prohibited religious ceremony. "We followed down the dry gulch, and what we saw was terrible. Dead and wounded (Indian) women and children and little babies were scattered all along where they had been trying to run away. The soldiers had followed along the gulch, as they ran, and murdered them

[1]From *Black Elk Speaks: Being the Life Story of a Holy Man of the Oglala Sioux* by John G. Neihardt. 1932. By permission of the publishers, William Morrow & Company, Inc.

in there. Sometimes they were in heaps because they had huddled together, and some were scattered all along. Sometimes bunches of them had been killed and torn to pieces where the wagon guns hit them. I saw a little baby trying to suck its mother, but she was bloody and dead."

Black Elks' narrative of Wounded Knee brought to its end his reminiscence. "After the conclusion," Neihardt writes, "Black Elk and our party were sitting at the north edge of Cuny Table, looking off across the Badlands ('the beauty and the strangeness of the earth,' as the old man expressed it). Pointing at Harney Peak looking black above the far sky-rim, Black Elk said: 'There, when I was young, the spirits took me in my vision to the center of the earth and showed me all the good things in the sacred hoop of the world. I wish I could stand up there in the flesh before I die, for there is something I want to say to the Six Grandfathers.'"

They took Black Elk to Harney Peak. I quote further from Neihardt's record, both because it is so fine in expression and because it is so representative:

Having dressed and painted himself as he was in his great vision, Black Elk faced the west, holding the sacred pipe before him in his right hand. Then he sent forth a voice; and a thin, pathetic voice it seemed in that vast space around us.

"Hey-a-a-hey! Hey-a-a-hey! Hey-a-a-hey! Hey-a-a-hey! Grandfather, Great Spirit, once more behold me on earth and lean to hear my feeble voice. You lived first, and you are older than all need, older than all prayer. All things belong to you—the two-leggeds, the four-leggeds, the wings of the air and all green things that live. You have set the powers of the four quarters to cross each other. The good road and the road of difficulties you have made to cross; and where they cross, the place is holy. Day in and day out, forever, you are the life of things.

"Therefore I am sending a voice, Great Spirit, my Grandfather, forgetting nothing you have made, the stars of the universe and the grasses of the earth.

"You have said to me, when I was still young and could hope, that in difficulty I should send a voice four times, once for each quarter of the earth, and you would hear me.

"Today I send a voice for a people in despair.

"You have given me a sacred pipe, and through this I should make my offering. You see it now.

"From the west, you have given me the cup of living water and the sacred bow, the power to make life and to destroy. You have given me a sacred wind and the herb from where the white giant lives—the cleansing power and the healing. The day-break star and the pipe, you have given from the east; and from the south, the nation's sacred hoop and the tree that was to bloom. To the center of the world you have taken me and showed the goodness and the beauty and the strangeness of the greening earth, the only mother, and there the spirit-shapes of things, as they should be, you have shown me and I have seen. At the center of the sacred hoop you have said that I should make the tree to bloom.

"With tears running, O Great Spirit, Great Spirit, my Grandfather—with running eyes I must say now that the tree has never bloomed. A pitiful old man, you see me here and I have fallen away and have done nothing. Here at the center of the world, where you took me when I was young and taught me; here, old, I stand, and the tree is withered, my Grandfather!

"Again, and maybe the last time on this earth, I recall the great vision you sent me. It may be that some little root of the sacred tree still lives. Nourish it then, that it may leaf and bloom and fill with singing birds. Hear me, not for myself but for my people; I am old. Hear me that they may once more go back into the sacred hoop and find the good road, the shielding tree."

Long ago I would have suspected an element of the histrionic in Black Elk's words; or that Neihardt was partly inventing so balanced and rich a harmony; or that Black Elk was a solitary and exceptional mystical genius. Years of being among Indians of many societies, as one vitally related to them, have shown me otherwise. Perfection of speech goes not where literacy goes, for average men; it goes where unwritten language goes. The poetic imagery among tribal Indians was and is as unfailing as Homer's imagery. Black Elk's telling of his life shows that he gave all that he had to the Sioux, his people; and they received and matched all that he had in response.

The Sioux are Plains Indians and famous fighters. The Shawnees are forest Indians and also famous fighters through their history. Shawnee society appears never to have numbered more than two thousand members, but its warriors fought all over what is now Kentucky, Indiana, Ohio. Tenskwatawa, the Prophet, and Tecumseh, his twin brother, who just after 1800 tried to rally all Indian tribes against the white invasion, were Shawnees. They failed, and subsequently the Shawnees were split asunder, the "Absentee Shawnees" settling in Texas, whence they were driven out into Indian Territory (Oklahoma) in 1839. The Absentee Shawnees numbered fewer than five hundred souls, and it is their world which is described by Thomas Wildcat Alford, and recorded by Florence Drake.[2]

Alford's memories commence after the millenniums of Shawnee warfare had ended, but the turbulence and peril en-

[2]From *Civilization* by Florence Drake. 1936. (One of the 26 volumes in the *Civilization of the American Indian* series.) By permission of the Publishers, University of Oklahoma Press, c1936.

veloping the Shawnees had not ended. They were being swept into that forced land-allotment, designed to dispossess the pacified Indians and to wither their community life, which did in fact largely accomplish its ends. What was their inward, spiritual condition? What was the human relationship within the little group?

Alford quotes, in Shawnee, the two basic rules by which he grew up.

"Do not kill or injure your neighbor, for it is not him that you injure, you injure yourself.

"Do not wrong or hate your neighbor, for it is not him that you wrong, you wrong yourself. Moneto, the Grandmother, the Supreme Being, loves him also as she loves you.

"Standards of conduct were just as rigid as the laws of any other people, but force was seldom used to enforce good conduct. *Each person was his own judge.* Deceitfulness was a crime. We lived according to our own standards and principles, not for what others might think of us. Absolute honesty toward each other was the basis of character . . . Indian parents gave few commands, because they were advocates of freedom of action and thought, but absolute obedience was exacted . . . All our histories, traditions, codes, were passed from one generation to another by word of mouth. Our memories must be kept clear and accurate, our observation must be keen, our self-control absolute . . . A child would strive with all his might to win praise (from a parent or elder), while he would be indifferent to bodily punishment.

"Our people appreciated skill or knowledge of any kind, but naturally they thought more of the wisdom that formed the background of our racial life."

The sundered bands of the Shawnees met again after more than half a century of separation. "Although the two bands had been separated for more than fifty years, each had held so tenaciously to its creeds, customs and traditions that neither had changed at all. They took up their life together with no jar or discord and again they were an undivided people."

The Shawnee's life was spacious, unhurrying; deeply rooted, which many uprootings did not starve because the undying society, not any material condition, was their soil. It was a life of joyousness and unfailing nobility through the whole of a very complex human relationship; of freedom within flexible orderliness; and of such a love for the Shawnee social institution as plants and creatures have for the sunlight, the giver of life. And in Alford's account there is not one note of hate, bitterness or fear toward the white oppressor, only this remark: "If cunning and deception were resorted to in dealings with white people, it was pitted against something that the red man felt powerless to cope with on common ground—something for which he had no name." Thus would Inca or Aztec have spoken.

Two more examples are given of that almost deathless inwardness of the Indian societies which mastered the ruin that seemed to overwhelm them through the hundreds of years. One is found in the story told by the Osage Indian, Tse-shin-ga-wada-in-ga, or Playful-calf, to Francis La Flesche.[3]

The date is 1912, just before, in Oklahoma, the fatal flood of gold (from oil discoveries)—$265,000,000 in sixteen years—started to drown the 2,000 Osages.

"My son," said Playful-calf, "the ancient Non-hon-shin-ga have handed down to us in songs, wi-gi-e, ceremonial forms, symbols, the many things they learned of the mysteries that surround us on all sides. All these things they learned through their power of 'wa-thi-gthon,' the power to search with the mind. They speak of the light of the day by which the earth and all living things that dwell thereon are influenced; of the mysteries of the darkness of night that reveal to us all the great bodies of the upper world, each of which forever travels in a circle of its own unimpeded by the others. They searched for a long time for the source of life, and at last they came to the thought that it issues from an invisible creative power to which they applied the name 'Wa-kon-da.' "

After a few moments of silent reflection, the old man continued: "Many of the sayings of the Non-hon-shin-ga who lived long ago have come down to us and have been treasured by the people as expressions coming from men who have been in close touch with the mysterious power whom the people had learned to worship and to reverence. Moreover, the men who uttered these sayings had long since departed for the spirit land and were regarded by their descendants as Wa-kon-da-gi, that is, sacred and mysterious persons. These sayings had been transmitted in ritual form, and during the passage of years had been jealously guarded against desecration by those persons who succeeded in memorizing them and had taken care to teach them only to such pupils as manifested a proper spirit of reverence for things sacred."

One day, as Playful-calf was reciting to La Flesche titles of the songs, there was a prolonged pause, while La Flesche waited pencil in hand. This pause was unusual for such a wide-awake

[3]From *The Osage Tribe: Rite of the Wa-Xo-Be* by Francis La Flesche. 1928. Bureau of American Ethnology.

man as Playful-calf, and La Flesche wondered if the old man
had suddenly been taken sick. When he looked at Playful-calf's
face, there were tears on his cheeks. When Playful-calf had composed himself he looked at La Flesche with a smile, and said:
"My son, a sudden remembrance of the old Non-hon-shin-ga
brought tears to my eyes. They were kind to us, those old men,
when I was working hard to learn from them the sacred songs.
As they sat around the fireplace, I fed the fire to make it shed
light and warmth, and I ran to the spring to fetch water for
them when they were thirsty. By these little services I won their
affection, and they were gentle and patient with me when they
taught me."

In his report La Flesche describes the symbolic beauty and
profundity, and the extreme complexity, of one of the ceremonies he later was allowed to witness and which Playful-calf
explained to him as it went along. "The object of Playful-calf
in having me witness the ceremony did not fail of its purpose,"
wrote La Flesche, "for gradually it became clear to me that the
rite as a whole was of a cosmic character; that it was a dramatization of the movements of certain cosmic forces whose combined
power brought forth material life upon the earth and set it in
perpetual motion." The ceremony was in fact a sacred dance-
drama and a prayer; through its perfect, tranquil but intense enactment, not the individuals alone, but the tribe, commingled
with the universe and contributed, not merely received, meaning and power.

A final example of the all-surmounting inwardness of the
tribal societies comes from New Mexico. In 1926 I was present
with a friend at an Indian gathering at which we were the only
whites. A diary entry which I made the following day, was given
to the Indian committees of the House and Senate in support
of a bill (which became law) insuring to the tribe, for a hundred years to come, the exclusive use of its sacred area in the
National Forest. Various opponents had hinted that the secret
occasion out in the mountain-wild was an orgy of pornography
and sadism, and therefore the tribe, after much hesitation, had
asked the two of us to come for this one time. The diary note
follows.

Twelve miles from the Pueblo, at 10,500 feet elevation, on the
flank of Taos Sacred Mountain, is the first of two ceremonial
grounds. Three hundred members went up to the ceremony. The
Pueblo contains a few over six hundred souls.

They went as whole families, including babes-in-arms a year
old. A few of the tribe walked; these were old men, reproducing

the custom of times before the horse. Some were unable to go, being held at the Pueblo by community tasks or by work in the fields.

There appeared some alterations due to historical contacts with the whites. The great lean-tos, built by the old men and women, had canvas for roofing, instead of buffalo hides. There were some woolen blankets in place of the ancient cotton; and in some cases, not the complete moccasin but store-shoe tops on moccasin soles. The horse provided a striking esthetic addition. Two hundred or more horses were pastured in the five-acre glade. Until nearly midnight, belated arrivals were coming in, riding through absolute blackness on the steep, craggy and disused mountain trail which has led to the ceremonial ground for thousands of years. Far off the horses would sense the coming horse, and the high, far-flung whinny of welcome from hundreds of horses would wing across the human song. All night this silvery whinnying from hundreds of throats was flung across the ceremonial ground.

Otherwise, what transpired was unchanged from immemorial age. Even the Plains Indian elements of Rio Grande Pueblo Indian culture were largely absent; no feathered bonnets, for example, were worn. No white eyes, nor even alien Indian eyes, had witnessed this occasion before; and after the cry to the Spirits had been sent forth in the opening song, we two witnesses were as nonexistent; and when at dawn we and the tribe departed opposite ways, there was no saying of good-by.

First, and throughout, was the supreme esthetic quality. Yet concerning it, as concerning stranger impressions of that night, descriptive words are nearly useless. Log fires threw a rising and falling glow on robed moving masses of human forms and on great aspen trunks. The lean-tos caught every glow. They were made of whole, thirty-foot trees, brought from outside the ceremonial ground, the tree-trunks two feet apart; and resting on them, great canvases. They rose from different levels of ground, tier behind tier, irregularly centering toward the fires. Under the lean-tos had been built dais-like structures; and there in the fire-glow clustered all who were not at any moment dancing. Here the gorgeousness of the Pueblo color-hunger was seen; women and infants wore colors which in the transfiguration of the fire-glow were rich as Chinese decorations. All the tribe's wampum, silver and turquoise was worn.

The fires lit the dance ground. Here were no colors, other than the fire's own color reflected from white or dusky robes. Here, with personal qualities shrouded, moved scores, hundreds of ghosts. They moved like masses of smoke, like wind made visible, like masses of cloud heaving over this (to the Indians) sacred mountain. No casual motion, no gesture of one to another, ever appeared; all was a mass rhythm; but an evolving rhythm which changed a hundred times during the night. Among the figures was a woman who danced all night with her baby on her shoulder.

The song went out from fifty, sometimes a hundred singers. From ten o'clock until dawn, there was never a full minute's interlude. Only once were the dancers still. That was when the mass singing ceased and one powerful voice for seven minutes sang alone.

How in many Pueblo sacred dances the oblivion of self and the corresponding inrush of power becomes almost terrifying, is known to all who frequent the dances. But even the Red Deer Dance is brief, its intensity faint, compared with this dance. The occasion as a whole was a summoning by the tribe of many spirits of the wild, elements or cosmic kin known from ages gone by; and a summoning from within the breast of capacities and loves which had formed the ancient life and must sustain its present and future. As the hours moved on, a displacement of human and mystical factors seemed to take place. The rejoicing was not only a human rejoicing; and that marvelous ever-renewed, ever-increasing, ever-changing leap and rush of song was not only human song. A threshold had been shifted, forces of the wild and of the universe had heard the call and had taken the proffered dominion. That is what the tribe believed; that is how it seemed—physical actuality in a thunderstorm or amid ocean breakers seems no more certain. Empirically, it can only be said that a strange release of energies took place, that the dynamic potentiality of ancient beliefs was realized, and that there was expressed a rejoicing, passionate and yet almost coldly exalted, and the fleshly raiment appeared to fall away.

On this night at this place, the spirit of Pueblo religion could have been mistaken by none. Forces or beings normally invisible, only half-personal yet connecting with the hidden central springs of the empirical life, are a dominating fact in the Pueblo (in the tribal Indian) mind. The Indian's relationship to these forces or beings is not chiefly one of petition or adoration or dread, but of a seeking and sharing in joy. It is a partnership in an eternal effort whereby, from some remote place of finding and communion, the human and the mechanical universes alike are sustained. A tribal religious illusion? Not the Indians nor can we prove or disprove it till the world ends. A primitive animistic fiction? Nevertheless, a fiction thus late (perhaps thus soon) endowing a disinherited race with an eagle's wings.

It seemed that among the necessary illusions or fictions since man, the creator, began, there could have been none more adequate for gathering all of a race's life into one self-transcending, quietly and permanently nourishing passion, than this fiction unloosed and re-affirmed in this place which might have been a Grecian temple. But a Grecian temple before the dance and song were gone, before the mural colors had faded from pillars and roof, before the oracle was stilled and Pan was dead. And before the Attic social age had passed away.

CHAPTER 10

Conquest North of the Rio Grande

NORTH of the Rio Grande, the Indian record begins in Labrador. There, in 1501, came the Portuguese explorer Gaspar Cortereal. He kidnapped fifty-seven Indians to be sold as slaves, but on the way home his own vessel sank in a storm and he and his men and the Indians chained in the hold were drowned together. A second vessel reached Portugal with seven Indians remaining alive. The Portuguese had found the natives curious, hospitable, helpful. (That was to be true of every initial contact in North America thereafter.) They gave the bleak country the name Labrador signifying "the place with an abundance of labor material."

Next on the record is the old man Ponce de León who came to Florida seeking his fountain of youth. The Indians received him in a friendly enough way. But when he returned, eight years later, he found that their attitude had changed. For in the meantime other Spanish adventurers had ravaged the shores of the Gulf of Mexico. And the year previous one Lucas Vásquez de Ayllon, an *encomendero* who had played his part in the depopulation of Haiti by way of slavery in the mines, had raided the shores of Chicora (now Georgia and South Carolina) and kidnapped more than a hundred Indians. One shipload of these was engulfed on the voyage to Haiti and the rest perished in the mines. So, when Ponce de León came again to Florida, the Indians warned him not to land. He landed and was killed along with many of his men, and the expedition beat a retreat.

The next great expedition was that of Hernando de Soto, who had been one of Pizarro's men in the conquest of Peru. There on one occasion he had displayed a sense of honor, crying out to Pizarro against the murder of Atahualpa, the kidnapped Inca emperor. Yet when he was welcomed by the North American Indians who were living in prosperity and peace, he outraged their hospitality.

While he was being fed and otherwise assisted by the Indians in what is now Arkansas, de Soto decided it was time "to make the Indians stand in terror of the Spaniards." Not many leagues away the unsuspecting Nilco Indians had their abode, "five or six thousand of them" living in one large town. De Soto sent his forces against the Nilcos and so surprised them that, according to *The Narrative of the Expedition of de Soto* by "The Gentleman of Elvas," "there was not a man among them in readiness to draw a bow . . . About one hundred men were slain;

any were allowed to get away badly wounded, that they might
rike terror into those who were absent." Some of the Spaniards
lled all before them, young and old, according to the record.
In the Creek country (Georgia), a beautiful "Princess" re-
ived de Soto with ceremony and gifts. Promptly he kidnapped
er as a hostage. Again and again, having been received with
ospitality, he kidnapped the headmen or chiefs. He burned the
llages, laid waste the cornfields, dragged Indians with him
om place to place in chains as carriers, and applied torture to
xtract information. These are not stories told by the Indians.
hey come from the source material as recorded by de Soto's
ompanion and eulogist, the Gentleman of Elvas. The lurid
ourse ran on until 1542, when "on the twenty-first of May,
eparted this life the magnanimous, the virtuous, the intrepid
aptain, Don Hernando de Soto, Governor of Cuba and Ade-
antado of Florida."

De Soto had discovered the Mississippi River, and Indians
om the Georgia coast to beyond the Mississippi had discov-
red the white man.

The next large episode of penetration and conquest, and
ightly the most famous of them all, is that of Coronado, whose
xpedition traversed Arizona and New Mexico, discovered the
rand Canyon of the Colorado, made contact with all the
ueblo city-states, penetrated deep into Texas, and traversed
Kansas to discover that mythical Quivira "whose cacique slept
n the afternoons under a tree, lulled by the music of golden
ells run by the wind." Quivira proved in fact to be the habitat
f the friendly Wichita tribe and a place of no gold; so the
omantic Indian who had led Coronado through hundreds of
eagues of fantasy was garroted.

The principal source document of Coronado's adventure is
hat of Pedro de Castenado, a private soldier in Coronado's
rmy; and it is one of the best documents of the conquest epoch.
Castenado brings to life the Great Plains, the Indians of the
Plains, and the unlimited herds of buffalo; the superb white
wolves and the armies of jack rabbits traveling with the buffalo.
His descriptions of Pueblo Indian life at the first white contact
re invaluable.

Coronado was seeking gold, and he found none. He and his
men, and the friars who accompanied them, were not intent on
proselytizing. Most of the time, with one glaring exception,
hey practiced moderation toward the tribes.

Had Coronado discovered gold, we might have a different
tory. Since he did not, the expedition bears a favorable record.

Seeking only gold, Coronado had no wish for *encomiendas* o
repartimientos. Failures, he and his men returned to Mexico
Yet it is important to record the fact that Coronado did no
torture Indians to make them divulge where gold might be.

In general, Coronado kept faith with the tribes during h
short time with them. He received everything from them, gav
them back nothing except forbearance and some defective an
wholly useless brass cannon. But unwittingly he gave them th
horse, extinct for ages on the American continents. And i
Spain he gave a measure of skeptical good will from the tribe
at the northern border of her empire. Thus, Coronado's achieve
ment endured. Apart from an immense increment to geography
including human geography, he supplied the first contributio
to a sense of mutuality between the races, a sense whose de
velopment over the generations was to make some parts of th
American Southwest a case apart in the bitter record of India
relations.

Let us turn now from the Spaniards to the English, and t
Sir Richard Grenville, immortalized as the captain of the littl
Revenge which battled the whole fleet of Spain and went dow
off the Azores coast. Grenville landed with seven ships in 158
in what is now Virginia. He explored as far as the presen
Roanoke River, meeting hospitable Indians everywhere. Ye
when one of his Indian hosts stole a small silver cup, Grenvill
sacked and burned the Indian's village. Thus, the Englishma
started his course in that land which "still retained the virgi
purity and plenty of the first creation, and its people their prim
tive innocence of life and manners."

The white settlement of Virginia actually began in 1607
Jamestown lay within the territory of the Powhatan Confed
eracy. Through the years when he could have struck the tin
colony with overwhelming power, Powhatan (Waukunsene
caw) withheld his blow. Before he died in 1622, wave upo
wave of new settlers had shifted the balance of power foreve
The succeeding chief, Opechancanough, attempted the delaye
onslaught, and failed. He attempted it again in 1644, when h
was past ninety. Then the Powhatan Confederacy went dow
in flame and blood. Opechancanough, taken prisoner, and dy
ing from age and fatigue, was needlessly shot by a guard. Hear
ing the murmur of the crowd around him, the aged chief re
quested that his eyelids be held open, that he might see th
Governor. Gazing on the white leader he said, "Had it bee
my fortune to capture the governor of the English, I would no

eanly have exposed him as a show to my people."

In Massachusetts there was peace between white man and
ndian for more than ten years after the Mayflower's landing in
520. During the three previous years, an unidentified sickness
ad depopulated the eastern shore from Penobscot to Narra-
ansett Bay. "The woods," remarked Cotton Mather, "were
most cleared of those pernicious creatures, to make room for a
etter growth." Massasoit, chief of the Wampancags, signing
treaty with the Pilgrims in 1621, remarked, "Englishmen,
ake that land, for none is left to occupy it. The Great Spirit . . .
as swept its people from the face of the earth."

But the Massachusetts settlers eventually pressed westward
hile the Dutch settlers pressed eastward from the Hudson
iver. Crushed between them, the Pequot Indians of the Con-
ecticut River valley made a gesture of self-defense. "A mas-
acre!" came the cry. Before this, that devout professional sol-
ier, John Mason, who had left Massachusetts, his sword having
een hired by the Dutch, had been engaged in harrying the
equots. Now from Boston there came to his support three
essels with men and guns. This was in the year 1637. It was
ot that Dutch and English loved one another so much. That
core was to be settled after the Red Man had been put to rest.

Unsuspecting, the Pequots were sleeping within their palisade
t a spot near the present New London. Daybreak was glimmer-
ng on their seventy wigwams. Mason approached with his re-
lenished forces in the night. His men rushed the wigwams and
indled them with torches. As the Pequots fled through the
urning wigwams they were riddled with musket fire. "God is
ver us," Captain Mason shouted, "He laughs His enemies to
corn, making them as a fiery oven." Dr. Cotton Mather fur-
ished a written account of the massacre: "It was supposed that
o less than six hundred Pequot souls were brought down to hell
hat day."

The Dutch were less assured of being God's chosen people
han were the Puritans, but they had not much more mercy on
he Indians. They did, however, establish the precedent of buy-
ng from the Indians their tribal land—a program to become
mportant later. They paid the Indians seventeen dollars for
Manhattan Island. Up to the year 1826, the United States and
he predecessor colonies had paid to the tribes an average of
.147 cents an acre for their purchased lands, which were later
e-sold to whites for two dollars an acre.

The French and the Quakers provided the redeeming ex-

ceptions to the record of these European invaders. The French
came to trade, not to possess the land. They sought the good
will of the Indians, adopted their modes of life as their own
often made permanent marriages in the New World. And the
French Jesuits came, saintly men and hardy men who proved
be discerning anthropologists and careful chroniclers as well
The Quakers, in Pennsylvania, cultivating peace in their own
breasts, and seeking the experience of the Spirit, found the Indians wholly congenial in the early years.

Yet these brighter hues of the French and the Quakers were
not to be enduring. "Imperial" interests overrode their pristine
intentions. French and British rivalries, economic and political
were intense; each strove to unleash the Indians against the
other; nearly all of the tribes found that they had no choice
except to take sides. None who held power on either side—
French or English—could withhold himself from the overriding
polity; if not offensively, then defensively, they must hurl the
Indians against their imperialist opponent, and this soon came
to mean hurling Indian against Indian.

William Penn's successors played this kind of power politics
along with the rest, only more successfully; and the reason for
their success was a significant one. The reason was that their
esteem and affection toward the Indians was genuine and active
The Indians responded in kind; and the Quakers honestly
sought to fulfill their own part of every bargain. So, though they
wanted peace, the Quakers, through binding to themselves and
thus to England members of the Iroquois Confederacy, contributed decisively to the smashing of French power through the
so-called French and Indian Wars.

This factor of power politics incalculably multiplied the Indian intertribal wars, and turned them into wars of extermination. Tribes were shunted pell-mell onto the hunting and planting grounds of other tribes. They had to stake all upon the
victory of one or another of the European powers. They did
stake their all again and again. They cast decisive weight into
the European struggles for a continent. The victor always
abandoned them after his use for them was over. Such is the
approximate fact, yet with an exception—in the long run, a
very important one. Because the tribes were indispensable
pawns in her own imperial game, England forged out a policy
toward the tribes, and that policy later became the basic Indian
law of the United States.

The British Crown in 1754 took over from the Colonies the
power of dealing with Indians, under this imperial policy: The

ribes were independent nations, under the protection of the
Crown; Indian lands were inalienable except through voluntary
urrender to the Crown; and any attempt by an individual or
group, subject to the Crown, or by a foreign state, to buy or
eize lands from Indians, was illegal.

Having framed this policy, the British Crown did more than
give lip-service to it. Repeatedly, violations of the policy by one
and another of the Colonies and by individual whites were rebuked and annulled. Hence, hatred of the Crown increased
among the "Borderers," the whites at the westward verge of
American settlement who were seizing the Indian lands. It
could be argued, and may be true, that England lost the war of
the American Revolution through trying to be faithful to this
policy, which thereafter became the policy (often submerged,
but ultimately triumphant) of the United States. At a far earlier
date, Spain temporarily lost Peru, and all but finally lost it,
through trying to be faithful to comparable policies.

So, through joining in the struggles for empire, though so
much of his blood and all his lands were lost, the North American Indian achieved an affirmative recognition of himself and
his societies. Far on in time, as we shall see, this recognition
persisted. This recognition was to become applied policy, as it
had long since become basic law, in the United States. The tragic
ordeal of the Indian was perhaps not in vain; it may turn out to
be an inspiration (as it has been in romantic literature) for all
mankind.

CHAPTER 11

Iroquois and Cherokees

THE MOST important Indian grouping on the
continent, north of Mexico, from the very beginning of European conquest on through and after the American Revolution
was the Confederacy of the Iroquois. I think no institutional
achievement of mankind exceeds it in either wisdom or intelligence—accepting the limits of its time and place. Our knowledge of this Confederacy is now, I think, complete—thanks to
the lifelong studies of one of America's great ethnologists, the
late J. N. B. Hewitt.[1]

[1] Fundamental work on the Confederacy's history and meaning was accomplished
many years ago by Lewis H. Morgan; other important work was done by Arthur
C. Parker.

The Confederacy came about sometime around the middle of the sixteenth century, or over fifty years after Columbus discovered America, but about fifty years or more before James town and Plymouth Rock—to say nothing of New Amsterdam and Quebec.

Ostensibly, it was a league of five tribes (the Tuscaroras driven from the south, joined in later to make the sixth)—Mohawk, Seneca, Oneida, Cayuga and Onondaga. The plan was to renounce warfare as between one another and to present an alliance against a warring world. For two centuries, or until the so-called French and Indian Wars, this Confederacy or League of United Five Nations was completely successful.

Viewed through the light of the full knowledge we now possess, the Confederacy was much more than a successful alliance for the purpose of keeping the peace among the most powerful of the North American tribes.

It sought universal, perpetual peace. It was Deganawida who was the motivating force. He was a man who lived not earlier than the sixteenth century; symbol and dream enveloped his memory, even as the memory of the Christ became enveloped. He was of virgin birth; his mother, Djigonsasee, "She of the Doubly New Face," guided and assisted him, and Hiawatha, a wizard who experienced a second birth through Deganawida's influence, was his speechmaker. Deganawida was a spiritual genius, uniquely endowed with *Orenda*, an inner power more strong than the natural powers of man. This Orenda knew how to reveal its truths through ceremonials, rituals, mystic parables.

Thus Deganawida (who suffered from an impediment of speech among a race of great orators) went with his intuitive vision fully wrought out, equated with every existing structure and value of the tribes, and cast into a logico-esthetic mold, to each of the five tribes who had so long warred with one another. Only the Onondagas remained unconvinced; the others made their union conditional on that of the Onondagas. Then Deganawida, the statesman, proposed that the Onondagas be made the Firekeepers in the proposed League Council—the chairmen, the moderators whose task was to find the way to happy unanimity. The Onondagas accepted, and the Confederacy was formed, to last in full vigor and harmony through more than two wildly storming centuries, and to last forever among the destiny-pointing ideas of mankind.

The code of the Confederacy read: "I, Deganawida, and the Confederated Chiefs, now uproot the tallest pine tree, and into

e cavity thereby made we cast all weapons of war. Into the
pths of the earth, deep down into the under-earth currents of
ater flowing to unknown regions, we cast all weapons of strife.
'e bury them from sight and we plant again the tree. Thus
all the Great Peace be established."

The Confederacy was one of delegated, limited powers; and
ith exhaustive care and success, it was so structured that au-
ority flowed upward, from the smallest and most organic
its, not downward from the top. From this source came the
bility of the Confederacy during the century and a half when
l of the maddening stresses of white contact were focused
on it as upon no other Indian grouping; and hence, its far-
eing statesmanship, recognized by the Colonies, France and
gland. The Confederacy was a nation which enhanced the
erty and responsibility of its component parts down even to
e minutest member.

"When the five Iroquoian tribes were organized into a con-
deration," wrote Hewitt, "its government was only a develop-
ent of that of the separate tribes, just as the government of
ch of the constituent tribes was a development of that of the
veral clans of which it was composed. The government of the
an was a development of that of the several brood families of
hich it was composed, and the brood family, strictly speaking,
as composed of the progeny of a woman and her female de-
endants, counting through the female line only . . . The sim-
er units surrendered part of their autonomy to the next higher
its in such wise that the whole was closely interdependent
d cohesive. *The establishment of the higher unit created new
ghts, privileges, and duties.*" [2] (My italics.) According to
ewitt the new rights, privileges and duties were created for
e higher level as well as for all the lower levels which com-
osed the higher; since power flowed always from the base to
e summit, not the other way.

*All power, but not all initiative and responsibility, thus
owed.* Like nearly all Indians, the Iroquois knew that creativity
d effective social action were matters of leadership. Develop-
g and choosing leaders, and relating leaders to each other
d to the people, was a preoccupation of nearly all tribes. It
as only that the Iroquoian peoples possessed values and
echanisms which were in part their own; and in the Con-
deracy, these values and mechanisms were stated and institu-

[2]From *A Constitutional League of Peace in the Stone Age* by J. N. B. Hewitt.
18. Smithsonian Institution.

tionalized close to perfection. To use exhaustively the leadersh
capacity of each component tribe; to conserve the rule of un
nimity in legislative decisions; to make of this unanimity
creative, not merely a precautionary, principle; to utilize at t
top levels, where the fate-making actions were thought out, a
not only at the lowest level where all authority was reposed, t
womanhood of the tribes; and to keep in intimate union t
leadership at all levels, male and female leadership with t
electorate from whom all power flowed (the mothers)—su
was the aim and for generations the achievement.

The Five Nations came into the epoch of white contact as
institution perfected and whole. Its forty-nine "chiefs" we
selected by the mothers of lines of descent which possess
hereditary chieftainship rights, subject to confirmation by pop
lar vote (male and female) in each tribe and to subsequent co
firmation by the whole body of chiefs. Women "Trustee Chie
tainesses" similarly were chosen, and they were part of the co
federated council. The mothers exercised the right of initiativ
referendum and recall. To insure that those "uterine familie
not possessed of hereditary chieftainship rights were not e
cluded from Confederacy leadership, the Council itself selecte
"Pine Tree Chiefs" on the basis of proved merit without rega
to hereditary right; these were installed in the same way as th
other chiefs. In addition, such families as did not hold heredita
chieftainship rights chose sister families as their representative
and in effect joined with them in exercising the basic authoritie

Each tribe, through its chiefs, cast a unit vote in the Counci
Four tribes—the Mohawk, Seneca, Oneida and Cayuga—vote
the fifth, the Onondaga, acted as moderator or chairman, calle
"Firekeeper." Each group of chiefs, in the order named abov
discussed separately a given question. Unanimous decisio
were simply confirmed by the Firekeeper; decisions not unan
mous were discussed by the Firekeeper to the end of discoverin
common ground or some new solution, and then were remande
to the four voting units. This procedure made of legislativ
process a path to discovery, not to deadlock.

The peace aims of the Confederacy were universal. Throug
adoption by a "uterine family," any Indian on the continer
could enter the confederation, and many did, voluntarily c
through capture. The whole prospect was changed throug
settlement by the whites with their imperial contests only fift
years after the Confederacy had been perfected. The Dutch, th
French, and the English solicited the Confederacy and threa

ened it. They set the tribes at their rival's throats and at Indian throats along the whole frontier and a thousand miles inland. The Confederacy chose the Dutch alliance; the Dutch armed its member tribes with gunpowder weapons, and the Confederacy established hegemony over a half of all the territory east of the Mississippi.

That which had been completely intended as an enterprise toward universal peace became irresistibly re-directed into an enterprise of daring yet cautious diplomacy and of cohesive, swift efficiency in imperial warfare and Indian civil warfare. The alliance with the Dutch became the alliance with England, and sealed the fate of the French. The world events which Deganawida could not have foreknown ruled out the dream and the purpose.

"Policy," it is fashionable to remark among sociologists of these current years, "is only behavior." The action and the event—these alone have efficient reality; the idea and intention can be disregarded. The policy, then, of Deganawida, was rather resistless war than living peace, for so the future event constrained and so the action had to be. How strange, insular, this current sociological fashion, with its implied derogation of the Buddha, the Christ, and all the other sources of illimitable influence. An idea and an intention, among the Iroquois, wrought out a social institution, a system of greatness in human relationships, a system for evoking maximum genius and for socializing it, and a role of women in society, which well may stand today as the most brilliant creation in the record of man. Then from a world unknown, a ravenous race swept in a dark age for the native life which was hurled into the pit by cannon, by rum, by money, by unconscionable intrigue.

Deganawida would speak for most of the Indians since the white man came: Events and action are not the all; ideas, ideals and intentions are the master facts; they saturate events, and trans-substantiate their meanings; and they outlast.

More than any other tribe, the Cherokee Nation furnished the crystallizing thread of United States government policy and action in Indian affairs. The Cherokees were the largest of the Iroquoian tribes; but they never joined the Confederacy, and we never think of them as being Iroquois. In the years before Great Britain's power ended, the British Crown had intervened repeatedly to check the seizure of Cherokee lands by the "borderers." Thus it came about that in the war of the Revolution the Cherokees allied themselves with the British.

Not until 1794 did they stop fighting. The treaty which they then made with the United States was kept by them as a sacred thing.

The Cherokees met every test of peacefulness, of practicality, of Christian profession and conduct, of industry and productiveness, of out-going friendliness to the whites, of "progress" in domestic order and in education. They even offered little resistance to marriages between young men of the whites and their young girls. One of their great men, whom we know as Sequoia, and whom we have idealized, invented an alphabet considered second only to our European system in the various schemes of symbolic thought representation, and the tribe quickly became literate in our European sense. The Cherokees wrote a constitution of the American white man's kind. They established a legislature, a judiciary and an executive branch. A free press and public schools were set up. Again and again the tribe surrendered great areas of its treaty-held land. Over and over again, however hard pressed, it kept the faith.

Yet, in the years that followed, the treaty was breached both in the letter and in the spirit by the United States over and over again. And it is clear that nothing the Indians could have been or not been, could have done or not done, would have changed the white man's heart and will. The remnant of their lands included seven million acres, mostly mountain country in the region where Georgia, North Carolina and Tennessee converge, what is now called the highland country. The Cherokees had to be removed even from these last fastnesses.

In 1828 Andrew Jackson was elected president. He was a "borderer" and had been a famous Indian fighter. Immediately he put through Congress an act called the Indian Removal Act which placed in his own hands the task of leading or driving all Indian tribes to some place west of the Mississippi River. At about the same time gold was discovered in the Cherokee country. The Georgia Legislature passed an act annexing—confiscating—all Cherokee lands within the state, declaring all laws of the Cherokee Nation to be null and void, and forbidding Indians to testify in any state court against white men. The Cherokee lands were distributed to whites through a lottery system.

In 1830, through John Ross, its chief, the tribe vainly appealed to President Jackson. Then it appealed to the Supreme Court. The Court refused to take jurisdiction; the tribe, it ruled, was not a foreign nation. "If it be true," said the Court, "that the Cherokee Nation has rights, this is not the tribunal in which these rights are to be asserted. If it be true that wrongs have been inflicted, and that still greater are to be apprehended, this is not the tribunal which can redress the past or prevent the future."

The conscience of the Court was troubled by this Pilate-like decision. Two years later, it had an opportunity to reconsider. Three white missionaries refused to swear the oath of allegiance to Georgia while resident in the defined country of the Cherokee Nation. They were arrested, chained together, and forced to walk twenty-one miles behind a wagon to jail. Two Methodist preachers intervened against the brutality; they were chained with the others and thrown into jail with them. The missionaries were tried and sentenced to four years hard labor in the state penitentiary. The case came up before the Supreme Court, and the Court, in effect reversing itself, ruled that Indian tribes or nations "had always been considered as distinct, independent, political communities, retaining their original natural rights . . . and the settled doctrine of the law of nations is, that a weaker power does not surrender its independence—its right to self-government—by associating with a stronger, and taking its protection.

"The Cherokee nation, then, is a distinct community, occupying its own territory, with boundaries accurately described, in which the laws of Georgia can have no force, and which the citizens of Georgia have no right to enter, but with the assent of the Cherokees themselves, or in conformity with treaties, and with the acts of Congress."

President Jackson retorted to the Court: "John Marshall (the Chief Justice) has rendered his decision; now let him enforce it."

So Georgia, and the whole of the Federal Government apart from the helpless Court, continued their policies toward the Cherokees. The whites could prospect for gold anywhere, the Indians not at all, though the land was their own. The President's commissioners harried some of the Cherokees into signing a treaty giving up the 7,000,000 acres still theirs for $4,500,-000 which would be deposited "to their credit" in the United States Treasury. The leaders and people had been immovable, but in an arranged meeting attended by some 400 of the tribe's 17,000 members, the fictional treaty was extorted. The Senate quickly ratified this "treaty."

Three years passed and the Cherokees were still upon their land. Then came General Winfield Scott with 7,000 troops and a non-military rabble of followers to invade the Cherokee domain. Cherokee men, women and children were seized wherever found and without notice removed to concentration camps. Livestock, household goods, farm implements, everything went to the white camp-followers; the homes usually were burned. After this the long trek to Arkansas in mid-winter was begun. An eye-witness in Kentucky reported: "Even aged females, apparently nearly ready to drop into the grave, were travelling with heavy burdens attached to their backs, sometimes on frozen ground and sometimes on muddy streets, with no covering for their feet.

Of about 14,000 who were herded onto this "trail of tears," as it came to be called, 4,000 died on the way. While a hundred Cherokees a day were perishing of exhaustion and cold on that dreadful road, President Van Buren on December 3, 1838 addressed Congress: "The measures [for Cherokee removal] authorized by Congress at its last session have had the happiest effects . . . The Cherokees have emigrated without any apparent reluctance." The financial costs of the trail of tears were charged by the government against the funds credited to the tribe pursuant to the fraudulent treaty.

As the final company of the Cherokees started on the long trail, their leaders held the last council they would ever hold on their home ground. They adopted a resolution which ought to be remembered forever. They did not ask pity for their people, because they knew there would be no pity, and asking pity was never the Indian's way. They did not reproach or condemn Georgia or the United States Government. They did not quote John Marshall's decision, since that decision, for them, had been written on water. To the violated treaties and fraudulent treaties they made no reference; for they had now learned that which General Francis C. Walker was to phrase immortally when, in 1871, writing as Commissioner of Indian Affairs, he described the white man's view concerning honor toward Indians: "When dealing with savage men, as with savage beasts, no question of national honor can arise. Whether to fight, to run away, or to employ a ruse, is solely a question of expediency." Their treaties, the Cherokees had learned, had been "ruses" of the white man. So the resolution, passed in what then seemed to be their final hour, was addressed to no man, and leaned on no consideration, except the principle of justice which they believed was undying:

"The title of the Cherokee people to their lands is the most ancient, pure and absolute known to man; its date is beyond the reach of human record; its validity confirmed by possession and enjoyment antecedent to all pretense of claim by any portion of the human race.

"The free consent of the Cherokee people is indispensable to a valid transfer of the Cherokee title. The Cherokee people have neither by themselves nor their representatives given such consent. It follows that the original title and ownership of lands still rests in the Cherokee Nation, unimpaired and absolute. The Cherokee people have existed as a distinct national community for a period extending into antiquity beyond the dates and records and memory of man. These attributes have never been relinquished by the Cherokee people, and cannot be dissolved by the expulsion of the Nation from its territory by the power of the United States government."

That was all. Then these men of true greatness, through fraud and violence stripped of everything, set forth on the bitter trail to a place which was to be no lasting home.

To this point the Cherokee narrative, with changes only of detail, is the narrative of all the tribes east of the Mississippi from 1800 to 1840. All, within varied but always amply structured and consecutive societies, held anciently owned lands under treaty guarantees. Always, the treaties were nakedly violated by the United States, or changed or nullified through statute or proclamation, or whittled down or annulled through fraudulent deals by commissioners.

Like the Cherokees, the others of the "Five Civilized Tribes" —the Choctaws, Chickasaws, Creeks and Seminoles—were shoved into the area which became Indian Territory and is now Oklahoma. Through extreme tenacity, remnants of the Choctaws, Seminoles and Cherokees eluded or fought off the deportation. In a seven-years' war, from 1835 to 1842, the Seminoles in Florida held at bay armed forces thrice exceeding the number of their whole population in a war which cost the United States 1,500 lives and $20,000,000, and in the end were left alone; they inhabit the Florida Everglades still. Their war chief, Osceola, when negotiating under a flag of truce in 1837, was kidnapped; imprisoned at Fort Moultrie, he was dead within a year; but the Seminoles never yielded. Of the Cherokees, a few hundred escaped and joined the wildcats and bears in the Great Smoky Mountains, where they were forgotten until, with the years, one by one they emerged to toil for the whites. Variously they re-acquired 56,000 of their seized 7,000,000 acres, incorporated themselves under the North Carolina state law, and ultimately were brought under Federal jurisdiction again. The Choctaw remnant, landless share croppers in their homeland until a few years ago, are still in southern Mississippi, culturally Choctaws still.

In Indian Territory, now Oklahoma, the Five Civilized Tribes were planted on ample lands. The new treaties pledged them exclusive, everlasting possession of their *communally owned* domains; it pledged that their tribal governments would be left in authority forever. I resume the Cherokee narrative, which stands for the rest.

No longer were there rival European imperialisms, using the tribes against one another and therefore respecting the societal integrity of each allied tribe. There was only the United States: treaty-bound with the tribes, guardian over them, and through Supreme Court decisions vested in its legislative and executive branches with "plenary" authority over Indians.

Until 1849, the Bureau of Indian Affairs of the government was an office in the War Department. The Army, to its cost and frequent humiliation, had learned what it was that made the Indians cohesive, resistant and recuperative. It was their tribal societies. Hence the Army reached the decision to dispose of them. The decision was one of military and political convenience, and was acted upon rather than proclaimed, being in thorough conflict with the pledges contemporaneously written into each new treaty when the antecedent treaties had been voided, and in categorical conflict with the ideal, basic Indian law of the United States which the Supreme Court never tired of re-announcing.

Through the decades of Army rule over Indian affairs, the unproclaimed decision, "The tribal societies must die," was implemented through the divide-and-rule technique. Lines of cleavage were felt out within the given tribe; and the events of the Indian removal had insured that lines of cleavage would exist in every tribe. The cleavage among the Cherokees ran between their minority of "Old Settlers" on the one hand (the "Old Settlers" were those who had gone voluntarily to Indian Territory in advance of the enforced removal), along with the few hundred who had signed the fraudulent treaty of removal, and on the other hand the Cherokee National Party, headed by John Ross, the great chief of the tribe. The minority faction numbered 6,000, the Ross faction 12,000. Both factions desired to heal the tribal wound, to re-institute the tribe, harmonious and whole, for its promised everlasting self-rule in its promised everlasting new land. The Army, representing the United States, threw its whole pressure-power behind the minority, thus procuring for a decade a condition of smoldering civil war within the Cherokee Nation.

But the healing, building will of the Cherokees was too persevering, resourceful and strong; the divide-and-rule strategy failed; the Five Civilized Tribes, every one, including the Cherokees, accomplished each its re-integration.

The control of Indian affairs was moved out of the War Department in 1849 and into the Interior Department. The choice, to subordinate Indians to the Interior Department rather than to create a new, civilian department wholly concerned with Indian matters, was a fateful choice; along with other factors, it insured for nearly all of the tribes a deeper doom than any that had gone before. For the Interior Department in those times was the agency of Congress in the "liquidation" of the American national estate—in the turning over to individuals, at the lowest possible price, public lands, including their timber and minerals, which was to say most of the lands west of the Mississippi. The Interior Department assimilated the Indians, their lands, societies, communities, families, personalities and very souls, into its "liquidation" preoccupation and technique. It transformed the Army's unproclaimed policy and strategy of tribal dissolution from an unformalized, somewhat episodic practice to a proclaimed policy, even into a kind of religious, fanatical profession. Elaborately implemented, followed through amid financial corruption with compulsive ruthlessness, the Interior Department prosecuted "Indian liquidation" right on into the dawn of the 1930's.

During the American Civil War, a majority of the members of the Five Civilized Tribes joined the Confederate side. When the war ended, every Southern state was permitted by the victorious Union to keep its every prerogative; but because some of the Five Tribes had aided the Confederacy, Congress in one stroke canceled every treaty under which the Five Tribes lived. Then new treaties were negotiated; they required the surrender by the Five Tribes of all their lands in western Indian Territory. Nearly two score of other Indian tribes from the woodlands areas and the plains were driven from their homelands and put down on some of this land extorted from the Five Tribes. The rest was "thrown open" to white settlers.

Still intact in eastern Oklahoma, within boundaries still containing nearly 20,000,000 acres, the Five Tribes and their governments remained. How, by methods not entailing new Indian wars, and within forms of law, could their residual lands be taken and their governments and societies wiped from the book of life? Many annual reports of Commissioners of Indian Affairs and Secretaries of the Interior, and many debates in Congress, revolved about this question. Indian wars had become unpopular. Between 1862 and 1867, wars with the Sioux,

Cheyenne and Navajo alone had cost the United States Government $100,000,000. The Commissioner of Indian Affairs in 1868 officially estimated that the cost per Indian killed was running at $1,000,000. Yet the Indian lands must be taken away, the Indian societies must be destroyed. How? The question applied to all Indian tribes, and the Five Civilized Tribes among them. A number of converging methods were adopted, and the Cherokee record shows one of them in action. It was the most universal and fatal of all the methods.

Tribal society and the communally possessed land were two aspects of a single fact. The earth lived; individuals of the tribe were members of one another and part of the earth. Individuals had no wish to own some one, detached piece of the land; they were co-owners of it all. But they were not even co-owners; they were co-operators with the land, defenders of it, at once its guardians and its children. "What," the famous Tecumseh had exclaimed, "Sell land! As well sell air and water. The Great Spirit gave them in common to all."

This, therefore, was the solution of the problem which vexed the statesmen: Each individual Cherokee should be forced to accept as his own one little piece of the tribal land. He should have no right, title or interest in any other piece. When each Cherokee had been forced to accept the decreed parcel of land, all land left over should be declared "surplus" and sold by the government to whites. The tribal society's interest in the individualized land should be terminated as a matter of law and of administration. With individualization of the land, guardianship of it should pass from the tribe to the Bureau of Indian Affairs.

Such was the "land allotment" system. By the time it had become fully formulated as a project (the early 1880's), all ethical scruples had been disposed of. The tribal societies were barriers against civilization, spiritual prisons of their members, insuring hell-fire for most of them after death. The de-tribalized Indian on his individual parcel of land would become thrifty, a go-getter; and if he did not, then it would be right to have created the situation wherein his sins would overwhelm him. The most eminent of the rationalizers of Indian allotment, and of forced individualization generally, was Carl Schurz when he was Secretary of the Interior in the early 1880's.

The Cherokees knew all that was intended by land allotment, and all that it would accomplish. Like the other tribes, they resisted it to the end. Once more they laid their case before the Supreme Court. The pending land allotment, they pleaded, was violative of their treaty guarantee "that the lands now occupied by the Cherokee Nation shall be secured to the whole Cherokee people for their common use and benefit." It was expropriative and confiscatory. It was a means of killing their society and government, which had received in successive treaties the guarantee of perpetual existence and self-rule. Their individual members did not want to receive title to a parcel of land and have their title to all the land annulled. They would be utterly ruined if allotment were carried through. From its Olympian remoteness, the Court rejected the plea. Allotment was within the authority of Congress and the Executive; it was they, not the Court, who must decide how to exercise guardianship; bad intentions were not to be presumed by the Court. Sixteen million acres were allotted to the members of the Five Tribes; 4,346,000 to the Cherokees. In about twenty years, all except 1,500,000 acres had passed to whites; the Cherokees had 400,-000 acres left.

As the Five Tribes' lands melted away, whites crowded in; the tribes became a minority in their own land. Did their governments have to perish? The answer of present years is no. They would have had to change; but priceless structures, serving the needs of mutual aid, of personality development, of social continuity, of the conservation of status, and of productivity on many lines, could have outlived the deep wound of land allotment.

But the United States was determined that no native social structure should live. By successive acts of Congress, the Five Tribes were shorn of their governmental function; their courts were abolished; their tribal taxes were abolished; the sale of their public lands and buildings was ordered; their legislatures were forbidden to remain in session more than thirty days in any one year. The public funds of the tribes were impounded into the United States Treasury. By the date of the "final act" of 1906, passed by Congress as a gesture of respect toward a few uncrumbled walls, the house of government of the Five Tribes had been demolished utterly. There still remained the Federal guardianship over the residual individualized properties, the pledged immunity from taxation (pledged in exchange for the surrender of vast areas of land), and the federally supplied social services. Under Oklahoma political pressure, these national commitments were diminished or abandoned one by one. The local looting of Indians became a principal business in eastern Oklahoma, continuing with brazen openness until past 1925, and not wholly ended even yet.

Meanwhile the Cherokees who remained in the East returned one by one from the wilds, years after the Removal, and acquired lands amounting to one per cent of the domain that had been taken from them. They virtually owned these lands individually but placed the title in a tribal corporation. Just a month before the time of this writing, I revisited the Eastern Cherokees. I have not encountered such poised, quiet, merry children, such old people of sage and witty happiness, since I revisited the Pueblos, two years ago.

Seventeen per cent of the total population of the Eastern Cherokees had gone into the armed forces in World War II. They fought on every front, and the battle deaths were high. Returning, the G. I. boys and men had flung themselves into the problems of their homeland. A thrilling work of balanced land-use and conservation, with the healing of erosion-wounded lands, was going ahead. The tribe had planned its long future, and on several lines was advancing into it.

CHAPTER 12

California and Plains Indians

THE INDIANS of California were under Spanish domination from 1769 until 1845, when California became part of the United States. When the Spaniards came, there were about 200,000 Indians in the area, speaking twenty-one languages in many dialects. They were a hunting and fishing people, not warriors. Tribal boundaries were severely respected. They existed within hundreds of distinct societies whose adaptations, motivations, structures and views of nature and man were ample for their needs. Sir Francis Drake's classic description of the coast tribes around the present San Francisco might be applied to them all: Arcadian people, he found them, whose natures could hardly be told save through the language of music; peoples joyously hospitable who seemed as free as birds, whose speech and colors were like the warbling and plumage of birds.

When the Franciscans came to California, their Missions brought together some 25,000 of these Indians who were then taught agriculture and crafts. But within the Missions they lost their old religions and traditions and tribal ways. Mortality was always high among these Indians during the sixty-five years the Missions endured; but swift death overtook them after the Missions ended in 1834. Most of the tribes that were wholly devoted to Mission life have long since become extinct.

Juan Rodriguez Cabrillo had explored the Southern California coast three hundred years before, and had found a dense population. Childlike they were, these natives, but athletic, precise, completely efficient toward their practical ends, within their unending dance and song. For how many thousand years had this man-nature garden of all bright colors grown? More than ten thousand years.

A military post was established at Santa Barbara in 1782, and a Mission four years later. The Indians usually entered the Mission by choice, but they were held there through force; the military insisted on forcible confinement because the Indians, who quickly learned to farm, fed the garrison.

In the first years the Indians lived in huts in the open. Later they were confined within a walled space, locked from nine in the evening until morning prayers. "Every six months men and boys received a pair of breeches, and every seven months a shirt," David Banks Rogers says. "The women and girls were allotted a chemise and shirt each, every seven months. With this wardrobe the hitherto naked savages were required to keep themselves modestly arrayed under pain of severe penalties for any lapse." The penalties took the form of the stocks, the shackles or the lash.

How galling physical punishment must have been to them, we may realize when we read in the early chronicles that there seemed to be no form of chastisement whatsoever in use among the natives before the coming of the white man. We know from the sources that at Santa Barbara Mission the women were punished by sentence of from one to three days in the stocks. If they proved obstinate or ran away, they were lashed in the woman's apartment by the hands of another woman. With the men, it often went much harder.

Death walked the Mission compound. After thirteen years there were eight hundred and sixty-four living Indians and six hundred and sixty-two deaths had occurred. The Indians, according to Rogers, "knew the fatal tendency of their new environment."

Many causes for the awful failure of the California Missions have been assigned, but the significant cause for all time to come is plain. It was the total, instantaneous suppression of the native societies, the willed destruction of those marvelous ecological complexes within which native life had gushed and bloomed in its millenniums. Verily, in this case, the thing which Las Casas did not know, which the Franciscans did not learn, which governments are only starting to learn now, contained the doom of the Indians.

In 1845 California became part of the United States, and four years later came the gold rush, bringing with it a diseased, local exaggeration of the national feeling toward foreigners, a hearty contempt for people and institutions that were different. This racial scorn and the greed fostered by the gold fever seared the Indians into charred remnants of people. The 110,000 to 130,000 California Indians of 1850 were fewer than 20,000 by 1880.

Disease was a factor; wanton murder which the white community did not view as murder at all; enslavement. But the principal cause was a more subtle and more dreadful thing, as C. Hart Merriam, a profound student of the California Indians, has pointed out; it was the gradual but relentless confiscation of their lands and homes, forcing them to seek refuge in remote and barren localities where health, even life itself frequently, could not be sustained. There was a cause more subtle and dreadful yet—a psychological depression resulting in the will to die, for their societies were slain.

Beginning in 1851, the United States negotiated treaties with 119 of the tribes. The Indians surrendered more than half of California (treaties were not negotiated with tribes occupying about one-half of the State) and accepted, in return, perpetual ownership of 7,500,000 acres. Through California pressure, the Senate in Washington denied confirmation to the treaties; the treaties and the record of the Senate's action were placed in the Senate's files, there to repose until 1905; the Indian Bureau, administrative guardian of the tribes, never breathed to the Indians what had transpired; the Indians remembered the treaties; they knew them by heart; they fulfilled their part of the supposed agreements only to witness the sale to whites, by the government, of every acre of the 7,500,000 pledged to them.

It was among the Plains Indians that the policy of annihilation of the societies and then of the individual Indian personality was carried to the farthest extreme.

Most of the Plains region came to the United States through the treaty of the Louisiana Purchase in 1803. Contact between the government and most of the Plains tribes dated from the close of the American Civil War. Beginning about 1870, a leading aim of the United States was to destroy the Plains Indians' societies through destroying their religions; and it may be that the world has never witnessed a religious persecution so implacable and so variously implemented. The successive and evolving reactions of the Indians to the irresistible proscription supplied a moving chapter to the religious history of mankind.

The assault against the tribal and intertribal religions was part of an all-out offensive against Indian land and society. The offensive, including its religious part, reached far beyond the Plains region, but nowhere else was it so intense. The main features of what may be called the secular part of the onset can be briefly indicated.

First, there was military assault, on slight pretexts or no pretexts at all, and the government exploited tribal rivalries in order that Indians should kill Indians. The limited and disciplinary war-customs of the Plains turned into total warfare, aimed at annihilation, with the United States Army as the driving power. The tribes were finally beaten, however, not through overwhelming numbers or superior armament (though these existed) but through starvation after the whites had destroyed the buffalo.

Treaties and agreements were made, and in a few years unilaterally broken by the United States. Here, as almost universally with Indian compacts, the record of the Five Civilized Tribes was duplicated.

The buffalo was destroyed. That revelry of slaughter, which had no sportsmanship in it, was recognized as a war measure against the Indians and was deliberately encouraged.

Thereafter, the tribes were imprisoned (it was technically and factually an imprisonment) in separate, diminished reservations, where they had no choice but to live by government rations. Treaty and statute had made the even-handed distribution of these rations obligatory; but in practice, and openly, as a matter of rule, the distribution was used to starve the Indians who would not forswear their religion and their tribal customs and loyalties. In addition, all authority was taken away from the tribal leaders who refused to serve as puppets under the Army and the Indian Bureau.

To kill the Indian traditions and to break the relationship of the generations, Indian children were seized at six years and were confined in "boarding schools" until past their adolescence. In vacation time they were indentured to whites as servants. In the schools the use of the native languages was forbidden; everything reminiscent of or relevant to Indian life was excluded; the children were forced to join whichever Christian church, through the favor of the Indian Bureau, had entrenched itself in the particular school.

Finally, forced land allotment operated among the Plains tribes as among all Indians, except for a few tribes in and outside of Arizona and New Mexico. It physically disrupted the extended family by attaching each household, even each individual, to a segregated parcel of land. The non-agricultural Plains tribes were furnished neither the training, the agricultural credit nor the capital goods requisite for a shift-over to farming. Perforce, as soon as restrictions against sale were lifted, the Indians sold their parcels to whites. Where they did not sell, the allotment in question was split into heirship equities with all collateral heirs included. There soon were a hundred heirs to a single allotment, and a given Indian found himself part-owner, with equities of a few dollars or a few cents, of twenty or fifty scattered parcels. No recourse remained except to sell the heirship lands or lease them in blocks to white cattlemen.

The Indians of the whole country lost 90,000,000 acres to whites through the direct and indirect workings of land allotment in the years from 1887 to 1933; but in addition, they lost to whites the *use* of most of the allotted land still Indian-owned.

All of these processes went forward within a governmental service dominated by political patronage and saturated with corruption. This single fact about the government's Indian record is so well known that it is here mentioned for one reason only. The friends of the Indian attributed his mounting ruin to corrupt, bad men. Across nearly fifty years, exposures, campaigns and drives within and without the government were focused toward getting a personally honest, in place of a personally dishonest, Indian Bureau. The policies and the system itself were not questioned except in terms of the personal morality of Indian commissioners and Indian agents.

Then, as early as 1905, by virtue of civil service and of elaborate fiscal controls, financial corruption became less important in the government Indian service. Outside the Five Civilized Tribes and Osage areas of Oklahoma, in the rest of the Indian country and in the administration at Washington, personal probity became the rule, not the exception. But the mounting ruin of Indians went on and accelerated with each passing year.

The purification of Indian administration had indeed its consequence. Given the policy, the system, the philosophy and the law of Indian affairs, it actually speeded the destruction of the Indians. A secondary consequence was important: The disappearance of personal scandal from administration compelled the Indians and their friends in public and private life to seek other causes for their distress. They found these causes in the policy, system, philosophy and law of Indian affairs, and they converged their efforts toward changing these impersonal facts. Short of that fundamental change, they realized, no reform could make any lasting difference at all. I myself participated across eleven years in the struggle for fundamental change; only one time, and in relation to one individual within the Interior Department, did I have occasion to charge or to suspect a corrupt financial motive.

It was not individual corruption but collective corruption; corruption which did not know it was corrupt, and which reached deep into the intelligence of a nation. It was such a collective corruption that dominated the Plains Indian record and nearly the whole Indian record of the United States. Collective corruption is more effectually carried into deed through agents not personally corrupt.

The onslaught against the religion of the Indians took the form of regulations against religious practices and ceremonies. The master-expression of Plains Indian religion was the Sun Dance. And to forbid the Sun Dance was to forbid tribal existence and to cut the tap-root of Plains Indian personality.

Viewed socially, the Sun Dance was the integrative and structuring institution of the Plains tribes. Viewed psychologically, it was the culminating discipline, forthgiving and sharing, which structured the personality of the young, renewed the personality of the old, opened the mind's windows to a noble world-view, and drew in power and joy from the tribe and from the universe to the individual breast. Viewed creedally, it asserted verbally, but far more richly symbolized and implied, the union of men in God.

The Sun Dance appears as an invention—an exquisitely perfect one—at the social level. With the acquisition of the horse, the life of the Plains tribes—Cheyenne, Arapaho, Sioux (Dakota), Crow, Blackfeet, Kiowa and others—became profoundly modified. No longer could the sub-groups composing a tribe stay in continuous physical contact with one another. The little sub-groups, with all their possessions, men, women and children journeying together, and with large herds of horses, needs must scatter over vast areas in pursuit of the buffalo. Yet the significant and valued flow of life was tribal. The Sun Dance was the invention which met this dilemma.

In the summer, at breeding season, the buffalo gathered in large herds; and in the summer, the grasses were lush, so that the concentration of the thousands of horses was possible. Therefore, at that time the scattered sub-groups all drew together; and the Sun Dance was the celebration. The whole tribe camped in one immense circle; the circle of tepees symbolized tribal unity. A priest, or director, possessor of a "sacred bundle," and imbued with knowledge of all ceremonies and meanings, assumed the religious and in some cases the political control of the encampment.

Near the encampment's center a sacred tepee was pitched; there, the rites preliminary to the main ritual were carried out. Those being initiated received their instruction, and there was smoking, feasting, praying, and the shaping of the objects to be used in the great ceremony. Meantime, the women held their own joyous and sacred gathering; and a virgin of exceptional character was selected by the priest or director to fell the tree which should serve as the Sun Dance pole.

The Sun Dance lasted four days and nights, within an immense brush lodge circular in form. Ritualized ordeals were undergone in the dance, and no participant ate or drank for the four days and nights. "The Ceremony was rich in symbolism," Donald Collier writes. "Besides the sun, other powers of the earth and sky, the thunder, the stars, mother earth, and the four cardinal directions, were represented in song, dance and painting, and the symbolism of war and the buffalo were prominent throughout."

There were numerous minor ceremonies, mock battles between the soldiers' societies of the different kinship groupings, and ceremonial hunts. Every age-level participated, every operation cut across all of the sub-groupings, and every homely practice of every day was brought into relation with the core-values and the cosmic yearning of the tribe.

Donald Collier writes further: "All of these things combined during the brief Sun Dance period to give an intense and joyful feeling of tribal unity. This tribal unification was the more effective because it stemmed from a period into which was crowded so much happy activity. At the end of this period the tribal organization ceased to exist, and the people moved off to their encampments. But as they resumed their usual activities, they felt strongly the fullness of life, and the greatness and unity of the tribe." Between Sun Dances, the tribe actually did cease to exist, except within the soul; it existed there as the road into the universe, a two-way road.

First, in the Sioux country, the Army crushed the Sun Dance with armed force. Then the missionaries influenced the Bureau of Indian Affairs to impose regulations against not only the Sun Dance but all "pagan" ceremonies which, they believed, impeded the progress of the Indians toward Christian civilization. The Interior Department framed a criminal code forbidding Indian religious practices and establishing penalties. Enacted in 1884 and enriched in 1904, this code stood in force and effect until 1933.

Of course, this code of Indian religious crimes could not be enforced everywhere. To crack down the Navajo "sings" in remote deserts, the Pueblo vigils and the rituals in the inviolable kivas, and Seminole rituals in the deep Everglades, the solitary keepers of visions on the Mojave desert, was a task beyond the government's resources. Not until the middle 1920's, as we shall later see, was the universal suppression of Indian religions, through the direct use of force, projected by the Indian Bureau. Prior to that date, outside the Plains area, the main means of persecution was not to shoot or jail adult worshipers but to immolate the Indian children in boarding schools and there compel them to join Christian churches.

But among the Plains tribes, the very nature of the Sun Dance, and of successor religions to the Sun Dance, made forcible suppression easy. The Sun Dance was a merging of every individual with the annually resurrected tribe in a social-cosmic worship. Merely to forbid the tribe to meet together at all was to kill the Sun Dance. That was done to the Sioux, and the military enforced the prohibition. With the buffalo gone, merely to withhold rations from those who insisted on meeting together was to confront them with actual death from starvation; and that was done. Failing these methods, the outright massacre of Indian communicants was practicable, for the Indians were now disarmed in the face of the white soldiery. The famous battle of Wounded Knee in 1890 was an outright massacre.

The Sun Dance was destroyed forever.

But the life of the Spirit, taking the various forms of what we call the religions of the world, and accompanied by ritual and ceremony, often by dance and song despite the Puritans, often by a severe asceticism despite the rotund bishops of so many persuasions, often by sackcloth and ashes in renunciation of this earthly life, is difficult to suppress. Among these Plains Indians and the Indians marginal to the Plains—those who could not en masse become good Christians by order—new religious cults evolved.

In Oregon there came into being the society of "The Dreamers," whose principal sentiment was an impassioned affirmation of the union between man and his mother earth. The Dreamers' religion appears in our white history through the figure of Chief Joseph of the Nez Percé tribe. Its religion was one of nonresistance to evil. "The earth is part of my body and I never gave up the earth," said Tochulhulsote, one of the chief priests and spokesmen. "I have only one heart," said an Umatilla chief. "Although you say: Go to another country, my heart is not that way. I am here, and here is where I am going to be. I will not part with my lands, and if you come again I will say the same thing. I will not part with my lands."

In 1877, General Howard of the United States Army, as a step toward dispossessing the Nez Percé band, threw Tochulhulsote, the principal Dreamer priest of Joseph's Nez Percé band, into jail. The Dreamers had no choice but to yield, and Joseph selected for the temporary confinement of the band a place in the Lapwai Valley of Idaho. While the Nez Percés were gathering their stock for removal, a band of whites attacked them, ran off the cattle and killed one of the Indians in charge. Then desperation broke through all religious restraint; the Nez Percés went to war. With his hundred warriors Chief Joseph in three weeks killed 58 white soldiers in a series of running fights. Impeded by more than 350 women and children, Joseph undertook to cut through three white armies which surrounded him and win his way to Canada.

Again, again and again, Joseph encountered detachments of the Army and cut them down or drove them off. At least, after a journey of more than a thousand miles, with his warriors reduced to fifty and starved and exhausted but still carrying their wounded and the women and children, within fifty miles of the Canadian line, he was intercepted by General Miles with fresh forces. He fought on until forty of his fifty warriors were wounded, the others killed. Then he surrendered upon the express pledge that with his survivors "he would be taken to Tongue River (Montana) and be kept there until spring, and then would be returned to Idaho." General Sheridan, into whose hands Joseph passed, violated the pledge which General Miles had given, and the surviving Nez Percés were sent to Indian Territory, where disease and hunger reduced the entire band from 450 to 280 in seven years.

So perished the religion of The Dreamers.

Beside Puget Sound in the State of Washington there arose a curious cult, among the Squaxins, somewhat resembling our early Shakers. They considered the church which they founded under their leader, Squ-sacht-un, known as John Slocum, as a Christian church, embodying all that was best in the Catholic, Calvinistic and Red Indian traditions. As with the Shakers, one of their first tenets was absolute non-violence. "Banishment, chains and imprisonment" were their lot.

The Ghost Dance religion was overwhelmed by the horrible massacre at Wounded Knee. Its prophet was a full-blood Paiute Indian, Wovoka, born about 1856, the son of an earlier Paiute prophet. Wovoka spoke no Indian tongue except Paiute, did not know the sign language, and never had been out of Nevada. But delegations from all over the Plains came to him. He knew some English, and worked for a white rancher.

On January 1, 1889, in the course of a severe illness, and on the day of a total eclipse of the sun, Wovoka entered into a trance. He seemed to be dead, and then he was reborn. His soul had been taken into the heavens, and there he saw God, "with all the people who had died long ago engaged in their oldtime sports and occupations, all happy and forever young." God told him that his own time was not yet; he must go back to earth and tell the Indians that they must be good and love one another; they must live at peace with the whites, and work, and put away all war. God did not promise that the Indians would come again into their own on earth; but in heaven they would come into their own.

Just what it was that drew them to Wovoka, who spoke none of their languages, living far off under the snowcapped Sierras bounding Nevada, is nowhere made clear. But they came as disciples, and their desperate troubles of the soul acted upon him. His prophecy changed. Not only in heaven, but on earth the millennium was to come, and it was to come soon. It was to come with earthquake when the risen dead, already arrived at the boundaries of earth, led forward by the Regenerator who would appear vast as a cloud and vague as a cloud, should suddenly be among men. Then the aged, weary earth, whose bonds with its people had been cut by the white man, would die. The races would die. The white man, if reborn, would be reborn into some other world. The Indians would be reborn into this world and land, their own, and heaven and earth would be confluent as of old.

Pacifism remained the soul and body of the doctrine. Be quiet yet a little while, Indians, all Indians; war is forever done, for you; the overruling spiritual power needs no help from you, except love and quiet in your souls. The end is near, is near . . .

Thus, like a great south wind, a boundless hope blew across the Plains.

But the white man was not idle. Out of his guilt, and from the Atlantic to the Pacific, he passed the word along: A new religion of war is sweeping the warlike tribes of the Plains; Indian uprisings are at hand. The eastern newspapers contained stories of the rumors, along with fictions of uprisings and massacres. The army reinforced its posts in Indian country. The end came swiftly; at Wounded Knee, on December 29, 1890, 98 disarmed warriors and 200 women and children were massacred. A religion of redemption, of active peace and of love, went down in blood.[1]

Yet, in spite of innumerable such destructions of mystical-social institutions, profound and strange, Indian religion lived on. Today it has been re-institutionalized, into an expanding, intertribal spiritual development known as the Native American Church. Incorporated some twenty-five years ago, the "cult" of the Native American Church dates from about 1870 among Indians in the United States. Its communicants number perhaps 25,000. In its ceremony, peyote, a cactus product, believed holy and miraculous, is eaten. Both Pre-Columbian and Christian elements are merged in its creed, ethical code and ceremonies. The synthesis is a creative one. Communion of souls one with another and with the Godhead, and charity and continence, are its controlling aims and tenets. Peyote, ceremonially used, brings a sense that barriers are melted away and that the human flows into the Godhead. Also it acts upon the centers of vision of the brain and produces or releases into consciousness illusions of beautiful colors and forms. Havelock Ellis characterized it as "the most intellectual of the drugs." Some four hundred books and technical papers, in many languages, are devoted to the "cult" and to peyote as a physiologically reactive substance. The extensive research finds peyote to be "not habit-forming or deleterious."

Alfred Wilson, Cheyenne Indian of Oklahoma, was head of the Native American Church, and until the day he died at sixty-

[1] *The Ghost Dance Religion* by James Mooney. 1892-93. Bureau of American Ethnology.

eight, he worked for the Church. When death came in February, 1945, he was in Washington on behalf of his congregation, seeking to persuade white men to repeal those state and federal laws which implement the persecution of the Native American Church.

Alfred Wilson was representative of much that is Indian and also more than Indian. When he said, "We will all go to prison, and stay there, or suffer anything, but we will not go away from our religion"; when he confronted the drive to exterminate by physical means an Indian religion, a drive carried out by white men and other Indians—by those who themselves had experienced persecution; when he renewed the offer of his congregation, made in previous years, to submit itself and its members to unlimited scientific investigation, biological, psychological, anthropological, because he had faith in science as well as in his religion; and when he did all these things in a spirit of disinterested love, then he represented a universal wisdom—while at the same time an Indian cause and an Indian wisdom.

His belief came from deep religious experience which was also philosophical realization at the same time. It made him love all sensate life and rejoice in it all. D'Arcy McNickle, a Flathead Indian, wrote of Alfred Wilson, after a talk with him.

"Alfred talked at length about the meaning of peyote and about the whole field of religious experience. The remarks which I here put down as a continuous statement, actually were very scattered, but they are carefully accurate.

"The Indian, he said, stresses the importance of 'I am.' By this he meant that the individual is a manifestation of the breath or energy of God. He is earth, but the earth part is only that which makes him visible; the part which is his real life, which makes the 'I am,' is that which we call the breath of God. Man, because he partakes of this spiritual essence, has a mind reaching beyond the conscious mind. It is that which flows into him from the deity and which is his to use during his lifetime. This mind, going beyond the conscious mind, is an active, thinking reality, and this active, thinking reality also makes or influences the conscious mind. When a man is sick and his brothers meet with him and hold a peyote ceremony, they are lending for his use their immaterial minds. The cure which they try to bring about is an insertion of the immaterial mind in the body and into the tangible, and it is achieved through reinforcing the sick man's unconscious, immaterial mind with their own.

"Peyote itself is a part of that immaterial mind—a part of the breath or spirit.

"Indians do not speak of the beginning as Christians do. They know nothing of the beginning, nor will they say that there is to be an ending. It is here. Nor will Indians say that there is a hell. They cannot conceive of such a thing. They say this: That men must follow the right path of living. They must live according to the laws of nature, which are moral laws. If they fail to do that, they hurt themselves and that is all the punishment there is. They point to the Milky Way, which is a path across heaven, but which has a branch leading off into emptiness. If man fails to live according to the laws of nature, he goes off on that side branch which ends in emptiness."

This faith and knowledge in Alfred Wilson enabled him to be quietly happy within whatever discouragements, infirmities and defeats, and to live and strive as the head of a persecuted religious group without the need to judge his persecutors. It enabled him to be as wise as he was charitable, and out of inner security to have no need for self-justification in his own eyes or anyone's eyes. Being thus wise, and inwardly secure and without the need for compensations, Alfred Wilson knew that the law of life and its way is action and service.

That "integrative" study which members of the cult first invited in 1924 and which Alfred Wilson again invited, still waits to be carried out. A rich opportunity for discovery waits. Meantime, white and Indian Christian missionaries, and some Indian tribes of Pre-Columbian orthodoxy, go ahead with their assault upon the Native American Church; and oblivious to the Bill of Rights and to the older, sacred value of liberty of conscience, they have lobbied the legislatures and have obtained penal statutes with which to scourge the Native American Church.

Alfred Wilson lived and died in the effort, not yet successful, to establish for his own congregation the most fundamental of American liberties, freedom of religion. He knew that persecution strengthened his congregation. But he strove also as an American, and as a man of universal qualities, and as an agent of civilization.

CHAPTER 13

The Final Struggle Commences and Prevails

BY THE year 1892, the Indian wars had ceased. The apocalyptic religions had been killed. The impersonal systems of Indian expropriation were fully under way—including land allotment and sale of the allotments; throwing open on bargain counters the unallotted residuum, so-called "surplus lands"; leasing, for short terms, allotted farm and grazing lands, under profligate conditions. Indian-built and Indian-maintained irrigation systems serving subsistence farming were destroyed, and irrigation systems built at great cost (the cost had exceeded $50,000,000 by 1924) and destined for the commercial use of outsiders were substituted. Indian-owned timber was clean-cut. (In 1917, the Assistant Indian Commissioner explained to the Indian Committee of the House that since the Indians were being liquidated it was policy to liquidate their forests at the same time, even though these forests were the protecting cover of watersheds.) Indian tribal funds (in an amount totaling more than $100,000,000 between 1900 and 1930) were diverted to meet the costs of the Indian Bureau. The Court of Claims, pursuant to Congressional direction, "offset" all past government expenditures nominally meant to benefit the Indians, including the costs of despoiling them, against awards which they might win through suits against the government. And in Oklahoma, individualized Indian estates were looted through a system of local white "guardians" named by the Oklahoma courts pursuant to Congressional grants of power. (To 2,000 Osages, Plains Indians with no experience in money economy, and battened upon by the white population, in sixteen years following 1915 there was paid out in cash, by the government, $265,000,-000 in royalties from Osage oil. Ninety per cent of this total went "down the wind" of ruined Osages and corrupted and corrupting whites.

On the whole, these interlocking, impersonal despoliations moved toward their end silently. Outside of eastern Oklahoma, lurid scandal was rarely involved; and as I have explained, personal financial corruption within the Indian Bureau had become the exception, not the rule. The individual Indian, who in all but a very few cases was denied by law the right to organize corporately or politically, was helpless against the silent storm. The white missionaries and denominations were silenced; nay, they were made ancillary to the impersonal despoliation. They worked among the tribes by the grace of the Indian Bureau; the largest group of them was heavily subsidized by the Bureau from Indian-owned funds. The enforced proselytizing of Indian children in the schools derived its authority from the Bureau. Anthropologists conducted studies among nearly every Indian group; but they, like other investigators, journalists or "agitators," proceeded under Indian Bureau license (factually when not technically), and were subject to forcible ejection from Indian country without reason assigned. Various espionage statutes, not successfully defied until 1922 and not repealed until 1933, when combined with the other conditions, blanketed the Indians and Indian country in the silence of a living tomb.

Yet outside the Indian Bureau, unattended by it or by great pressure groups or committees of Congress, a change in the climate of opinion was dawning. Individuals influenced this change. The government was running its Indian schooling "to break up the Pueblos," but President Theodore Roosevelt visited the Hopi peoples and extolled their way of life, "as precious as anything existing in the United States." He spoke for the conservation of resources, particularly of forest resources, though his words and actions did not reach to the Indian forests. Natalie Curtis, Mary Austin, Ernest Thompson-Seton, and a score of others of distinction spoke out. The surviving and, in a few tribes, newly exfoliating, ancient arts and crafts, were discovered by museums and schools. Then came World War I. The Indians, not then citizens, and exempt from the draft, volunteered by thousands, and made a record that was generally acclaimed.

Other changes in the climate of opinion were taking place, which had a latent relationship with the Indian in the United States. Mexico's revolution swept through bloody changes to its end, and projected a bold, far-reaching Indian program. North Americans became aware of the millions of Indians south of the Rio Grande. Movements of folk dance, folk art, folk drama, folk craft arose among our own people. The geographical frontier was done; it had been pushed to the Pacific Ocean; thus the Indian in the white mind was freed from his symbolic stigma as the opponent of the expanding frontier; he need be viewed as the enemy no longer.

No knowledge of these changes in the climate of opinion reached the Indians; and the Indian Bureau, imprisoned within its own system of dogma and device, did not suspect that these changes were taking place. Commencing in 1917, an increased frenzy of "liquidation" seized the Bureau. Swift as were the legalized devices of expropriation, they were not swift enough; the Bureau rushed beyond the law, and forced upon Indians throughout the allotted country the acceptance of fee-patents to their lands. This drew the land onto the local tax rolls and allowed its immediate sale to whites. The yearly supply bills of Congress for a quarter century thereafter carried appropriations to pay damages for this lawless policy. The Plains tribes had been building themselves into the cattle industry. The Bureau persuaded and where necessary coerced them to sell their breeding stock; and then (in World War I years and thereafter) it pressured all the lands into white leaseholds. It leased the semiarid grasslands to be broken to the plow, and soon thereafter to be washed or blown away.

When Warren G. Harding became President, he made Albert B. Fall his Secretary of the Interior. Oil had been struck on the Navajo lands, which still remained tribal, and apart from the Doheny and Sinclair oil scandals, the Teapot Dome affair and other jockeying over oil, another oil scandal, though an impersonal one, developed over the Navajo homelands.

Fall and the Indian Bureau concocted the so-called "Indian Omnibus Bill" which the House passed and which the Senate Committee on Indian Affairs reported favorably. Indian leaders drew up a petition and found a champion, Robert M. LaFollette, the elder, of Wisconsin, who succeeded at the eleventh hour in killing that bill on the Senate floor.

The intentions of the bill and its provisions may be briefly summarized.

The bill sought to individualize all tribal assets, not previously individualized; to pay to each individual in cash the appraised value of his atom of the assets; to have then quitclaimed to the government all future responsibility to these Indians. Many treaties would have been torn into scraps of paper by this one act of legislation; an orgy of loot would have been released, particularly against the tribes of Arizona and New Mexico, but also against the Klamaths of Oregon, the Menominees of Wisconsin, and the remaining tribes who had escaped allotment. For them the pittance in money they would receive would scarcely have compensated for the loss of their homes and lands and tribal unities, the roots of both their individual and communal beings. Before Fall could renew his pressure for this bill, he had been driven from office.

Let us consider some of the other factors. Two-thirds of the Indian lands which still remained tribal were held by the Indians under Presidential decree, as distinguished from treaty. Oil was struck in the Navajo lands within the "Presidential decree" rather than the "Treaty" area of the tribe. Fall ruled that the oil belonged to the government, to dispose of as it might choose, and not to the tribe. The effect was to deny that the Indians owned some sixteen million acres of their own land, title to which had been confirmed in them by Executive Order. The Fall administration then set in motion an open drive, aimed principally at the Pueblo tribes, for the suppression of all the native Indian religions still existing.

Finally, although first in order of time (I have held it back because it requires more lengthy discussion), Fall pressed the notorious Bursum bill with all the powers at his command; and the Senate enacted it. Then a storm broke. The Pueblos determined to battle with all their resources.

The Pueblos of New Mexico hold their lands in common under grants from the Spanish Crown. Some of the grants were made direct to the tribes; others were made to whites who then sold title to the tribes. These grants were confirmed to the Pueblos by the Court of Private Land Claims of the United States during the 1890's. Hordes of non-Indians had encroached and continued to encroach on the Pueblos' grants. They usurped or helped themselves to the Indian-built improvements. For example, these lands had been irrigated by the tribes since hundreds of years before Columbus. Some of the tribal city-states lost the use of 90 per cent of their irrigated lands. But they refused to disperse.

The Supreme Court had ruled, in 1871, that the Pueblos were not "wards of the United States" and that their lands were not under government guardianship. Nevertheless, Congress appropriated the funds for Indian agents there, and for two large boarding schools where the young of the tribes would be detached from their homes and the break-up of the city-states be expedited. The Bureau did nothing to help prevent the continuing encroachments until 1913. Then it brought the question of Pueblo guardianship before the Supreme Court anew, and the Court reversed itself. Federal guardianship, it held, was complete, and had been continuous since New Granada had been taken from Spain. Hence, all encroachments, at least since 1848, had been illegal; the Pueblo title was perfect and unimpaired.

In 1918, through political chance, Richard H. Hanna, who at an earlier date had been Chief Justice of the Supreme Court of New Mexico, became government attorney for the Pueblo tribes. Hanna, a man of real greatness, later to become famous as a defender of the Indians, insisted at this time that the government must move to recover the Pueblos' lands from the white dispossessors. He was allowed to file suits to quiet title. Delays were interposed by the Interior Department through the Department of Justice at Washington, and the suits dragged on until Harding became President and Fall became Secretary of the Interior.

Fall's bill in the Congress, known as the Bursum bill, was simple enough. It transferred the Pueblo title from the Indian owners to the white squatters. For good measure, it brought the internal affairs of the city-states under the jurisdiction of the United States District Court. This last might not seem so bad from an outside point of view; but it actually meant the attempted establishment of a religious inquisition, for the internal affairs of the Pueblos are completely involved in their religions. Among the Rio Grande Pueblos, the rule of secrecy is inviolable. Under the Fall-Bursum bill, the Indian Bureau would have been able to keep the priests, governors and other principal men of these tribes in jail for contempt of court, or whatever, for most of their lives.

No Pueblo Indian knew of the existence of this bill. It had been carefully guarded from its inception, and the press had missed it in the pressure of other matters. The Indian superintendents knew; but no one of these public servants hired to protect Indian interests and supposed to represent the Indian just as a lawyer is expected to defend his client—not one of them wanted or dared even anonymously to "leak" information to the Indian leaders—not even to a single Indian. During those days the tribes were immured.

As it happened, I was down there at the time—eleven years before I became Indian Commissioner. Antonio Luhan, of Taos Pueblo, guided and introduced me to the meeting that resulted in the discovery of the Fall-Bursum bill. In meetings lasting far into the night, the Fall-Bursum bill was read and explained and analyzed in English, in Tanoan (Tiguan), Tewan, Keresian and Zunian; it was so read at the meetings while old men of the tribe moaned, knowing it was a sentence of death.

At Cochiti Pueblo, Alcario Montoya started off the battle. He said: "We must unite as we did once before." He was referring to the ancient Pueblo rebellion of 1680, before there was a

United States, an uprising which had driven every white man out of New Granada. He did not mean by force of arms, which would have been ridiculous. He meant *before the law*—the law, guardian of justice, even among the white races and among all races.

And thus there came into being the Council of All the New Mexico Pueblos, which was to be the spearhead of the struggle of all the tribal Indians everywhere until after 1933. At Santo Domingo Pueblo, November 22, 1922, the All-Pueblo Council met—its second meeting in 242 years. All of New Mexico by that date was aflame over the Fall-Bursum bill; the artists and writers of Santa Fe and Taos joined in encouragement and deeds.

At Santo Domingo Pueblo it is usual for a family to live in a single great room; its beams are whole trees, blackened with age, and its walls within and without are snow-white, but hung with red chili, dried meat, and red, blue and dark-green dried corn. There are no beds, tables or chairs; the fireplace and the outdoor adobe oven, beehive-shaped, make the kitchen. One of these homes was the council chamber. The 123 Indian delegates were the religious and political headmen of the 19 tribes; they grouped themselves by languages, so that discourse proceeded simultaneously in English, Spanish and the four distinct root-languages of the New Mexico Pueblos. To the few whites who were present—they included Stella Atwood, and Mary Austin, and myself—the little assembly had a feeling of immensity. Far horizons seemed to stretch onward, and power seemed to flow from out remote ages. An element in the Pueblo world-view is that there exists a dimension not apprehended spatially and not subject to spatial description or limitation. That dimension is *intensity;* and it can be partly symbolized by the image of the indrawn and outflowing breath, in the instant present, of all time that ever was, all racial time and cosmic time, race and cosmos, personality and cosmos being one. To me, on the day of this All-Pueblo Council meeting, resumed after 242 years, there reached a certain sense of understanding that was to be renewed at many an Indian council meeting in years to come. Compared to Indian council meetings, our own legislative assemblies operate within a frame of reference exceedingly narrow, and take into account facts exceedingly few, and draw upon shallows of thought and emotion exceedingly thin

The Council framed an appeal. "The time has come when we must live or die," the Council said, and went on to tell briefly about Pueblo life (the telling, as nearly always with tribal Indians, being of present life as related to an unextinguished, dynamic past and to the "long hope," the racial hope). They acted to send messengers to the United States, a delegation of seventeen of their representative men.

The Pueblo delegation went to the people of the country. It was superlatively skillful in presenting its case at gatherings in many cities, and even before the Stock Exchange of New York. Its case was an affirmative one. The governors of the tribes carried with them their silver-headed canes, symbols of authority bestowed by the Spanish Crown and long after by President Abraham Lincoln. Their organization, as wrought out after the great rebellion of 1680, represented the solitary flowering in full perfection and achievement of the Laws of the Indies and the philosophy of Bartolomé de Las Casas. Here was social continuity unbroken since the Stone Age, and here was Christianity deeply felt, at peace in the same breasts with pre-Columbian religions yet more deeply professed. Here was what John Marshall had intended for all Indians.

The Senate recalled the Fall-Bursum bill from the House, on motion of Senator William Borah, of Idaho; the stated ground was unusual within the tradition of Senatorial "courtesy." The Senate implied that it had passed the bill on the strength of a misrepresentation, innocent or otherwise, by its sponsor. Then in Congress a two-year struggle commenced—actually, an eleven-year struggle before the single issue of the Pueblos' lands had been concluded; but the battle front extended to the Indians everywhere and to the whole law, policy and system of Indian affairs. In March, 1923, the Fall Indian Omnibus bill was killed. In that same month the Senate's Indian Committee, again on the basis of a misrepresentation, reported favorably a Pueblo Lands bill which was only a little less ruinous than the Fall-Bursum bill had been. By that date, the Pueblo delegation had returned home. The Senate committee was misled to believe that the Pueblos, the General Federation of Women's Clubs, and the newly formed American Indian Defense Association, had been brought to endorse a bill-draft which transferred Pueblo title to whites, without compensation, but under a due-process-of-law formula whose despoiling outcome Congress would decree in the bill. The Pueblos, the Women's Clubs and the Defense Association repudiated the bill and denounced it and it died. But *de facto* the white squatters and settlers remained on the Pueblo lands, and many Pueblos continued to starve.

When Albert B. Fall passed from office, to be indicted, tried and imprisoned, all his piracies had been smashed; he had filled the role of the indispensable villain in the drama, needful at its beginning. But the Indian Bureau moved automatically, implacably on. Its strategy of counterattack became manifest within a few months after the Pueblos had struck their first blow. The campaign followed these lines: The Pueblos and their friends were racketeers, taking money from the sympathetic public under false pretenses. They were anti-American, and subversive. In fact, they were "agents of Moscow." They were cultists of Indian paganism; and the pagan cults were horrible, sadistic and obscene. They were seeking to discredit and weaken the United States Government.

The Indian Bureau controlled ramifications of influence very far-reaching. Through the Home Mission Boards, it lined up the Protestant denominations in blanket apologetic acclaim for the Bureau and the Indian system. It immobilized the Franciscan order, which in 1922 had gone into action for and with the Pueblos. By 1924 it had split the General Federation of Women's Clubs wide open, had pushed Stella Atwood out from her chairmanship of the Federation's Indian committee, and had annexed the Federation's national officers to its own cause, although some of the State Federations battled on. It swung the Board of Indian Commissioners behind itself. This Board had been set up by President Grant as an unpaid body of virtuous men. The Bureau financed a competing, Bureau-controlled Council of All the New Mexico Pueblos. This never accomplished anything, but was symbolical. Opposing groups of white seekers of Indian welfare, including eminent names, found themselves, with some bewilderment, maneuvered into partnership with the Bureau.

But the tribes' insurgence widened and deepened far beyond liberal white sentiment toward them. It reached to the Great Plains tribes, to the Columbia Basin and the inter-mountain Indian country, to the Indian remnants in California. The tribes now had their common agenda for Indian affairs revolution; but wisely they decided to form no single, all-Indian nationwide organization. The American Indian Defense Association "serviced" them legislatively and through research and publication; but each of the hundreds of tribes, except the confederated Pueblos, characteristically strove ahead autonomously, each upon its own, yet in concert. The pressures which the Indian Bureau's system could command, and which it employed extravagantly, sometimes temporarily silenced one or another tribe, but the Indians' front was never broken. Thus the struggle continued for eleven years.

Commencing with the Pueblos' actions of 1922, the destruction of the native religions that yet lived was viewed by the Indian Bureau as a *political* necessity. The religions made the tribes strong, and made the individuals of the tribes immune to intimidation or corruption. The Bureau's new onslaught fell upon all the Pueblo native religions and upon the expanding, intertribal Native American Church. Federal and state enactments against the Native American Church were lobbied through by the Indian Bureau. Toward the Pueblo religions, methods more lurid were used.

The Bureau sent out inspectors. These men collected pornographic gossip about the tribes, among whom no pornography existed at all. Much of the gossip was unprintable. The Bureau submitted it for scrutiny to no Indian and to no ethnologist. The foul pages, numbering 193, were photostated and turned over to various emissaries under the seal of confidence, as well as to leading editors, churchmen and heads of women's organizations. I got my personal copy from the editor of the *Saturday Evening Post,* entirely innocently on his part.

Then the Bureau struck publicly. These "agents of Moscow," the Pueblos and their friends, according to the Bureau's publicists, were likewise the emissaries of pagan religions unspeakably bloody and foul, though, as a matter of common knowledge, the Pueblos were "pagan" but Christian too. Unprintable pornographic exhibits were circulated by the Bureau in 1923.

But Indian pressures continued, and increased, and the Pueblos went ahead as the spearhead. Then, in 1926, the Indian Bureau moved from defamation to action. Commissioner Charles H. Burke visited Taos Pueblo, and notified the old men in council assembled that they were "half animals" through their pagan religion. The Bureau forbade the withdrawal of Pueblo boys from school for their initiation ceremonies. The Pueblos as a body announced themselves ready for jail or any other penalty; the initiation ceremonies would go forward. Then the whole governing body of Taos Pueblo was thrown into prison for violating the Bureau's religious crimes code. The Pueblos struck back. They took their case to the religious press of the nation, and again addressed Congress.

Representative James A. Frear of Wisconsin went to the tribes to find out for himself. He became their irrepressible spokesman in the House Indian Committee and on the House floor. Senator William A. King of Utah pressed for a Senate investigation of Indian matters as a whole. Public indignation increased; publicity was widespread. The Federal District Court in New Mexico sent the jailed Taos Indian leaders back to their homes.

In 1924, a defective yet not wholly inoperable Pueblo Lands Act was passed by Congress. It "loaded the dice" against the recovery of their lands by the tribes, but directed that compensation be paid them under certain limiting conditions. The Act provided that a Pueblo Lands Board be set up to execute its terms. In this Board's proceedings, the Pueblos fought, under the handicap of a biased Board and a statute loaded against them, every step of the way. Richard H. Hanna became their attorney. Not until 1933, the first New Deal year, under a changed Indian Bureau, did the Pueblos finally win their battle for their lands. Then Congress, amending the defective Lands Act of 1924, and redressing the stubborn parsimony of the Lands Board and of the Federal District Court, granted a reasonable compensation to the tribes for their lands lost under the Lands Act; and it forbade the expenditure of any of the tribal funds thus created (about $1,300,000) without tribal consent.

In 1926, Congress reversed the Albert B. Fall order which denied the Indian title to the Executive Order lands (some 16,000,000 acres), which had been repudiated in 1924 by Attorney-General, later Supreme Court Chief Justice Harlan Stone.

In 1927, under the mounting pressures, and in the face of a threatened Senate investigation of Indian Affairs, Secretary of the Interior Hubert Work invited the Institute of Public Affairs of Washington (the Brookings Institution) to make an investigation. The investigation was made, at a cost of $125,000 privately supplied. Its results were published in a truly monumental book in the field, *The Problem of Indian Administration.* That was in 1928. The findings and conclusions supported the case the Indians had made. Before that publication, the Senate had overridden the resistances of the Indian Bureau and adopted the King resolution, launching the Senate's investigation of Indian affairs.

That investigation blasted the record wide open. The Senate's committee traveled to every part of the Indian country, and the tribes were ready with their case. After one year, Commissioner Burke, in a public outcry, charged that Senator Pine of Oklahoma, Republican, and I were in a conspiracy to destroy the authority of the United States government in Indian affairs. The Senate committee demanded evidence; Burke had none to give; he resigned. The Assistant Indian Commissioner, Edgar B. Merritt, who had dominated Indian affairs since 1912, followed Burke in two months.

This abbreviated account of the years from 1922 to 1929 leaves many interrelated struggles of the Indians and their friends undescribed. The prolonged battle by the State of California, for instance, on behalf of its Indians. That began in 1924. The struggle, ultimately successful, to block the Indian Bureau's and the Montana Power Company's attempt to confiscate the giant power site of the Flathead tribe; the struggle, ultimately successful, to prevent the transfer of the Walapai tribe's lands, without compensation, to the Santa Fe railroad; the struggle to bring to an end the starvation of Indian children in the government boarding schools (where the Bureau was feeding them on as little as seven cents per pupil per day); and the struggle to force the Indian Bureau to allow the Indians to receive technical aid from other branches of the Federal Government—these are examples. They fade into history, and only this significance is given them now—that they were prosecuted as episodes and vehicles of one integrated effort, withal an effort dispersed among more than two hundred tribes. The tribes were counseled and helped by more than a hundred of the best legal and public affairs brains in the country, individuals whose names, even, are not mentioned here; and the integrated program had few and simple principles.

These principles were: That Indians were entitled to the traditional American liberties, which included freedom of conscience, freedom of communication, freedom to organize politically and economically; freedom to use their assets productively, and to control them; access to the benefits of the general government (to which, indirectly and also directly, the Indians had contributed more of material wealth than any other population group); and freedom to draw upon the wellsprings of whatever genius, fed from the mountains of whatever past, might be theirs.

The four years 1929–33, under Herbert Hoover as President, Ray Lyman Wilbur as Secretary of the Interior, and Charles J. Rhoads as Indian Commissioner, witnessed some amelioration. W. Carson Ryan, as the new Educational Director of Indian Service, brought the most modern of educational thinking to bear in the schools. By intent, under him the schools no longer strove to break the relationship of the generations, to stifle the flow of language in young minds, or to blight the Indian cultures. In the area of broad intent, Secretary Wilbur and Commissioner Rhoads affixed their signatures to policy statements that went far. They described the ruining work which land allotment had done and was doing. They called for tribal organization under statute, particularly tribal corporate organization. They pointed out the injustices and the waste of time and life involved in the piecemeal, niggardly and so often hypocritical adjudication of tribal claims for money damages against the government. They did not, however, move any of these programs into attempted legislation. They did not check the diversion of nearly five million dollars a year of Indian capital funds into the running costs of the government's Indian Service. They allowed Indian Service to continue to avert its gaze from the huge process of soil erosion which was destroying the basis of Indian life. They did not appeal to the spirit of the Indian. They *did* put a stop to the pyramiding of debt against Indians in the process of building costly structures needed by whites; and they obtained from Congress the authority to remit unjust and wastefully imposed indebtedness of the tribes to the government. The ebb tide of Indian life had ceased to run; the flood tide, held back by the old system, was slowly coming in.

The tribes were patient for two years, and then resumed their pressures. Nothing less than the basic changes which they had been seeking since 1922 could give them their chance. They knew this from the long dark generations before 1929. "Terminate the executive absolutism," they insisted (to paraphrase words of theirs). "Terminate it by law. *Enfranchise our societies.* Empower and implement our own collective life. Benignant absolutism which perpetuates absolutism is malign, not benign."

CHAPTER 14

The Indian New Deal[1]

IN MARCH, 1933, Franklin D. Roosevelt entered into office as President of the United States. Harold L. Ickes became the new Secretary of the Interior. I was appointed the new Indian Commissioner.

I had been learning a great deal about the American Indian himself, and about other men and women who knew the Indian, for over twelve years; and my staff and I, always with the firm support of Harold L. Ickes and the active and personal interest of the President, formulated a set of principles that have remained dominant. They may be summarized this way:

First, Indian societies must and can be discovered in their

[1] Parts of this chapter are taken from the writer's "The Indian Administration as a Laboratory in Ethnic Affairs." *Social Research*, Vol. 12, No. 3. 1945.

continuing existence, or regenerated, or set into being *de novo*
and made use of. This procedure serves equally the purposes of
those who believe the ancient Indian ways to be best and those
who believe in rapid acculturation to the higher rather than the
lower levels of white life.

Second, the Indian societies, whether ancient, regenerated or
created anew, must be given status, responsibility and power.

Third, the land, held, used and cherished in the way the particular Indian group desires, is fundamental in any lifesaving
program.

Fourth, each and all of the freedoms should be extended
to Indians, and in the most convincing and dramatic manner
possible. In practice this included repeal of sundry espionage
statutes, guarantee of the right to organize, and proclamation
and enforcement of cultural liberty, religious liberty, and unimpeded relationships of the generations.

Fifth, the grant of freedom must be more, however, than a
remission of enslavements. Free for what? Organization is
necessary to freedom: help toward organizing must be extended
by the government. Credit is necessary to freedom; co-operatively managed credit must be supplied. Knowledge is necessary
to freedom: education in terms of live local issues and problems
must be supplied through activity programs in the schools;
technological and business and civic education must be supplied
to adults; professional and collegiate training must be opened
to the post-adolescent group. Responsibility is necessary to freedom: one responsibility is perpetuation of the natural resources,
and conservation must be made mandatory on the tribes, by
statute. Capital goods are necessary to freedom, and responsibility must be applied to capital goods: a tribe that handles its
revolving credit fund irresponsibly must know that shrunken
credit will be its lot tomorrow.

And now, the sixth principle: The experience of responsible
democracy, is, of all experiences, the most therapeutic, the most
disciplinary, the most dynamogenic and the most productive
of efficiency. In this one affirmation we, the workers who knew
so well the diversity of the Indian situation and its incalcitrancy
toward monistic programs, were prepared to be unreserved,
absolute, even at the risk of blunders and of turmoil. We tried
to extend to the tribes a self-governing self-determination
without any limit beyond the need to advance by stages to the
goal. Congress let us go only part way, but the part way,
when administrative will was undeviating, proved to be enough.
Often the administrative will was not undeviating, often the

administrative resourcefulness was not enough, often the Gulliver's threads of the land allotment system and of civil service and the appropriation systems kept the administrator imprisoned. The establishment of living democracy, profound democracy, is a high art; it is the ultimate challenge to the administrator. The Indian Service since 1933 has practiced the art, has met the challenge, in ways varied enough and amid situations diversified enough to enable one to give a verdict which seems genuinely momentous: the democratic way has been proved to be enormously the efficient way, the genius-releasing and the nutritive and life-impelling way, and *the way of order*.

The seventh principle I would call the first and the last: That research and then more research is essential to the program, that in the ethnic field research can be made a tool of action essential to all the other tools, indeed, that it ought to be the master tool. But we had in mind a particular kind of research impelled from central areas of needed action. Since action is by nature not only specialized but also integrative of specialties, and nearly always integrative of more than the specialties, our needed research must be of the integrative sort. Again, since the findings of the research must be carried into effect by the administrator and the layman, and must be criticized by them through their experience, the administrator and the layman must themselves participate creatively in the research, impelled as it is from their own area of need. Through such integrative research, in 1933, the Soil Conservation Service directly originated in the ecological and economic problems of the Navajo Indian tribe. In current years integrative research (the administrator and layman always participating) has pushed far back our horizons of knowledge and understanding of a whole series of the tribes, and has searched our policies, administration, personnel and operating methods to their foundations. I add, in passing, that such research invariably has operated to deepen our realization of the potentialities of the democratic way, as well as our realization of our own extreme, pathetic shortcomings.

In 1934 the Indian Reorganization bill was laid before Congress, where the hearings on it lasted several months. Some people ridiculed this bill because it contained 52 printed pages. They forgot that it was offered as a successor to the greater part of several thousand pages of Indian law. Until 1934, Indian tribes rarely had been consulted on the legislation introduced for their supposed benefit. In preparing this bill, however, the Indian office first sent to all the tribes questions concerning the Indian problems deemed to be central. Then the bill was furnished them all. Finally, congresses of Indians were held in all the regions, gatherings in which practically every tribe in the United States was represented.

As originally introduced in Congress the bill had six main parts.

1. The Indian societies were to be recognized, and be empowered and helped to undertake political, administrative and economic self-government.

2. Provision was made for an Indian civil service and for the training of Indians in administration, the professions and other vocations.

3. Land allotment was to be stopped, and the revestment of Indians with land was provided for.

4. A system of agricultural and industrial credit was to be established, and the needed funds authorized.

5. Civil and criminal law enforcement, below the level reached by federal court jurisdiction, was to be set up under a system of courts operating with simplified procedures and ultimately responsible to the tribes.

6. The consolidation of fractionalized allotted lands, and the delivery of allotments back into the tribal estate, was provided for under conditions which safeguarded all individual property rights and freedoms.

The first four parts of the Reorganization bill, as listed, became law. The fifth and sixth parts were lost. The fifth part may have been fortunately lost, because the tribes, under the enacted parts of the bill and under court decisions defining the unextinguished, inherent powers of Indian tribes, are coping with law and order more effectively with each passing year. But the loss of the sixth part was a major disaster to the Indians, the Indian service and the program. Congress has not yet righted that blunder of 1934. The fractionalizing of allotted Indian lands rushes on; the real estate operation of leasing these atomized parcels and collecting and accounting for and paying out the hundreds of thousands of vanishing incomes becomes increasingly costly, and increasingly a barrier against productive work or thinking in the allotted jurisdictions; millions of their best acres remain unusable to the Indians.

In the meantime, however, the Indian Service and the tribes are struggling to reverse the flood that is eating away the Indians' land-base. This is being done through voluntary exchanges and relinquishments, which require contact with each of the all but innumerable heirs—fifty heirship equities may vest in one Indian, and one allotment may have hundreds of scattered heirs. Despite the difficulties, the wasting flood has been checked and reversed in a few jurisdictions. It is only where this occurs that there can be a beginning of the positive program of using Indian lands through Indian effort. The situation was fully recognized in the report of the House Sub-committee on Indian Investigation, issued in December, 1944. In passing so lightly over this very important subject I wish only to add that in this matter, too, the Indians are wrestling with a problem widely encountered in other lands. One of the heavy drags on the agricultural economy of Asiatic India, for example, is the ever-increasing fractionalization of farm holdings. The formulae that are being successfully used here in the United States (but far too gradually, in the absence of the Congressional authority sought but not obtained) have application in Europe and in Asia.

The Reorganization bill, as finally enacted, contained a requirement that every tribe should accept or reject it in a referendum held by secret ballot. Those who accepted the act could organize under it for local self-government. Through a subsequent referendum they could organize themselves as federal corporations chartered for economic enterprise. Ultimately, about three-fourths of the Indians of the United States and Alaska came within the act. A related enactment, the Johnson-O'Malley Act, also passed in 1934, provided for the devolution of federal power to states and other political subdivisions, and for the enlistment of private agencies in the Indian task, through a flexible system of contracts and of grants-in-aid.

The Indian Service, on the basis of this legislation and impelled by the principles enumerated above, has striven to the end that every one of the particular programs—conservation, the cattle program, community organization, schools, the credit program, health, the Indian branch of the Civilian Conservation Corps and the other depression-years programs, the arts and crafts work—that every particular program should serve the primary aims of freeing or regenerating the Indian societies, and infusing them with the spirit of democracy, implementing them with democratic tools, and concentrating their attention upon their basic practical exigencies. Year after year, and cumulatively with the years, we who were doing the work observed sadly our partial failures, here and there our complete failures. Yet we also witnessed a development that has far outweighed the deficiences.

We have seen the Indian prove himself to be the best credit

risk in the United States: of more than $10,300,000 loaned across ten years, only $69,000 is today delinquent. We have seen the Indian beef-cattle holdings (nearly always they are managed co-operatively) increase 105 per cent in number of animals and 2,300 per cent in yield of animal products; and we have seen this increase take place on ranges that in varying measures were gutted by erosion caused by overgrazing twelve years ago, and now, in general, are overgrazed and gutted no more. We have watched scores of ancient tribal systems reorient themselves toward modern tasks, while more than a hundred tribal democracies have been newly born and have lived and marched out into life; these democracies are political, industrial and social. We have witnessed the Indian peoples giving themselves with ardor and discipline to the war; 25,000 of their young people have served in the armed forces, with the highest volunteering record, we believe, of any population in the country. Finally, we have seen the Indian death rate more than cut in half, and for this achievement the expanded and improved clinical services supply only a partial explanation: the changed anticipation, from death to life, the world winds that blow at last within what were the reservation compounds, the happiness and excitement of democratic striving and clashing and living—this is the significant explanation of a 55 per cent decrease in the death rate in less than ten years.

Indian affairs can be viewed not only as of significance in themselves; they can also be seen as an ethnic laboratory of universal meaning.

The story of Acoma, a pueblo in New Mexico, is the story of how a sky city came down to earth and the stone age overshot the modern mark. It is also a story with a lesson for us all today.

Twenty-two years ago the Indian Bureau had been driving hard against the Pueblos' religious unity. The particular issue was an attempt by the government to forbid Pueblo boys from going through the initiation vigils and disciplines during which they were taught the mystic lore and were made into men. Acoma wanted to know what to do about this issue, and three of us went there from California. We hired an old Ford for the occasion and drove across the desert to the so-called town of McCarthy's in search of the Governor of Acoma.

An Acoma boy met us on the way and ran ahead to notify the Governor. There he learned that the Governor had departed on foot for Acomita, fifteen miles east. The boy ran to Acomita; but on arriving he mistakenly told the Governor that we were journeying to meet him at Old Acoma, the sky city. The three towns mentioned form a triangle, and each is fifteen miles from the other.

When we reached McCarthy's, a little while before sundown, we learned that the Governor was at Acomita. We drove to Acomita. There we learned that he had departed on foot for Old Acoma to greet us; when the boy runner had given him the mistaken information the Governor had been at Acomita only a few minutes, having run there on some Governor's business from McCarthy's. The Governor, a Carlisle graduate, was seventy years old.

It was night now, but moonlight. We drove to Old Acoma. And when we had climbed to that city of dreams, up the long sand dune that breaks against its higher crags, we learned that the Governor had discovered his mistake and had run back to McCarthy's. So we drove to McCarthy's, lost our way, our headlights went off, and shortly before dawn, by the light of a waning moon, we tumbled down the steep rocky road from the higher country and found ourselves at McCarthy's. We were tired and we hoped to sleep. But there in his house sat the Governor, his Principal Men around him. He had run forty-five miles, but had not thought of rest. Coffee and bread were awaiting us, and we launched into a meeting that lasted till afternoon. Then the Governor said to us, "Now you friends go to my inner room and sleep. I've got some irrigation ditches to look after."

This incident, rather than the greater subtleties, intensities and mysteries of Acoma, comes to my memory as I try to summarize what happened there in subsequent years. Acoma lives by virtue of the Ancients. They are within the wills of the living men of Acoma; the future must be saved for them. But equally true of Acoma is Swinburne's image of the world wave which "rolls under the whitening wind of the future." Our conventionalized apprehensions, semantically and mechanistically thought-bound, do not quite apply to Acoma. Its deepest solemnities are shot through with gaiety; merrymaking surrounds the rituals and vigils upon whose efficacy life, and the Planet itself, are believed dependent. Through the deep-based security and assurance of the Ancients, Acoma is carefree, and it delivers itself to joy and to work, with nothing held back. The eagle soaring, the patient beast at the plow, the desert cactus and the plum and peach blossom, the old Governor who runs all night, deliberates all day and then goes to tend the ditches, who is not tired and does not scold the boy who told him wrong—all these are Acoma, but, sociologically, none of them is symbol enough. Acoma is also a primary social group which is at the same time a complex city-state whose life-giving democracy strikes across and beyond all the forms; it is a summation of the stimuli of an enormous past whose nurture and motivation are institutionally insured and wrought into happy, dauntless personalities; and it is a capacity for social action in the face of new emergencies.

In 1933, Acoma had about a thousand people, and its numbers were growing. Irrigation farming could not be much extended. The cash crop and main sustenance was cattle and sheep, but the government had encouraged maximum livestock numbers, and Acoma's lands were seriously eroded, the erosion accelerating each year. In its wounded condition the range could support 8,500 sheep units without being further wrecked. The sheep units on the land numbered 33,000.

In the West, overgrazing is the principal cause of soil wastage, and at Acoma it was the only cause. Overgrazing results not from greed and shortsightedness alone, but from the failure to use ecological and social knowledge, and from economic and social pressures that may sometimes appear remote. Ranges close to the Spanish-American villages in New Mexico are often hideously abused, and they have to be abused, because the villagers, who require at least a minimum of livestock for their subsistence, have been pushed off by the big commercial grazers from the ample ranges they used two generations ago. On the vast Navajo reservation the truly appalling soil wastage is due to the circumstance that for many decades the government encouraged and practically compelled the Navajos into a one-crop economy, sheep and goats, and, though their population was multiplying, Congress forbade them to extend their landholdings, as it forbids them now. Acoma was in a similar plight. Though conservation had been made mandatory upon Indian lands, under the Indian Reorganization Act, we knew that the exigency must be met, if it could be met at all, by methods having nothing to do with compulsion.

Since 1933, soil conservation has called into being a new integration of subject-matters and disciplines, natural and human. The soil conservation operation is conceived complexly, and as a process covering a rather long time. To be specific, soil conservation necessitates range-rest, reseeding, contour furrowing, water spreading, the vegetative healing of gullies and canyons. It requires a new enterprise and resourcefulness in animal genetics. Of livestock-owning populations that are near the subsistence level it demands changed methods of herd management and marketing and, usually, a shift for a long or brief period— usually long—to a more diversified economy. All this has deep-reaching effects, social as well as natural. The mere reduction of livestock may affect rather profoundly the status system within a social group. It strikes at individual security and it smashes headlong into habitual practices and expectancies.

In the light of these facts the significance of what Acoma did becomes manifest.

The Soil Conservation Service had ascertained the Acoma facts. The responsibility of finding the answer fell upon the superintendent of the United Pueblo Agency. That superintendent, I may mention, was a woman. In 1936 she invited the officers of Acoma, and in time the whole population, into conferences with her staff and the Soil Conservation staff. There the appalling fact was told them, that if their lands were to survive they must reduce from 33,000 to 8,500 sheep units. This was no command from the government. There was no fiat, and there would be none. Acoma was merely being furnished the facts, and it would also be furnished technical assistance, if desired. The conferences lasted through days, weeks, months. Gradually they broadened and deepened, and passed from point to point, until much of what was known about soil saving was known by the Acomas. The whole deep, living past of Acoma, with the vision of the ages to come and of the land to be saved for those ages, slowly absorbed the new facts and adopted their challenge. The thing was done. Acoma effected the crushing reduction, went through with all the sacrifices, applied conservation science through its whole gamut. And Acomas saw the ranges begin to heal, saw the weight and fleece of the residual animals increase, saw their sales prices soar through collective marketing.

The Soil Conservation districts, now numbering thousands, came into existence subsequent to Acoma's achievement, and came to be one of the most creative expressions of democracy in our American world. Acoma, with Laguna pueblo nearby, and the vast Navajo territory to the northwest, was the pioneering Soil Conservation area, and none in the white world has approached it in severity of sacrifice and brilliance of accomplishment.

Yet elsewhere in the famous watershed of the Rio Grande River, with its white cities, pueblos and villages of Spanish-Americans, the soil-saving effort has smashed into more resistant habits and vested interests. That valley and all its human treasure is doomed to ruin within the lifetime of men living now, unless the accelerating soil wastage of the whole watershed is stopped. It is not being stopped yet, although all the technical and organizational ways are known.

I have given a good deal of space to Acoma, not only because concrete and narrative statement is better than summary and abstract statement, but also because in the light of later experience it seems to me to represent more than just Acoma, or Indians in the face of modern challenges, or soil conservation democratically pursued.

For one thing, the refusal to use coercion, and instead the procedure of patiently waiting and skillfully endeavoring until the Pueblos' own central will took a painful task unto itself, had several specific rewards. Acoma did not develop bitterness and resistance toward social programs, toward technicians and "theorists," but on the contrary, developed confidence in them, and enthusiasm. Again, assuming that the soil conservation job had to be done—and it certainly had to be done—the government saved itself unknown amounts of money, probably millions, by using social science and relying on the principle of democracy. Further, no divorce was created between the old, lasting life, its consecrations and hopes, and the new life; instead, the old life created the new, and no dichotomy arose at all, no split in the community organization, no conflict between fundamentalism and science, and *no conflict between world-views*. The Acoma personality saved itself whole.

For another thing, Acoma refuted the stubborn error that Indians are segregated within their societies, immured within them from the world. It was within their society, for their society, by virtue of its powers, that the people of Acoma flashed beyond the world-present into the world-future.

I have emphasized the complex, the really multi-dimensional character of soil conservation science. It is ecological, drawing upon all the social sciences and requiring that the mind and the will shall dwell upon wholes—complex wholes—and shall contemplate a long time-process. I believe that the Indians of Acoma have a personality structure and bent of mind similar to that discovered among the Hopis 250 miles northwest of Acoma.

This personality structure and bent of mind become manifest quite far down in the age scale. If any one word can describe their quality it is the word *holistic*—the capacity to entertain complex wholes, and to maintain the complexities in a dynamic equilibrium. It is what one might anticipate from knowing the age-old nature of the Pueblo city-state: its necessary struggle, never intermitted, to survive in a desert environment amid foes pressing from every side, where abortive judgments might bring death; this struggle never exclusively extroverted, however, but always, as its first and last reliance, attending to the deepening of will and consciousness within the individual, and profoundly persuading man that the universe itself is dependent on the human intensity of thought and of will, achieved within tranquillity. In such city-states the holistic and artistic bent of mind is the very inmost fact and the guarantor of survival power. Such is the bent of mind which can easily master the complexities of the soil conservation program.

This discovery which we have made among the Hopis, even if it does not prove to hold good for all the Pueblo tribes, modifies our perspective upon these tribes. We see them as being not backward in time but forward in time; competent not merely to deliver their individuals into a civilizational level which the country knows now, but into a civilizational level far beyond the American standard of today. If our perspective be thus changed, if we see these tribes in this way, our administration, our education, our system and required quality of personnel, are indeed challenged. It is the *future* Indian service that must meet the challenge. So far it has not met it, except in spirit and by intention.

Now another and contrasting story, this one about the Navajos, those most magnetic of all Indians. When Kit Carson destroyed all the three thousand fruit trees in Canyon de Chelly and the Navajos were exiled to eastern New Mexico, they numbered probably 12,000. That was in 1863. Today they number 55,000, and they increase at more than 2 per cent each year. Their 16 million desert and semi-desert acres rival in beauty any of the scenic splendors to be found on our globe. There is a great forest, too, and underground there is oil, and there are 60 billion tons, more or less, of low-grade coal.

But the land itself, as distinct from these timber and mineral resources, could not support 5,000 whites. For several decades the government urged the Navajos toward sheep and always more sheep, even forbidding them to sell the breeding ewes. A huge overload of stock developed, and erosion on a monstrous scale. The Navajos have the money (from oil) to buy new land, and they offer to pay the local taxes on any land they buy, but Congress holds their cash; the Budget Bureau, too, is loath to see the Navajos pay local taxes. So new land remains unbought. A large irrigable area awaits a grant of irrigation construction money from Congress. Almost the first action of the administration which took over Indian affairs in 1933 was to send a Commission to the Navajo country. The Navajo tribal council met in July of that year, and the Commission reported direct to the council. Its report was not very different from the one that was subsequently made to Acoma pueblo in 1936. The tribal council was deeply shaken. It returned home, sought advice, and came again to say that facts were facts; erosion must be stopped; the stock overload must be reduced to carrying capacity.

That was twelve years ago. Today, on the Navajo reservation, anguish of a spirit is a wolf against the breast, and struggle rages, hardly less than any year before. There are no large lines of the endeavor which the Indian Service would erase if it could go back.

The Navajos are widely scattered over their lands, which equal a sixth of the total area of New Mexico. As a tribe, they are not a primary social group; their primary groups are many hundreds of extended families and little neighborhoods. Nor did they have in the past any consecutive organization of the tribe as a tribe. Their political government dates only from 1923, and until 1933 it was a yes-man government with severely limited powers.

It was this young, immature and hitherto narrowly circum-scribed institution of government that had thrust upon it the overwhelming and urgent problem of reducing stock and controlling soil erosion. Other responsibilities and authorities were extended to the tribal council at the same time, and reorganiza-tion and enlargement of the council were pressed. Then, in a little more than a year, the Navajos, like the other tribes, were required to choose, by secret-ballot referendum, under a uni-versal franchise, whether they would adopt or reject the Indian Reorganization Act. Acceptance would have made the conserva-tion of resources mandatory upon them. But the Navajos re-jected it by a very narrow margin, and thereby, for a decade, lost access to the credit fund, the land purchase fund and the system of orderly devolution of powers to the tribe, which were pro-vided for in the act.

Greatly telescoping the record, I set it down that again and again over the years the elected tribal council affirmed the con-servation program, enacted the implementing ordinances, strug-gled with the people over the issue and went into defeat at the next election. The struggles over this single subject so monopo-lized the field of debate and of decision that in nearly all other matters the political development of the tribe was stopped dead. In 1946 the tribal council operated without an executive com-mittee or any standing committee.

Of eighteen Navajo districts, all but five have reduced their stock to carrying capacity, and those five will soon do so. The sheep genetics laboratory of the Navajos has produced from the

ancient Navajo breed an offspring as hardy as his sires and
heavier in meat and fleece, which yields multi-purpose wool.
Stockwater and irrigation developments have increased the reservation's agricultural potential by the equivalent of as many
sheep as have been taken from the range. But the population
grows faster and faster—the human population. The Navajos
feel that they have submitted to conservation, not that they have
achieved it.

Nearly all of us see this as the most important fact: The
Indian Service has not had, or has not used, the means whereby
it could reach the intellect and the psyche and the social opinion
of the Navajos at the "grass roots." One who goes quietly there,
to the homes and little neighborhoods, and stays a while, encounters ample capacity to think, ample readiness to think and a
deep and often sad sentiment of responsibility toward the people
and their land. The barrier of language is a very heavy obstacle,
but a heavier one is the awareness in the wise Navajos themselves that whatever their perceptions and their understandings
may be, there exists no mechanism for translating the insights
and impulses into tribal decisions and actions. As for the Indian Service, driven, veritably hounded, by the exigent over-all
requirements, it has not often dared to pause and to try to think
through and feel through the problem of how the service and the
issues can be merged with each of the local communities, one by
one.

I do not present the Navajo record as one demonstrating the
failure of a democratic attempt which was energetically pressed.
I do not even ask whether it might have been a wiser course, in
this one case of stock reduction and range management, to have
used authority, frankly and absolutely (the authority existed),
and not to have cast upon the new and groping political democracy of the tribe so crushing a weight. Nor do I ask whether it
might have been better to take no notice, for a few years more
(as the prior administrations had taken no notice), of the dread
erosion situation, and to have devoted to community organization among the Navajos, and the development of subsidiary
natural resources, the energies which were flung lavishly into
the conservation enterprise—to have done this for a few years,
without hurling the administrative energies along the line of
greatest resistance, the stock reduction issue.

It is more useful to look forward. Conservation is very near
to accomplishment on the Navajo lands. An outlet for tribal
migration is likely to be achieved soon, and before very long

the decisive irrigation potentialities of the San Juan basin, in the northeast corner of the Navajo reservation, will possibly be realized. Therefore now (remembering that now is beginning as well as end) is the time for the Indian Service to pause, to go out and stay among the grass-roots communities, to start building diversely not eighteen land-use districts but hundreds of diverse Navajo local communities. No potency of Navajo life that existed in 1933 is absent today. Now as before, there is no people, anywhere, among whom *esprit* and *élan vital* are more regnant. The looming material disasters, which in 1933 and afterward seemed to demand the immediate and uniform action of those years, have been overcome or are almost overcome, and a wealth of knowledge and experience has been accumulated.

The ethnic laboratory of nearly three hundred Indian tribes has yielded richly, will yield more richly in the years ahead, and its yields do not conform with any one line of presupposition. Yes—there is one line of presupposition that it bears out. Making people free by helping them to confront real emergencies which they are capable of mastering is equivalent to the creation of new human and social energies. This effect is particularly dramatic when the freed peoples have been for a hundred years—as were our Indians—imprisoned within the fatalisms of unrealistic alternatives. This lesson, of world import, is taught equally by the contrasting Navajo and Acoma records. In the Navajo case a reliance placed on the historical political forms and dynamics of Europe and white America was confuted by the event. At Acoma, if the Indian Service had done less than cast the difficult load onto the whole pueblo organization the happy outcome would have been unlikely. Even if the particular practical result could have been won by the lesser means, the effect would have been to deprive the pueblo as an institution of a supreme opportunity. A truly deep democratic action was achieved at Acoma precisely by not seeking to persuade that action into a conventional European and white American mold.

This task of the guardian government, to make free the peoples who are its dependencies, demands not only sincerity of disinterested purpose but also deep knowledge of what those peoples are, and of the material environment within which they have their being. In particular (and this is true of all human life) what they are must be known in relation to what they must conquer. Here we verge upon social planning, which is just now beginning, and upon administration as art and science, which is also just beginning. In dealing with pre-industrial and pre-literate peoples, with colonies and dependencies, it has been the rule to rush in where angels would tread very cautiously. I mean, customary for dominant and guardian governments and religious and social missionaries and investment bankers thus to rush. Acoma and the Navajos, both, out of somewhat opposite records, raise their voices for knowledge and more knowledge, wisdom and more wisdom, and all possible freedom from the panic of haste, in the dealings which are upon us—the inescapable dealings—with the ethnic groups of Oceania and Asia, the Caribbean and Africa and our Western Hemisphere countries. Hundreds of millions of people raise or will raise the same voice that Acoma and the Navajos raise now.

It is no contradiction that even blunderingly making dependent peoples free to grapple with real emergencies is hygienic, life-releasing and life-saving. The apparent contradiction is canceled out with time, if the administrator is faithful to the spirit of science, to the spirit of that knowledge which he has not yet mastered. It is from the needs of action that knowledge is dynamically empowered. Imperfect action is better for men and societies than perfection in waiting, for the errors wrought by action are cured by new action. When the people acted upon are themselves made true partners in the actions, and co-discoverers of the corrections of error, then through and through, and in spite of blunders or even by virtue of them, the vital energies are increased, confidence increases, power increases, experience builds toward wisdom, and the most potent of all principles and ideals, deep democracy, slowly wins the field. This presupposition of the Indian administration since 1933 has been borne out by all of the experience.

Another conclusion that holds significance for dependencies everywhere pertains to the technical instrument, the Indian Reorganization Act itself. Over Indian matters, as over offshore dependencies, Congress still holds plenary power. But in the Indian Reorganization Act, and in some other related Indian statutes, Congress through general legislation has adopted self-restraining ordinances. The Reorganization act furnishes a flexible system for the devolution of authority from the government, including Congress, to the tribes. The Johnson-O'Malley Act furnishes the machinery for devolution from the federal institution to local subdivisions of government. The Pueblo Lands Act places the Peublo tribal corporations in control of the communal monies. It is true that all three of these acts explicitly or by implication affirm that federal responsibility shall

continue, no matter how far the devolution shall go. They contemplate that a single, integrated agency of administration shall
continue to exist, charged with the effectuation and defense of
the Congressional policies. At the same time, however, this
power of defense includes defense against Congressional attack
on the policies; and, in addition, the acts contemplate that the
single, integrated agency shall procure the needed services rather
than itself supplying them. The Reorganization Act offends
many prejudices and blocks the ambitions of many and powerful groups, and therefore it has been under attack within Congress every year since it was enacted. Yet it has not been repealed or weakened in any item. The act which freed the Indians
and moved the administration toward diversity of program and
method has proved to be also a conserving and stabilizing measure.

The policies established by legislation in 1934 have withstood
every attack, except the attack through appropriations. Increasingly in recent years the appropriations acts of Congress have
been made vehicles of covert legislation. The appropriations
sub-committees, especially in the House of Representatives, are
all but autonomous; the House gives only a fiction of delibera-
tive consideration to the annual supply bills. In numberless
cases Congress has concluded after careful deliberation that
such and such policies shall be law, and has then proceeded to
rubber-stamp appropriation bills which nullify and reverse the
policies.

Specifically, in the Indian field, land acquisition for Indians,
authorized by Congress, is blocked through the appropriation
bills; the situation is similar with respect to the expansion of the
Indian co-operative credit system. Congress legislated that Indian tribes and corporations should be given technical advice
and assistance in their operations, and then the appropriation
act nullified the legislation. The United States entered into
treaty with thirteen other Western Hemisphere countries, and
by the treaty pledged herself to maintain a National Indian
Institute; the House subcommittee on Interior Department appropriations has flaunted the treaty commitment. In general,
the appropriation acts have handicapped the Indian Service and
the Indians in the realization of every democratic, libertarian
policy that Congress has established as the law of the land.

This anomaly of our Congressional system has effects, of
course, far beyond Indians and dependencies and ethnic problems. Precisely because it is an evil of so universal a reach, we
may expect it to be corrected in times ahead. While it lasts, it

hangs like a gloomy shadow over the Indians and over territories and dependencies such as Alaska, the Virgin Islands and Puerto Rico.

From the Indian record we can draw these conclusions:

First, biological racehood, whether it exists or not, is without practical importance. There accumulate within and around races that are biologically distinguishable, and within and around races that are not biologically distinguishable, those in-group and out-group factors whose aggregate is called "racial." The factors are socially caused and socially transmitted.

Second, in ethnic matters, as in other vital matters, governmental intervention can be baneful or benign. In any field of human relations, when government tries to do the whole job, authoritatively and monopolistically, the result is baneful. The earlier Indian record is replete with evidence of this. But when government makes research an inseparable part of its ethnic operations, eschews monopoly, acts as a catalytic and co-ordinating agent, offers its service through grants-in-aid to local subdivisions, then government can be decisively benign, as the recent Indian record demonstrates. It is of national importance, and necessary to the good role of our Occidental governments in the world, that ethnic groups shall have equality of opportunity, shall be enabled to contribute their ideals and genius to the common task, shall not suffer discriminations, shall be free to breathe deeply the breath of public life. The Bill of Rights and the Constitution within the United States, the Charter of United Nations in the world, must be made good. It follows that governments and the federation of governments should and must concern themselves with ethnic matters, and that the methods should be right and not wrong.

Third, the individual fares best when he is a member of a group faring best. All human beings, in young childhood at least, are members of groups. The group is the tree and they are the fruit it bears. At least up to a certain age-level, the individual reft from his group is hurt or destroyed. The ruin inflicted on Red Indians through the white man's denial of their grouphood, and his leading them to deny their own grouphood, is only a special case of something that is universal. It may be that contemporary white life is being injured nearly as much by the submergence of its primary social groupings as the denial of Indian grouphood injured Indian life. If the primary social group in white life were regenerated for full functioning, through resourceful and sustained social effort, and were dynamically connected once more with the great society, the hygienic and creative results might be no less startling than those observed in the comeback of Indian societies.

Fourth, in ethnic groups of low prestige the apparent inferiority (acquired or innate) may mask an actual superiority. In most Indian groups the academic lag of children is pronounced, but if these children were given non-language tests that have been standardized on whites, they excel, even to a sensational extent. Their elder brothers excel when they are thrown into critical action, as they have been in the recent world war. In rhythm, so little regarded in our white society, the Indians excel. In public spirit they excel, and in joy of life, and in intensity realized within quietude. They excel in art propensities, and in truthfulness. These superiorities will be masked by an apparent inferiority until their group as a group moves into status and power. Then the mask will fall away. The application of this fact to underprivileged ethnic groups in general is readily apparent.

And last, the Indians and their societies disclose that social heritage is far more perduring than is commonly believed. On how small a life-base, on a diminished and starved life-base for how many generations, the motivations and expectations of a society, and its world-view and value system and loyalties, can keep themselves alive; how these social possessions, which are of the soul, can endure, like the roots and seeds on the Mojave desert, through long ages, without one social rain; and how they rush, like these roots and seeds, into surprising and wonderful blossom when the social rain does come at last. Perhaps no other ethnic groups have revealed this old, all-important truth so convincingly as the Indians have done. Indeed, this capacity for perdurance is one of the truths on which the hope of our world rests—our world grown so pallid in the last century, and now so deathly pallid, through the totalitarian horror. The sunken stream can flow again, the ravaged desert can bloom, the great past is not killed. The Indian experience tells us this.

CHAPTER 15

*The First Inter-American
Conference on Indian Life*

ABOUT 1915, one Dr. Manuel Gamio came
to supervise the excavations of the incomparable ruins at Teotihuacan. In 1917 he launched the most exhaustive, *integral* research project attempted up to that time in the Western world.
His program was to make an actually objective study, complete
and final, demographic, economic, sociological, of the peoples
of the Valley of Teotihuacan. Gamio had been a student of
Franz Boas at Columbia. His first findings were published in
1922 in three huge volumes entitled *La Poblacion del Valle de
Teotihuacan*.

Having completed his great work, Gamio wanted to go into
action. He had concluded that nothing less than "integral"
education—education brought to bear on the community as a
whole, involving itself with the whole life of the community
and conducted in all the deeper things by the community itself—
nothing less could meet the need, the desperate and profound
spiritual need, of Mexico and her Indians.

Such education he brought into being in the Valley of Teotihuacan. It included the schooling of the Indian children, but
went beyond to a health program, to an agricultural program,
to the revival of the arts and crafts. This enterprise, which President Obregón sponsored, which was financed by the fees visitors paid at the ruins, was terminated through political change
when Calles became President. But in the meantime, it had become known to the Indian populations of the Americas.

Coincident with Gamio's integral education enterprise, the
Pueblos of the American southwest had attracted the world's
attention. In their struggle to hold their institutions and religions from the Indian Bureau's death sentence, they had made

known what sort of integral education it was that had been practiced by Indians from Stone Age times.

In 1931, some of those in the United States who had joined cause with the Pueblos met with Mexico's workers in education. Jointly, they projected a clearinghouse of Indian data, internationally oriented. They agreed that it was the nations themselves which must be led to create and sustain the institution.

In 1932, under the leadership of the late Dr. Ernest Huber, of Johns Hopkins, a great anatomist and a passionate devotee of the Indians' cause, an inter-American group was formed in order to lay before the Third International Eugenics Congress the record of Indian life. A "Graphic Display of the Population Record of the Native Races of America" was prepared. It showed the Indians to be not a dying but a growing people.

In ensuing years, at meetings of the Western Republics at Montevideo and at Lima, actions were taken preparatory to the First Inter-American Conference on Indian Life. Bolivia was made the host country, but surrendered this honor to Mexico. On April 14, 1940, the Conference was inaugurated, at Patzcuaro. It was at Patzcuaro, four centuries before, that a sixty-year-old priest, Don Casco de Quiroga, had drawn the Indians into *hospitales,* where they lived and carried forward their numerous crafts, while they tilled the adjacent fields. All around the dreamlike lake on whose shore Patzcuaro is built, and back into the purple mountains, these *hospitales* were both the local self-government and the industry of the countryside.

Today there remains the original monastery, and the surrounding wall of the first of the *hospitales.* Within the wall there grow olive trees four hundred years old, of fabulous dimensions. The bones of Quiroga rest within the beautiful provincial museum maintained by the town of Patzcuaro.

This was the environment of the First Inter-American Conference on Indian Life. Nineteen Republics were present. From a number of the countries, opposing domestic elements were brought together. Specialists on Indian life attended from most of the countries, in addition to the official delegations; and Indian delegates came from countries as far apart as the United States and Bolivia.

Universally, through the ten days of the sessions, it was felt that a culmination had been reached and a new epoch begun. There was determination to get results; and though strongly contending philosophies and political situations held back no force of expression, there was in every critical matter a "give and take." All of the important actions when finally taken were unanimous.

Four sections worked throughout the Conference: social-economic, legislative, educational, biological. A subsection dealt with arts and crafts. The Indians held their own sessions apart, but participated also in the sectional and plenary meetings. The prepared papers of the Conference totaled 1,100 extra-length papers; they amounted to a cyclopedia on the living Indian. The "Acta Final," reporting only the resolutions and actions taken, filled 58 single-spaced pages.

Representative of the resolutions which were passed are these:

I. The nations of the Americas shall adopt and intensify the policy of offering the amplest opportunity for the display of the capacity of their Indian groups, to the end that the Indian cultures shall not die but shall endure to enrich the culture of each nation and of the world and contribute to the energies of the nations.

II. Where there exists an over-concentration of the ownership or control of land, the respective governments shall take appropriate measures, in accordance with equity and justice . . . : and we recommend that they adopt measures appropriate to their own situations to help the Indian populations in building up their economic life, providing them with needed land, water, credit, and technical facilities.

1. That each government shall establish an agency or an office with the object of concentrating attention upon the problems of the Indians, and of focusing upon Indian need in effective manner the services of the governments.

2. That such Indian agencies or offices should not monopolize the administration of Indian services, but should operate to focus upon the problems of the Indian all the resources of the governments as well as all the local resources.

3. That the offices of Indian Affairs should work with the Indians through indirect methods, utilizing the Indian groups as their media, or otherwise developing or utilizing cooperative organizations for the mutual aid and mutual defense of the Indians.

At the close of the Patzcuaro Conference, the nineteen governments in attendance established provisionally the Inter-American Institute of the Indian.

The Institute became definitive when ratified by the governments through treaty. The member governments now are: Mexico, the United States, Honduras, El Salvador, Guatemala, Panama, Nicaragua, Cuba, Santo Domingo, Colombia, Bolivia, Peru, Venezuela, Paraguay. The first Director of the Institute was Moises Saenz, educator and scholar of Indian life, from Mexico, at the time Mexico's ambassador to Peru. On Saenz's untimely death in 1942, Manuel Gamio succeeded him. This hemisphere does not contain a broader-minded man or a spirit more devoted than Manuel Gamio. I served as President of the Institute's Governing Board until May, 1946, and now represent the United States on that Board.

The Institute is supported by the several governments through quota payments; it is an autonomous part of the Pan-American system. Under the Treaty, each member country organizes and supports, within its own boundaries, a National Institute of the Indian, which is a branch of the International Institute. All of the National Institutes are now in being, and some of them are major forces in their countries. The United States has formed its National Institute. The Senate repeatedly has voted the funds for its operations but the subcommittee on Interior Department appropriations of the House Appropriations Committee has repeatedly refused them. Thus, in spite of the treaty-making Senate, the United States has breached the Inter-American Indian treaty.

At the Patzcuaro Conference, the achievements in Indian affairs of two countries stood out. These were Brazil and Canada (which did not attend the Conference nor join the Institute), in some respects at opposite poles, but for that very reason especially interesting.

Canada's Indian policy was, from the first, based on the English policy of respecting the Indian landholdings and keeping faith with the tribes. It was also concerned with conserving natural resources. The Hudson's Bay Company, formed by Charles II of England in 1670 to exploit all the lands watered by streams flowing into Hudson's Bay, was itself a conserver of Indian life and society. As such, and through the medium of the Indians, it became the earliest institution in the modern white world to apply itself to the conservation of natural resources. The resources were the fur-bearing animals; but these existed within the web which included the forest and the man. In the United States the web was reft asunder; in the Hudson's Bay area, after a good deal of early destruction, the web was permitted to regenerate itself, and is nearly intact today.

Canada made Indian treaties thriftily and never broke them; neither did Canada drive the tribes at one another's throats nor fight them. She formulated out of practice, a brief, flexible body of Canadian Indian law which is eminent for fairness of spirit and for common sense. She did not force land allotment on her

Indians; she did not appropriate their communal funds or divert them into her costs of administration; she did not tolerate corruption in her Indian Service. She provided an orderly, dignified transition for individual Indians, out of the tribal and into the general life, but she did not force the process by way of the many kinds of bludgeoning and confiscation employed in the United States. And this is still true in the present day.

However, a qualification must be added. Canada's "frame of reference" in Indian matters has been a narrow one, and until now has caused her somewhat to withhold herself from the movement of Indian regeneration which is reaching to the whole hemisphere. Canada's Indian goal is to make Indians self-supporting and to Christianize them. She does not, officially, acknowledge that Indian heritage and Indian society have greatness in them. They have usefulness, but except in the wilderness of the far North, they have no indispensability; and they have no generative, creative role. The Christian denominations, with their asocial view of Indian life; the keeping of faith in all practical matters with the tribes; and the movement of Indians as individuals into the prevailing economy—these influences and norms supply the framework of Canada's Indian policy.

Genius, vision, adventurousness are not greatly present in Canada's Indian record. But it means much that there is one Commonwealth in the Western world—there is only one—which from beginning to end has shown moral integrity in dealing with Indians and has kept the faith.

There is one other unblemished record, but the nation, Denmark, is not of the Western world. Commencing nearly two hundred years ago, Denmark recognized the Eskimos of Greenland and their culture as being permanent. Her scholars rendered the Eskimo language into written form. Not isolated from Denmark or the wider world, but united with them, are the Greenland Eskimos, by virtue of being sophisticated in a proud culture of their own.

The other outstanding country of the Western Hemisphere, in its dealing with the Indians, is Brazil where more than one million forest and jungle Indians are living today. In the early years after the white man came to Brazil, down to the 1890's, it had been taken for granted that an unbridgeable gulf divided the white man from the Brazilian Indian. The Indian had no rights at all, no value except as a jungle slave and a purchaser of firewater.

Within Brazil, advocates of the Indian began speaking persistently, as early as 1896. Their farthest-heard voice was Pro-

:essor Dario Velloza, in Curityba, but not until 1910 was broad
action achieved. In that year, by Presidential decree, the
Brazilian Service for the Protection of the Indian was established; its Director was General (then Colonel) Rondon—
Candido Mariano de Silva Redondo.

The task was gigantic; but the task was entrusted to a giant.
General Rondon was (and is, for he lives and works on, as his
eightieth year approaches) a man of greatness, intellectual,
emotional and moral. He was a man of achievement even before
1910, as a soldier, a civil engineer, a geographer and an ethnog-
rapher. Charged with building the telegraph circuit, he undertook to fulfill the commission without shedding Indian blood.
The jungle region was inhabited by wild tribes who had never
experienced anything but terror at the white man's hands. Many
of the tribes had become desperate in the struggle to survive at
all. Rondon built the telegraph line, and while building it, he
converted these fugitive, embattled tribes to friendliness as he
went along.

The Indian service which Rondon came to develop is an ex-
citing institution to the student of administration. Rondon, who
knew the jungle and its peoples and the modes of direct and
indirect slavery which had persisted for so long, sought through
research and experimentation to discover practical programs
valid for the societies and situations of the Indians. He established a limited number of "Indian Posts" widely scattered,
reaching into the remotest jungle and forest regions. Each of
these Posts he made into a center for "action-research, research-
action." Results were recorded, interchanged, and delivered to
the people of Brazil in written and pictorial form. Always, the
dimensions of the problem and task were kept to the fore. The
Indian service was a trial ground of an enterprise which must
be expanded and continued, directed at the salvation of a whole
race.

Rondon had no dogma of "segregation" and "assimilation"
or "individualization" or "collectivization." He knew that
humans must move into change from where they are, carrying
with them what they are; and he knew the meaning and value
of the native societies. He believed, and again and again in very
dramatic ways demonstrated, that the jungle tribes could comprehend anything they needed to know and could make profound adjustments without becoming disrupted. Through wise
speech, even Socratic discourse could be entered into with them.
This required, on the white man's side, knowledge, but more
than that, it required empathy—the power to identify one's own

thinking and feeling with the thinking and feeling of others. It required active love; Rondon lived and worked by Goethe's principle: Only through love is there understanding.

He sent his "call for creators" to the youth of Brazil, and enlisted a personnel of unusual endowment, intellectual and moral. He formulated a decentralized administration; each Indian Post and Community and Farm Center must find its own solution in constant interaction with the tribes. Every worker knew that the practical discoveries made would be faithfully relayed to the Brazilian people. From 1910 to 1930 there was continuity, under Rondon's magnetic leadership. But in 1930, from political causes, national support for the Indian service was reduced to a pittance. Many of the field station workers stayed on their jobs, throwing in their lot with the Indians. In 1939, national support was renewed, under a Policy Board which General Rondon headed and now heads. One of Rondon's understudies, the able and superior Dr. José Maria de Paula, serves as Director of the Indian Protective Service, now placed in the Department of Agriculture.

"Die if you need to; but kill, never." Such was Rondon's injunction to his workers. Sometimes they did die; even in immediate self-defense they never killed. And soon, the whole unencompassable jungle knew what was happening. The tribes congregated about the Indian Posts, now numbering 106. There they could have schooling, clinical service, implements and seed, learn new techniques of jungle agriculture and livestock husbandry. Extensive communal fields for the cultivation of wheat, flax, millet, cotton, manioc, rice, were cleared and improved, the tribes contributing the labor. Agricultural, fishing and hunting areas were demarked for exclusive use by the tribes. Meantime, the subtle adjustments of jungle life were carefully not broken down. And nothing, as an absolute, was imposed or "high-pressured" on the Indians. The methods were democratic and designed to win maximum permanent results through minimum official control and expense, maximum results made permanent through being achieved by the tribes themselves and thus organically incorporated.

I think there can be no question but that the Brazilian Indian service is the best equipped and most thoroughly committed of any of the Indian services; and taken as a whole, it is both the most inspired and down-to-earth, and probably the most economically operated. It is not ashamed to be moved by an "overbelief," an intellectual passion whose affirmations are not coercive on those who do not share it. Thus de Paula does not

sitate to speak of "this race which could not be exterminated
in more than four hundred years of oppression, whose deep-
rooted pride and independence could not even be diminished,
and whose personality, filled with noble sentiments of attach-
ment to the native soil, affection and devotion to the family,
and generous hospitality to the stranger, could not be weakened
. . Courage in fight, and abnegation and stoic resignation before privations and suffering, these are attributes sufficient to
constitute the strongest and most progressive race in the world,
if they had been properly encouraged . . . by the first colonists."

Rondon and his co-workers serve not only the Indians, but
the expansion of the culture and soul of Brazil.

Since the Patzcuaro Conference, interest in the Indians has
deepened and widened throughout the Western Hemisphere.
In recent years, revolutions in Ecuador, Bolivia, Peru, Guatemala—countries whose populations are two-thirds Indian or
more—have had elements of mass-movement in them, as had
the El Salvador revolution. Now they are reaching below the
political level, and across the narrow political boundaries of
previous years. They are not, as yet, Indian revolutions, but they
include genuine and deeply intended efforts to free and aid
the Indians. Should they fail, it might very well be that Indian-
centered revolutions would take their place. The awareness of
this fact is a potent awareness in Guatemala and in all the
Andean countries. It reinforces other governmental trends not
sharply revolutionary—trends toward the economic, bio-psy-
chological and political strengthening of the several Republics
viewed as wholes. Since 1940, these trends have been reinforced
by the systematic interchange, from all the nations of the West
to each nation, of the data of experimental social achievement,
including an interchange of personnel.

Consecutive, building effort often can take the place of advancement through revolutionary shock. There are ways other
than the direct struggle of social classes for the achievement of
basic, revolutionary, necessary changes. Not to use peaceful,
readjusting, building methods, in the Latin-American countries,
would mean continuity of revolutionary shock. Unless revolution passes into creative construction (as it did in Mexico under
Cárdenas, for example), even the basic revolutionary gains
cannot hold their own. These facts are strong in the consciousness of many Latin-American governments now, and they favor
the multiplication of social enterprise directed at the basic populations—the Indians.

Bolivia supplies an example. Ernest C. Maes, a Spanish-

American social scientist of New Mexico, formerly with the United States Soil Conservation Service, and later the emissary of the National Indian Institute of the United States to all of the South American countries, now serves as Counselor to the Ministry of Education of Bolivia. His experimental work, in part financed by the Inter-American Educational Foundation, is subordinate to the Bolivian government. In its essence the Bolivian enterprise carries forward that "integral education" which Manuel Gamio had demonstrated in the Valley of Teotihuacan twenty-five years before. It works not in one but forty-one population areas of altiplano and valley. Health education and agricultural education teachers and home demonstration agents work as permanent members of the staffs of forty-one rural school centers. Motion pictures are used, and a traveling theater. The social unit served is the inexpungeable Indian community; the whole life-problem of the Indian is being experimentally attacked in one unified effort; and the permanent structures of the communities are being integrated with the schools which are so much more than schools.

At the political level, an event of irrevocable significance took place in May, 1945, at La Paz, Bolivia. It paralleled the same kind of event, which had preceded it, in Peru. The First Bolivian Indian Congress assembled; 1,400 delegates came, from the highlands, the valleys and the tropics. Gone was the conventional image of the Andean Indian obsessed with an "inferiority complex" and so indrawn that he would not commune with the wider world. The All-Indian Congress concentrated on essentials; and an impressive identity of conception, among groups which had never met each other before, is evident in the record of the proceedings. At the end of the Congress, the then President of Bolivia (Villarroel) announced four decrees, consonant with the demands of the Congress. One decree abolished the system of *mita* (forced labor, principally in the mines) and the *pongueaje* by which hacienda owners forced their peons to supply the hacienda larder from their own starvation provender. Another decree prohibited the hacienda practice of using the children of the peons for house labor without pay. A fourth decree projected the establishment of a comprehensive Agrarian Code.

The diversity of the Indian events of the years since 1940 can be only suggested here. In the jungles of Nicaragua, for example, among the 20,000 Miskito Indians, we encounter the following enterprise:

Loaned by the United States Navy to the Inter-American Indian Institute, at the request of Nicaragua, Lieutenant Commander Michel Pijoan made a survey of the health of the Miskito people. He found that 90 per cent of the morbidity among these jungle dwellers was caused by nine principal diseases. He believed that the Indians themselves would be able to diagnose and cure these diseases through the means now known to medicine.

It was done. The native *curanderos* were assembled at the hospital of the region, a mission hospital directed by a first-rate doctor who understood and liked the Indians. They received for three months clinical, as well as verbal, training. Drugs were donated by the Wythe Drug Company. The *curanderos* returned to their home neighborhoods. The drugs were paid for by the Indian patients or their families; the proceeds went into a revolving fund to buy more drugs. The *curanderos* served without pay; the mission hospital supervised them. The Miskito Indians became better served—self-served—medically and in public health than were the city dwellers of many of the Latin-American countries. The Miskito Indian health service is fully operating today. The stimulus for this Nicaraguan enterprise came from Dr. Victor McGusty who visited America from the Southwest Pacific, and told of the sub-professional health system of Fiji. The mechanism for transmitting the stimulus was the Inter-American Institute of the Indian.

In Guatemala, overwhelmingly Indian in its population and in its unextinguished tradition, there are other developments. There, under the leadership of Antonio Goubaud Carrera, a richly trained social scientist who unites a daring imagination with hardest practicality, the "integral" methods of Indian work are being pressed through all the glittering plateau country—the thousands of Indian communities, the fifteen pre-Columbian language groups. A phase of the effort is the bold approach to the subject of bi-lingual education. The nations at the Patzcuaro Conference recognized this problem. Classroom teaching exclusively in Spanish and other European languages had left the millions of Mexican, Central American and Andean Indians illiterate in the European language. Small-scale demonstrations in the United States and Mexico had established (as the Cherokee Indians had established more than a century earlier) that initial literacy *in the native Indian language* made effective literacy. The subject was of extreme importance. Two-way literacy would stabilize, enrich and free from insularity

the Indian soul; it well could be the beginning of the output o.
great literature by Indians; it would speed the development of
the nations as integrations of plural, mutually reinforcing cultures. At Pitzcuaro, the nations recommended bi-lingual teaching in the schools. But in none of the countries was pedagogical
inertia ready for such a re-direction. The systems of schools
were not organized or oriented that way. In general, the great
adventure was nowhere seriously attempted.

Dr. Goubaud, through the Guatemalan National Indian
Institute, and with the help of a Negro specialist in linguistics
(Dr. Mark Hanna Watkins, loaned by Fisk University from
the United States) is exploring systematically this fundamental
problem of the Indian. He is exploring the other problems—
economic, hygienic, Indian group-structure, existing and possible administrative mechanisms—which are involved with the
language problem. Guatemala's technical resources are placed
liberally at his disposal. If continuity of time be granted—which
seems very probable now—Guatemala, which until yesterday
had no Indian welfare movement at all, well may become a
pioneering nation in behalf of all Indian cultures. That exquisite blend of Maya-Quiche culture with post-Conquest Spanish culture, which distinguishes the highland Indian communities of Guatemala, may enter an epoch of new springtide and
of national and world communion.

CHAPTER 16

Summary and Prediction

THE CONTROLLING fact of Indian life today,
and of present governmental Indian enterprise, is the triumph
of the *group life* of the Indians. This triumph contains within
itself the future of the Indians, and their renewed power to
benefit mankind. It contains within itself the triumph of their
individuals.

Across four hundred years, the struggle of the Indians in
behalf of their group life was waged as an enormous delaying
action. Indian groups numbering more than forty thousand social units on the two continents sustained this delaying action,

ach unit largely in isolation from the others. In the process of his struggle, deep changes took place in Indian life. The changes were not merely mechanical. They did not consist merely in the loss of this and that native "trait" and the acceptance of this and that European "trait." Rather, organic assimilation and vital synthesis took place.

There was no method of destruction that was not used against them, and most of them coped with all the methods of destruction. Legal proscription, administrative proscription; military slaughter; enslavement, *encomienda,* forced labor, peonage; confiscation of nearly all lands, forced individualization of residual lands; forced dispersal, forced mass-migration, forced religious conversions; religious persecutions which hunted down the social soul to its depths, and the propaganda of scorn; catastrophic depopulation, which mowed down the native leadership and the repositories of tradition; bribery of leadership, and the intrusion of quisling governments by the exploiting powers. Indian group life—Indian societies—outwore all the destructions.

Now, at last, the Indians' delaying action has changed in some countries, is changing in others, to a strategy of advance. The proscriptions are ended, or are being ended. The nations are accepting the Indians' societies as being unkillable and even indispensable. Rondon in Brazil, in 1910, first challenged the proscription, ended it, and built Brazil's Indian service upon the Indian groups. Mexico, in the unrolling of her last revolution, affirmed the ancient values. The United States, after 1933, radically enunciated and set in motion the policy of *social action vested in the Indian groups and executed by the groups from their own centers.* In Bolivia, Peru, Ecuador, the *comunidades,* numbering four thousand in Peru alone, are becoming incorporated into the social service and agricultural improvement programs, the educational systems, and the slow-starting yet insistently advancing agrarian revolution. But let us look at a few representative Indian societies of today for a view of the Indian's New World.

On the cold heights, at 13,000 feet elevation, the *comunidad* of Collana in Bolivia looks down from three leagues away upon La Paz, the capital. The Collanas number only some 600. Social management is entirely in the hands of the pre-Conquest *ayllu.* Each year there is carried out the reassignment of land to families; the cattle browse on the common range; the planting and harvesting are done by voluntary co-operation. Annually, the people elect their *alcade* and their *cabildo* (council). These officers regulate the use of all resources, and sit in judgment on all cases civil and criminal. No outsider is permitted to remain overnight in Collana. Since Inca times, there has been almost no change; only a loss of contact with the wider Indian world, which became dispersed or immured after the Conquest.

In Peru, near Jauja, is the *comunidad* of Muquiyauyo. Muquiyauyo is constituted by the union of four *ayllus*, each having its own elected officers. These sit in the council which meets each week; and the council includes all males over twenty years old. Offices are so rotated that every male finds himself in due time drawn into some responsible function of the government.

In Peru, any unused portion of an hacienda or church estate may be taken over by the government and offered for public sale. Muquiyauyo, out of its savings from wages earned at the mines, purchased a thousand acres of such land. On this new land, alfalfa was cultivated through joint labor. In ten years 70,000 *soles* were saved up; this saving was invested in a hydroelectric plant, built through contributed labor. The plant generates 4,400 volts; it supplies light and power to the *comunidad*, and supplies half of the electricity needed by the town of Jauja, four miles away. An electrically run flour mill grinds the corn of the *comunidad;* thus the women are released for leisure or for the crafts. Muquiyauyo has built, through community labor, a rural school for 300 pupils, and has presented it to the government. Here is witnessed the *mita* of Inca days, before the Spaniards perverted it. Every able-bodied male contributes labor to the public work. Women may substitute for the males of their families. Out of its communal fund, the *comunidad* furnishes to parents a bonus of five *soles* for each male infant born and two and a half *soles* for each female infant. When a child seeking additional schooling, or a young man or woman, seeking university training, leaves the *comunidad*, the communal treasury subsidizes him.

Muquiyauyo is one of the many *comunidades* (there exist, even, co-operative federations of *comunidades*) which demonstrate not merely the "staying" capacity of Indian societies but their competence for new adjustment. It has brought to life many of the ancient values, has modernized the immemorial man-nature co-operation, and has displayed readiness for innovation and the capacity to innovate.

In Greenland, the literate Eskimo culture, two centuries old, has produced novels, poetry, histories, drama, a free press, and a perfectly normal merger of the Eskimo way with the European Danish. In Alaska we find that most of the Eskimo communities carry forward distributive co-operation, modern style, with perfect, easygoing success. Yet their social forms and their personality types remain largely what they were before the earliest contact with any other modern men.

We go down to the warm southeastern Alaska coast and discover the Metlakatlans, a west-coast tribe which, within the memory of the living, was uprooted and driven in migration from Canada. We find a social organization which is an all-embracing co-operative commonwealth, wholly modern in its forms. Fishing and canning are a corporate enterprise; the municipality owns and operates all of its utilities, including electricity. When, here and there around the world, relief needs present themselves, Metlakatla sends its check unsolicited. Complete modernity, embracing the unforgotten past!

Then we come to the Hopi Indian society of the Northern Arizona plateau. In its beautiful but very difficult desert land, on its high rock-mesas swept by storm and brooded over by sun and stars which seem very near, the Hopi race has sustained an unbroken, undiminished continuity for more than fifteen hundred years. Its whole past moves on explicitly and consciously into its present; and all is magnetized from a future which draws the tribal soul as a work of art in process draws its creator. Through an immense, ceaseless action of the will, the Hopis believe that they help to sustain the universe.

Food and water must be wrested by the Hopis from a semi-arid land. Famine, through the centuries, has been an ever-present threat, and often a grim reality. Yet the Hopis have met the challenge of the desert on the physical as well as on the social and spiritual level. The desert forced them to develop a remarkably effective technology of dry farming. On the social level, it forced on them a democratic, co-operative social structure which tolerated no waste of human energy and no individual self-seeking.

Seen as a whole, the Hopis are a profoundly and intensely practical people. That nature-man constitution which they have built through their ages will incorporate any gain—any new tool or goal—which is contributive to Hopi destiny. Hopi inner life is not small or eccentric, but catholic and cosmic. The Hopi's world-view and art of self-making are not less congenial to the world's future than to his own past. The opportunity for teaching and for wise administration is immense and fascinating, *in terms of the Hopi*. But the mere intrusion of influence is mostly wasted effort; when successful, it is, in the degree of its success, only harmful. But creative social planning is within the Hopi's scope now as of old; and the modern social sciences can become the Hopi's tools not less than ours.

Antonio Garcia of Colombia has pointed out that the old as-sault against the Indian societies had been marked by two con-ditions. One condition, the more commonly taken into account, was the attempted extermination of the societies, and it failed. The other condition was the exclusion of the societies from the flow of national life—the flow of political power, of economic benefits and of technology. What would the Indian societies become, what would they achieve, if this second condition were reversed? Would their power to create, within the national and the world setting, prove to be as great as their power of re-sistance, of endurance and of inner regeneration?

I have certain predictions to make, growing out of my years of absorption with the Red Indian situation, my life with them, my efforts for them as Commissioner.

The Western Hemisphere nations increasingly will base their Indian programs on the Indian social groups. They will do this with greater boldness and inventiveness as experience is ac-cumulated, is recorded, and is interchanged among nations.

The Indian societies will keep their ancient democracy, some-times adapting it to the larger tasks which they will take to themselves, sometimes with no adaptation at all. There will exist productive Indian local democracies to the number of forty thousand or more—democracies social and economic, not merely political. These Indian social units will become federated within nations and over national boundaries. They will traffic with the other social groupings within the nations, particularly with labor, with conservation bodies, with research institutions, with organizations concerned with the arts.

These Indian societies will supplement their ancient co-oper-ative forms with modern co-operative forms; they well may be-come the major embodiment in our hemisphere of the co-operative movement of the world.

With the advance of "integral" education, including bi-lingual literacy, the realized mental potential and the social energy of the Indian societies, and their biological vigor, will increase by hundreds, even thousands of per cent. A large num-ber of their individuals will pass out into the general life of their nations, and they will pass into increasingly higher social levels. But they will not become divorced from the societies which formed them and gave them their orientation; and thus hey will play a part in the world of the future out of lessons drawn from the past.

As the Indian societies move from their four-centuries-long delaying action into a confident and rejoicing advance, expression along many lines of literature, of the arts, of religion and of philosophy will come into being. The ancient-modern Indian affirmation of the deathless man–nature relationship will flow into poetry and symbolic art of cosmic intensity, tranquillity and scope.

The movement will be inward and outward at one and the same time—inward to the world-old springs, buried or never buried, which still flow because the societies have not died; outward to the world of events and affairs.

There will come to dawn in the nations, the Indians playing their part, two realizations. The first, that their soils, waters, forests, wild life, the whole web of life which sustains them, are being wasted—often irreparably and fatally. The other, that their local community life, their local democracy, their values which are required for beauty, wisdom and strength—their very societies—are wasting away even as their natural resources are wasting. As these realizations increase, the nations will turn to their Indian societies increasingly, seeking the open secrets they have to reveal.

All these good things will come to pass if the nations will maintain and increase their enterprise and research into Indian need and Indian power. More slowly, less decisively they will come about even if the nations *regress* in their Indian programs. For the delaying action of the Indian societies and of that spirit they represent is ended. They have proved that they cannot be destroyed, and they are now advancing into the world.

INDEX

Ⓜ Ⓒ Ⓢ

Other MENTOR, SIGNET CLASSIC and SIGNET Books of Interest

☐ **THE DEATH OF THE GREAT SPIRIT: An Elegy for the American Indian by Earl Shorris.** A comprehensive history of the American Indian, from Sitting Bull to the Red Power Radicals of today. (#MW1355—$1.50)

☐ **AMERICAN INDIAN MYTHOLOGY by Alice Marriott and Carol K. Rachlin.** A collection of myths, legends and contemporary folklore from some twenty North American tribes, this profusely illustrated volume is one of the most comprehensive studies of Indian lore in America. (#ME1555—$2.50)

☐ **PEYOTE by Alice Marriott and Carol K. Rachlin.** A penetrating exploration of the controversial peyote religion, its institutionalization in the form of the Native American Church, its subsequent diffusion among the Indian tribes, and its relationship to other facets of Indian culture. (#MW1519—$1.50)

☐ **LAUGHING BOY by Oliver LaFarge.** The greatest novel yet written about the American Indian, this Pulitzer-prize winner has not been available in paperback for many years. It is, quite simply, the love story of Laughing Boy and Slim Girl—a beautifully written, poignant, moving account of an Indian marriage.
(#CW917—$1.50)

☐ **THE LAST FRONTIER by Howard Fast.** The classic story of the injustice suffered by the Indian at the hands of the American government. "A rich American novel."—The New York Times
(#Y6608—$1.25)